Teaching Anti-Fascism

A Critical Multicultural Pedagogy for Civic Engagement

Michael Vavrus

TEACHERS COLLEGE PRESS

TEACHERS COLLEGE | COLUMBIA UNIVERSITY

NEW YORK AND LONDON

Published by Teachers College Press,® 1234 Amsterdam Avenue, New York, NY 10027

Library of Congress Cataloging-in-Publication Data is available at loc.gov

ISBN 978-0-8077-6696-5 (paper)
ISBN 978-0-8077-6697-2 (hardcover)
ISBN 978-0-8077-8103-6 (ebook)

Printed on acid-free paper
Printed and bound by CPI Group (UK) Ltd, Croydon, CR0 4YY

The twentieth century, which was born proclaiming peace and justice, died bathed in blood. It passed on a world much more unjust than the one it inherited.

The twenty-first century, which also arrived heralding peace and justice, is following in its predecessor's footsteps.

—Eduardo Galeano
from *Mirrors: Stories of Almost Everyone*, 2009

We've seen a force that would shatter our nation, rather than share it.

Would destroy our country if it meant delaying democracy.

And this effort very nearly succeeded.

But while democracy can be periodically delayed, it can never be permanently defeated.

—Amanda Gorman, United States Presidential Inaugural Poet
excerpt from "The Hill We Climb," January 21, 2021

Contents

Series Foreword

In this sobering, timely, and informative book, Michael Vavrus describes why educators should be concerned about anti-fascist traditions and elements that mobilized in the United States after the presidential election of Barack Obama in 2008 and intensified during the presidential term of Donald Trump (2017 to 2021). In articulating his angst about the rise of fascism in the United States, Vavrus's views are consistent with writers such as Madeleine Albright (2018) and Fiona Hill (2021). Albright titled her book *Fascism: A Warning*, framing the crisis in stark terms. Hill (2021) fears that because of deepening inequality and increasing class stratification within the United States, we might be headed for the grim threats to democracy that now exist in Russia.

Fascism is characterized by governments that are hierarchically organized and that "maintain a totalitarian and regimented society through violence, intimidation, and the arbitrary use of power" (Shafritz, 1992, p. 220). The state is absolute, and individuals and groups are given little regard. A charismatic leader is also an important factor in the establishment and maintenance of fascism (Shafritz, 1992). Fascism is a complex concept with multiple dimensions and components. Practices that reflect fascist ideology and principles exist in Western democratic nations such as England, France, and the United States.

Vavrus describes fascist elements in the United States and events and developments that epitomize fascist ideology, including the White nationalist rally in Charlottesville, Virginia, on August 12, 2017, where neo-Nazism was on public display. James Alex Fields Jr., a self-professed neo-Nazi, killed 32-year-old demonstrator Heather Heyer when he drove his car into the crowd. Fields was convicted and sentenced to life in prison. Other events that echo nascent fascism in the United States include politicians who deny that the election of Joe Biden as president in November 2020 was fair and legal; the actions by state legislatures controlled by Republicans to limit the voting rights of citizens of color (Abrams, 2020); and the efforts to recall school board members who are accused of supporting teaching about racism and diversity in the schools (Saul, 2021). Most of the attacks on school board members accuse them, without evidence, of supporting the teaching of critical race theory (Lòpez et al., 2021; Wallace-Wells, 2021).

Vavrus argues that anti-fascism should be an essential part of a transformative and critical civic education that will reduce fascism and help students develop the knowledge, skills, and values needed to act to make their communities, the nation, and the world more just and democratic. The major purpose of this book is to describe the ways in which fascism has been manifested in the United States and other nations through time (especially in Italy from 1922 to 1945, and in Germany from 1931 to 1945), and how a transformative and critical civic education can and should become an antidote to it.

In this book, Vavrus describes and tries to reclaim the anti-fascist curricular orientation that the New York City Teachers Union and segregated Black educators incorporated into intercultural education in the 1940s. Vavrus also describes how fascist elements and activists developed in Europe and the United States during the 1950s and 1960s. He makes the important point that fascism is cyclical in the United States and other nations; it exists continually over time and within various historical periods. However, it becomes more and less intense in various times and epochs.

This book is an important addition to the Multicultural Education Series, whose major purpose is to provide preservice educators, practicing educators, graduate students, scholars, and policymakers with an interrelated and comprehensive set of books that summarizes and analyzes important research, theory, and practice related to the education of ethnic, racial, cultural, and linguistic groups in the United States and the education of mainstream students about diversity. The dimensions of multicultural education, developed by Banks (2004) and described in the *Handbook of Research on Multicultural Education* and in the *Encyclopedia of Diversity in Education* (Banks, 2012), provide the conceptual framework for the development of the publications in the series. The dimensions are content integration, the knowledge construction process, prejudice reduction, equity pedagogy, and an empowering school culture and social structure. The books in the Multicultural Education Series provide research, theoretical, and practical knowledge about the behaviors and learning characteristics of students of color (Conchas & Vigil, 2012; Lee, 2007); language minority students (Gándara & Hopkins 2010; Valdés, 2001; Valdés et al., 2011); low-income students (Cookson, 2013; Gorski, 2018); other minoritized population groups, such as students who speak different varieties of English (Charity Hudley & Mallinson, 2011); and LGBTQ youth (Mayo, 2022).

Racism and anti-Semitism are integral components of fascism. A number of other books in the Multicultural Education Series focus on *institutional and structural racism* and ways to reduce it in educational institutions, which is an especially relevant topic because of the national and international protests and dialogues about institutionalized racism that began after George Floyd, an African American man in Minneapolis, died when a White police officer pressed his knee to Floyd's neck for more than 8 minutes on May 25, 2020. Books in the Multicultural Education Series that focus on race include Özlem Sensoy and Robin DiAngelo's (2017) *Is Everyone Really Equal? An Introduction to Key Concepts in Social Justice Education* (2nd ed.); Gary Howard's (2016), *We Can't Teach What We Don't Know: White Teachers, Multiracial Schools*

(3rd ed.); Zeus Leonardo's (2013), *Race Frameworks: A Multidimensional Theory of Racism and Education*; Daniel Solórzano and Lindsay Pérez Huber's (2020), *Racial Microaggressions: Using Critical Race Theory in Education to Recognize and Respond to Everyday Racism*; and Gloria Ladson-Billings' (2021), *Critical Race Theory in Education: A Scholar's Journey*.

Vavrus argues compellingly that the study of fascist politics and anti-fascist responses can become the basis for a transformative and critical multicultural civic education. A transformative and critical multicultural civic education is an effective antidote to fascism. Fascism gives priority to the nation and national identity, whereas multicultural education sustains and honors the multiple identifies of individuals, including their personal, family, community, and cultural identities (Banks, 2020). The identities of individuals are recognized and sustained rather than eradicated in school programs that actualize multicultural education (Paris, 2012). Multicultural education also fosters democratic values and ways to actualize social justice within society, whereas fascism privileges the nation over the individual and perpetuates ideologies such as racism, anti-Semitism, sexism, and homophobism.

Michael Vavrus has made original, prescient, and influential contributions to multicultural education and teacher education for several decades. He has contributed two previous books to the Multicultural Education Series. *Transforming the Multicultural Education of Teachers: Theory, Research, and Practice* (2002) was one of the earliest books published in the series. His second book in the series, *Diversity and Education: A Critical Multicultural Approach*, was published in 2015. I am pleased to welcome his third book to the Multicultural Education Series and hope that it will attain the influence and visibility that it deserves.

—James A. Banks

REFERENCES

Abrams, S. (2020). *Our time is now: Power, purpose, and the fight for a fair America*. Macmillan.

Albright, M. (2018). *Fascism: A warning*. Harper/Collins.

Banks, J. A. (2004). Multicultural education: Historical development, dimensions, and practice. In J. A. Banks & C. A. M. Banks (Eds.), *Handbook of research on multicultural education* (2nd ed., pp. 3–29). Jossey-Bass.

Banks, J. A. (2012). Multicultural education: Dimensions of. In J. A. Banks (Ed.), *Encyclopedia of diversity in education* (Vol. 3, pp. 1538–1547). SAGE.

Banks, J. A. (2020). *Diversity, transformative knowledge, and civic education: Selected essays*. Routledge.

Charity Hudley, A. H., & Mallinson, C. (2011). *Understanding language variation in U.S. schools*. Teachers College Press.

Conchas, G. Q., & Vigil, J. D. (2012). *Streetsmart schoolsmart: Urban poverty and the education of adolescent boys*. Teachers College Press.

Cookson, P. W., Jr. (2013). *Class rules: Exposing inequality in American high schools*. Teachers College Press.

Gándara, P., & Hopkins, M. (Eds.). (2010). *Forbidden language: English language learners and restrictive language policies*. Teachers College Press.

Gorski, P. C. (2018). *Reaching and teaching students in poverty: Strategies for erasing the opportunity gap* (2nd ed.). Teachers College Press.

Hill, F. (2021). *There is nothing for you here: Finding opportunity in the twenty-first century.* Mariner Books.

Howard, G. (2016). *We can't teach what we don't know: White teachers, multiracial schools* (3rd ed.). Teachers College Press.

Ladson-Billings G. (2021). *Critical race theory in education: A scholar's journey.* Teachers College Press.

Lee, C. D. (2007). *Culture, literacy, and learning: Taking bloom in the midst of the whirlwind.* Teachers College Press.

Leonardo, Z. (2013). *Race frameworks: A multicultural theory of racism and education.* Teachers College Press.

Lòpez, F., Molnar, A., Johnson, R., Patterson, A., Ward, L., & Kumashiro, K. (2021, September). *Understanding the attacks on critical race theory.* School of Education, University of Colorado Boulder, National Education Policy Center. https://nepc.colorado.edu/sites/default/files/publications/PM%20Lopez%20CRT_0.pdf

Mayo, C. (2022). *LGBTQ youth and education: Policies and practices* (2nd ed.). Teachers College Press.

Paris, D. (2012). Culturally sustaining pedagogy: A needed change in stance, terminology, and practice. *Educational Researcher, 41*(3), 93–97. https://doi.org/10.3102/0013189X12441244

Saul, S. (2021, October 21). Energizing conservative voters, one school board at a time. *The New York Times.* https://www.nytimes.com/2021/10/21/us/republicans-schools-critical-race-theory.html?searchResultPosition=1

Sensoy, Ö., & DiAngelo, R. (2017). *Is everyone really equal? An introduction to key concepts in social justice education* (2nd ed.). Teachers College Press.

Shafritz, J. M. (1992). *The HarperCollins dictionary of American government and politics.* Harper Perennial.

Solórzano, D., & Huber, L. P. (2020). *Racial microaggressions: Using critical race theory in education to recognize and respond to everyday racism.* Teachers College Press.

Valdés, G. (2001). *Learning and not learning English: Latino students in American schools.* Teachers College Press.

Valdés, G., Capitelli, S., & Alvarez, L. (2011). *Latino children learning English: Steps in the journey.* Teachers College Press.

Vavrus, M. (2002). *Transforming the multicultural education of teachers: Theory, research, and practice.* Teachers College Press.

Vavrus, M. (2015). *Diversity and education: A critical multicultural approach.* Teachers College Press.

Wallace-Wells, B. (2021, June 18). How a conservative activist invented the conflict over critical race theory. *The New Yorker.* https://www.newyorker.com/news/annals-of-inquiry/how-a-conservative-activist-invented-the-conflict-over-critical-race-theory

Acknowledgments

There are many people who contributed to the conceptualization of this book. Among them are Jon Davies and Grace Huerta, my coteachers in two different academic programs during 2017 and 2020, respectively, in their support of incorporating an anti-fascism perspective into our curricular offerings to undergraduate students. The engagement displayed by students from an anti-fascist curricular strand was a motivation in the development of this book. Hallway and pub conversations with Steve Niva and David Price helped me to sharpen my orientation prior to delving into the research required for this book. I wish to thank both James Banks for his support of this book as a valid perspective on multicultural education and Brian Ellerbeck for his encouragement and recommendations throughout the publication process at Teacher College Press. John Bylander's, Jitendra Kumar's, and Julie Angel's close read of the manuscript provided invaluable copyediting critiques. The Evergreen State College library staff was incredibly helpful during the COVID-19 pandemic in assisting me in locating a wide variety of source material. Olivia Archibald was an important sounding board for many of the concepts in the book as well as in contributing helpful perspectives and contemporary news sources for me to consider. Moreover, Olivia's invaluable moral support helped to keep me balanced in light of the necessity to wade into research and accounts revealing abhorrent information, much of which is incorporated in the pages that follow.

Part I

"GOOD TROUBLE"

Part I follows the social justice advice U.S. Representative John Lewis gave during a college commencement address: "You must find a way . . . to get in good trouble, necessary trouble" (as cited in Hubley, 2016, para. 16). The opening chapters present what led to the writing of *Teaching Anti-Fascism,* along with the book's rationale and theoretical orientation, contested terminology, and organization of chapters. Each chapter contains brief cataloguing of historical and contemporary events that encourage responding by getting into "good trouble" with a critical multicultural pedagogy for civic engagement.

CHAPTER 1

"U.S. Gov't Is Soft on Fascism"

We cannot be soft on domestic Communism.

> —Richard Nixon to a 1954 American Legion meeting

Beginning with the Congressional elections of 1950, red scare tactics and rhetoric frequently were invoked to discredit liberals and individuals allegedly "soft" on communism, to extinguish…any form of social protest.…All segments of society, including the public schools, fell victim to this period of new and intensified red scare attack.

> —Stuart J. Foster, "The Red Scare: Origins and Impact"

The title for this introductory chapter originates from a bumper sticker I saw years ago when visiting the University of Wisconsin. I purchased two of the stickers from the student union bookstore. One I put on a vehicle I had at that time. The other I adhered to my office door where it remained for over 20 years until I relocated to a different office. I was attracted to the sticker's ironic play on the wording of the far right's Cold War (1947–1991) contention that America was soft on communism. The phrase "U.S. Gov't Is Soft on Fascism" captured what I had come to understand about U.S. politics, evident in the decades that followed World War II (1939–1945) and the "Red Scare" of the 1950s and 1960s. For some colleagues the bumper sticker's contention that the United States is soft on fascism seemed remote and a bit over the top. The new occupant of my old office eventually had the sticker removed during the 1st year of the presidential tenure of Republican Donald Trump (2017–2021).

It was during the early years of the presidency of Democrat Bill Clinton (1993–2001) when I acquired those stickers. During his campaign for president in 1992, Los Angeles had erupted in civil violence after police officers were acquitted for the brutal beating of a Black man that was videoed and distributed to a news outlet. Scores of people died in those riots, and multiple businesses were damaged. At the time, Clinton expressed empathy for the plight of African Americans and appeared as the candidate who could ameliorate racial discrimination and unrestrained police violence.

The Clinton presidency, however, turned out to be disillusioning for many who anticipated advocacy for a progressive political agenda. Instead, Clinton gave conservatives and the far right an agenda that fit their ideological leanings. The Republican Party disdain for social services for those in need found an ally in Clinton who lived up to a campaign slogan to "end welfare as we know it" that left millions falling through an already threadbare social safety net into the 21st century.

Taking on the mantle of the law-and-order trope, the Clinton administration lit a match that helped spark the largest per-capita prison population in the world. In 1996, first lady Hillary Rodham Clinton, who would eventually become the Democratic nominee for president in 2016, added additional fuel to this racialized inferno through a fictitious image of rampant juvenile crimes. By circulating a debunked narrative, she spread the unfounded panic that "there are certain kinds of kids that are called 'super-predators.' No conscience, no empathy, we can talk about why they ended up that way, but first *we have to bring them to heel*," a legacy that haunted her failed bid for the presidency in 2016 (Gearan & Phillip, 2016, para. 3, emphasis added). The distorted analogy of "super-predators" further inflamed a perception that a police presence was necessary in public schools—particularly those in low-income Black neighborhoods—all of which helped expand an unjust school-to-prison pipeline that continues to ensnare vulnerable adolescents. Such anti-Black dog-whistling rhetoric to garner votes created a false domestic enemy at the expense of young Black and Brown people. Two decades later in 2015, Bill Clinton admitted that he made "the problem worse" (BBC, 2015, para. 2): "The bad news is we had a lot of people who were essentially locked up who were minor actors for way too long" (para. 10). Unfortunately, school administrators had picked up the rhetoric of law-and-order toughness that resulted in hyper-disciplinary practices to the detriment of thousands of children and youth.

In *Fascism: A Warning*, President Clinton's secretary of state, Madeleine Albright (2018), a post–World War II immigrant from Eastern Europe, provides an overview of European fascism in the mid-20th century. Conceptionally, Albright surmised:

> To my mind, a Fascist is someone who identifies strongly with and claims to speak for a whole nation or group, is unconcerned with the rights of others, and is willing to use whatever means are necessary—including violence—to achieve his or her goals. In that conception, a Fascist will likely be a tyrant, but a tyrant need not be a Fascist. (p. 11)

The year before she became secretary of state (1997–2001), Albright was U.S. ambassador to the United Nations during an embargo on Iraq. In a 1996 nationally televised interview, Albright was asked, "We have heard that *a half million children have died.* I mean, that's more children than died in Hiroshima. And, you know, is the price worth it?" (L. Stahl, as cited in Mahajan, 2001, para. 1, emphasis added). Albright responded, "I think this is a very hard choice, but the price—*we think the price is worth it*" (as cited in Mahajan,

2001, para. 2, emphasis added). In the writing of her book on fascism, Albright was apparently so encapsulated by American exceptionalism that she failed to recognize her own fascist tendencies that contributed to President George W. Bush's eventual invasion and occupation of Iraq, a nation that never posed a direct threat to the United States (see Albright, 2004, para. 9).

The purpose in highlighting the Clinton administration is not to single it out as an anomaly. Instead, into the 2020s it serves as an example of how financially dominant political parties—whether Democrat or Republican—under the guise of *American exceptionalism* too often pay lip service toward advancing an egalitarian and fair world. The Clinton administration represents mainstream politicians who adhere to American exceptionalism and position themselves as ideologically neutral *centrists*. The political center is actually "an abstraction" because any ideology can discursively define the extremes in which to locate itself (Wallerstein, 2011, p. 6). In practice "liberal centrism is conservative" by failing "to offer weapons, let alone shields, against the *fascism of the state*, the *white supremacist* constellations it encourages, in the *micro-fascisms* that permeate daily life and habit" (Lennard, 2019, p. 4). All of which brings us back to the notion that the United States is soft on fascism.

COUNTERING A MASTER NARRATIVE OF AMERICAN EXCEPTIONALISM

American exceptionalism is a belief that the United States, from its colonial founding to the present, holds a special status in world politics that permits it to act independently without restraint or accountability. American exceptionalism results in a feel-good history that ignores its political tendencies toward fascism. A curricular approach centered on American exceptionalism distorts public school history textbooks when the focus is exclusively on positive accomplishments that conceal from young people a civic education with a holistic historic telling that also includes flaws and shortcomings of this discourse (Loewen, 2007). Hence, a purpose of this book is to bring the blackout of anti-fascism out of the shadows and into the light of the classroom. This requires countering an imposed master narrative of exceptionalism on civic reasoning and discourse and to bring to the forefront alternative perspectives that describe patterns of fascist politics necessary for a more accurate and historically honest civic education. The first two chapters initiate this process, whereas Part III presents more detailed cases.

A BRIEF CATALOGUING OF AMERICAN TENDENCIES TOWARD FASCISM

In *Teaching Anti-Fascism*, I include examples of U.S. fascist leanings and actions, anti-fascist and anti-racist resistance, and the effects on civic educational policy, teaching, and learning. Lest this civic history is forced down an

Orwellian "memory hole," for now a brief overview of U.S. fascist tendencies and anti-fascist actions are highlighted.

In the fight against fascism during the 1930s and 1940s, numerous public schools and teacher education programs took advantage of new transformative curricular materials devoted to anti-racism and anti-Semitism. In 1941 a New York far-right state legislative committee set in motion the purging of faculty from public schools and colleges for their pedagogy. Among those were numerous members of the politically left New York City Teachers Union and 50 professors from City College. The Teachers Union responded that the state was "*soft on fascism* and anti-Semitism" (Toloudis, 2015, pp. 575–576, emphasis added).

The U.S. government was only ever explicitly anti-fascist from December 1941 through the end of the war in 1945. A golden era of intercultural anti-fascist education ended 2 years after the end WWII. Cold War architects and far-right educators and politicians operated in sync with J. Edgar Hoover's (1924–1972) notoriously led Federal Bureau of Investigation (FBI) and its paranoid conflation of any whiff of communism with racial justice activism. The anti-communism era of the 1950s and 1960s squelched any anti-fascist civic education devoted to cultural inclusiveness and anti-racism. Now racial and cultural injustices were expected to be set aside and replaced by a color-blind Americanism of unified anti-communism.

The thought of any legitimate U.S. communist party or left-oriented movements that questioned the profit-hungry aim of capitalism in contrast to the human-needs orientation of socialism sent financial chills up the spines of the capitalist class. During this era of far-right extremism and the near hysteria about anyone with seemingly communist and progressive sympathies among the general population resulted in prominent screenwriters, actors, authors, and educators losing their jobs under the pretext of being communists and, thus, un-American. Governmental and school officials joined the dogmatic anti-communism, anti-socialist peddling of fear that created a hostile post-WWII era for any educators who sought to continue teaching with an anti-fascist lens focused on U.S. histories of racism and anti-Semitism. In New York an estimated 300 teachers "fell victim to the city schools' ideological purges" (Foster, 2000, p. 1). In Los Angeles, 30,000 teachers were required to sign "invasive loyalty oaths" to keep their jobs (p. 1). Across the nation books found subversive were censored or burned if they contained any discussions related to socialism or sexuality.

Throughout most of the 1950s and 1960s conditions resembling modern slavery existed for migrant Mexican farm workers in closely guarded agricultural camps and fields. African Americans lived under a constant cloud of Jim Crow violence. In 1956 the Alabama home of Dr. Martin Luther King, Jr. was bombed. The historic 1963 civil rights "March on Washington" that featured Dr. King helped galvanize public attention to the plight of people of color. Deemphasized or excluded from mainstream recollections and schoolbooks, the publicized purpose of the gathering at the Lincoln Memorial was for "jobs and freedom." In 1965, 34 people died and thousands were arrested after Black residents rioted over an incident of White callous Los Angeles policing that blew the top off long simmering experiences of use of excessive force by police. A year later in a Chicago suburb when Dr. King was nonviolently leading a march against racial discrimination, neo-Nazis threw objects that struck his head. In the spring of 1967, Dr. King delivered his "Beyond Vietnam" speech that tied U.S. apartheid conditions that many Blacks lived under to the military attacks on Brown bodies in Vietnam.

By the summer of 1967, Black segregated and heavily policed communities erupted into what euphemistically were labeled "race riots" rather than what they were: spontaneous pent-up insurrections against voter suppression, economic inequality, and unaccountable police violence on poor people confined in high-density neighborhoods. An estimated 159 riots that summer resulted in the National Guard and other military personnel in tanks patrolling urban streets (McLaughlin, 2014). In Newark, protesting young people were photographed carrying signs identifying themselves as "Youth Against War and Fascism" and calling for the removal of military troops from their streets (Gonsalves, 2017). In the Jim Crow South, far-right police officers and the Ku Klux Klan continued in their unrestrained brutality on Black and White anti-racist protesters. The following year, 1968, Dr. King was assassinated while in Memphis to support over a thousand Black sanitation workers on strike demanding humane working conditions and a living wage. A few months later anti-war presidential candidate Robert Kennedy, who had voiced advocacy for the civil rights of Latinx farmworkers, African Americans, and impoverished White rural residents, was assassinated in Los Angeles.

By the late 1960s and into President Richard Nixon's presidency (1969–1974), large numbers of young people pulled away the veil of America's illusion of a fair and equitable democracy. Thousands of young people in the fall of 1967 converged on the Lincoln Memorial in a march on the Pentagon to protest U.S. military brutality on the peasant population of Vietnam that was conducted under the Cold War narrative of stopping the spread of communism. A massive and sustained anti-war movement against an undeclared war on Vietnam and nearby southeast Asian nations resulted in students shutting down colleges and universities across the United States. Protests centered on higher education's complicity with governmental anticommunist propaganda, conducting research for the Department of Defense, and censoring political dissent and free speech on campuses. In May 1970, in response to anti-war protests, the National Guard opened fire on the Kent State University campus, killing four unarmed young people. Ten days later when Black students at Jackson State College were protesting racism, the Mississippi Highway Patrol shot "150 rounds in twenty-eight seconds," killing two and wounding 12 (Means, 2016, p. 157). In both instances "a majority of Americans blamed the students" (Lepore, 2020a, p. 73). What was labeled a "generation gap" during that turbulent era found significant numbers of young people questioning and acting against U.S. domestic and foreign policy of American exceptionalism that an older generation generally accepted. The resulting "counter culture" that emerged displayed a disdain for a crass consumerism promoted by capitalistic advertising and sought to prefiguratively create alternative communities centered around a sharing economy and participatory consensus decision-making.

In dramatic armed displays and provisions of breakfast programs for impoverished young people, the Black Panther Party for Self-Defense in the 1960s brought vivid attention to long-standing police use of excessive force and extralegal actions in Black communities and the neglect of poor and hungry school-age children. (The federal government eventually emulated the Panther's program and made free school breakfasts in public schools permanent in 1975 for students from low-income families.) A young generation of activists recognized an inherent self-defense legitimacy in the Black Panthers' naming of the police as "fascist pigs." Activists soon used *Amerika* as an alternative spelling for America to signal the fascistic and oppressive nature of policing and the military, especially toward African Americans and "third world" war victims.

During this period of social and political upheavals the nation witnessed the rise of the American Indian Movement, the women's liberation movement (second-wave feminism), and the movement for gay and lesbian rights. Parents pressed for civil rights for their children hidden from sight in draconian institutions warehousing those deemed too handicapped to attend public schools.

This time was also an era when significant numbers of the White working class males rejected movements toward a more inclusive and equitable society (Lepore, 2020a). A White supremacist discourse found political traction among Republicans, racist fringe third parties, and liberals who actually blamed Black families for their own poverty, disenfranchisement, unemployment, and segregated housing. Notably, liberal, conservative, and far-right actions and words *echoed the objections of fascist regimes* against any movements opposed to imperialism, skin-color racism, cultural racism, feminism, racial discrimination in schools and workplaces, and the closeting away of those outside the mainstream norms of mental and physical ability.

A decade later such a toxic anti-democracy political environment remained during the presidency of Republican Ronald Reagan (1981–1989). In 1985, the Philadelphia Police Department used tactics of fascist terrorists to drop military-grade bombs on a neighborhood housing a Black liberation group, killing adults and children and leaving hundreds homeless. The racially volatile era of the 1970s and 1980s was the backdrop to both the eventual Clinton presidency and multicultural education initiatives that surfaced more visibly in research, teaching, and teacher preparation programs.

Despite modest gains toward a more inclusive and equitable society during the latter half of the 20th century, inequality in wealth and income fueled by capitalism undermined the promised liberty and equality of a pluralistic democratic society. By the beginning of the 21st century, finance capitalism had already made easy credit available through a variety of venues and helped to create a nation of widespread vulnerable and dispossessed debtors. Naming capitalism as the primary culprit in perpetuating inequality and destructive environmental practices was viewed as anti-democracy and un-American by mainstream propaganda. Meanwhile, as corporate profits soar, we witness today in real time the rapid decline of the health of the planet; it is becoming unsustainable for the well-being of human beings and the natural world, a dismal scenario for the future of children and youth.

CIVICS MISEDUCATION

Black educator and historian Carter Woodson's 1933 *The Mis-Education of the Negro* emphasized that the education of African American students created a dependency on the whims of a White-ruled nation rather than helping young people become active citizens. Writing in the midst of White supremacist legalized segregation, Woodson (1933/2000) highlighted how living under "terrorism" functions so effectively that young African Americans "ceased to think of political matters as their sphere" (p. 88). Woodson noted how this miseducation for civic engagement affected White students as well—except that their future offered "actual participation in the affairs of government" denied oppressed Black adults (p. 88).

More recently, Giroux (2016) captured a similar sentiment by pointing to public schools as "'dead zones of the imagination,' reduced to anti-public spaces that wage an assault on critical thinking, civic literacy and historical memory" (p. 351). In mainstream public schooling, civic education is sanitized so as not to rock the status quo boat of American exceptionalism that might result in parent, community, and school board scrutiny and objections. Giroux (2019) further zeroes in on the educational lives of young people and the disconnect from the political world they find themselves living in:

> Rather than educating people to become active and critical citizens in the process of governing, the most important forms of education employ pedagogical practices that lie largely on the side of domination and work to prevent people from understanding how private troubles are connected to wider systemic structures and issues. (p. 715)

After 12 years of public education, millions of students graduate without the requisite knowledge, skills, and dispositions for civic reasoning and active citizenship to address social ills. Instead, the bully pulpit of far-right legislators and their media outlets want to determine the content of civic education, which most certainly excludes an anti-fascist multicultural education.

Carlos Cortés (2012) notes how "media function as nonschool teachers and create an informal nonschool curriculum about diversity" (p. 1461). During Trump's presidency miseducation about diversity, citizenship, and democracy proliferated through the growth of online media outlets that "allow the far right to create and quickly spread conspiracies, . . . destabilizing people's sense of truth" (Miller-Idriss, 2020, p. 55). In an investigation into Facebook, for example, Sheera Frenkel learned how social media giant Facebook—with a total value of $1.21 *trillion* of stock shares (Dennison, 2021)—granted access to a far-right group to plan and display weapons in online discussions leading up to the Capitol riot. Frenkel observed, "I had never seen a Facebook group grow so quickly, adding thousands of users within hours to this group in which they were sharing all sorts of falsified videos and documents about election fraud. It's very clear from our reporting that Facebook knew the potential for explosive violence was very real" for Trump's January 6, 2021, rally and eventual siege on the Capitol (as cited in Gross, 2021, para. 6).

To counter far-right conspiracies and "fake news," Garrett (2019) notes research that finds "students with formal media literacy education were better able to navigate information and less prone to biased interpretations" (p. 23). However, studies also find that in general "middle school through university students were . . . unsophisticated analyzers of online information" (p. 27). Furthermore, with far-right propaganda replacing the closure of local news outlets, students navigating media and trying to understand their role as knowledgeable active citizens are provided a civics miseducation via media conglomerates such as Facebook (see Alterman, 2021). Because the teaching of critical media literacy as a part of a civic education is rare, along with an absence of an anti-fascist education, young people can become more susceptible to distorted information that leads to far-right fascist politics.

Giroux (e.g., 2018, 2019) and Peter McLaren (e.g., 2020a, 2020b) are among the few educators who have consistently published tracts critically analyzing and sounding a much needed alarm about fascist tendencies and actions in our current era of miseducation. Yet, most critical educators, myself included, are concerned about what far-right extremism holds for education as we continue to draw attention to political inequities that harm the life opportunities of young people. However, a search of research databases and publications in the field of education, including multicultural and intercultural education, reveals an absence in curriculum and instruction devoted to contemporary expressions of fascism and histories of anti-fascism that can counter a civics miseducation. Collectively we have not published a synthesis of fascism, far-right extremism, and anti-fascism into a multicultural conceptual framework. To counter this absence, *Teaching Anti-Fascism* follows up on the warnings from Giroux, McLaren, and others by proposing a critical civic education that is not soft on fascism.

INTERSECTIONALITY, CRITICAL THEORY, AND ANTI-FASCISM

Intersectionality and critical theory are integral for the design of an anti-fascist civic education. An anti-fascist approach brings together under one conceptual umbrella disparate ideologies and material conditions often captured through the scholarship of intersectionality. Intersectionality moves beyond "single-axis thinking" that "undermines legal thinking, disciplinary knowledge production, and struggles for social justice" (Cho et al., 2013, p. 787) and brings "an analytic sensibility" (p. 791) to take up "larger ideological structures in which subjects, problems, and solutions were framed" (p. 795). Burley (2021a) explains, "Antifascism is a core response to the interrelated crises we currently face, from economic to ecological. . . . As these crises deepen, the threat of fascism will as well, and all intersecting social movements will have to reckon with it" (para. 10). The interdisciplinary nature of anti-fascism is inherently intersectional in both theory and practice in the long and continuing battle for social justice.

Critical Race Theory

As a critique of dominant narratives about society and culture, critical theory—from which *critical race theory* (CRT) developed—informs my standpoint. CRT begins with the premise that "racism is normal, not aberrant, in American society" (Delgado, 1995, p. xiv). CRT provides a way to understand how presupposed neutral legal and educational concepts such as "knowledge, truth, merit, objectivity, and 'good education' are in fact ways of forming and policing the racial boundaries of white supremacy and racism" (Roithmayr, 1999, p. 4). Cornel West (1995) emphasized the intersectionality of CRT that "compels us to confront critically the most explosive issue in American civilization: the historical centrality and complicity of law in upholding white supremacy (and concomitant hierarchies of gender, class, and sexual orientation)" (p. xi).

Critical Pedagogy and Multicultural Education

Critical theory informs a *critical pedagogy* for an anti-fascist civic education. Critical pedagogy is a dialectical process that tests assumptions and assertions for accuracy as part of an ongoing interrogation of political and historical claims, a process that can lead to social justice actions by teachers and students (McLaren, 2015). Following the lead of critical theory, critical pedagogy incorporates how knowledge, power, and social change intersect. With roots in critical theory, CRT, and critical pedagogy, the field of *critical multicultural education* is positioned to incorporate anti-fascism. Like anti-fascism, critical multicultural education not only acknowledges the place of identity recognition for the historically marginalized, but also takes a democratic socialist stance to equitably address basic human needs such as housing and health care and to counter an ecological crisis from capitalism's continuing degradation of the planet (see Gandesha, 2021; Vavrus, 2015). Anti-fascism is conceived as an action arm of critical multicultural education's attention to myriad forms of discrimination and oppression.

Critical Theory, Fascism, and Hope

Importantly, critical theory emerged as a critique during the rise of fascist regimes in the 20th century. More than 30 years ago Kellner (1990) encouraged critical theorists to expand connections "with new social movements and existing political struggles" (p. 31). Kellner's point clarifies that critical theory is more than critique but offers hope and emancipatory possibilities. Dinerstein (2020) explains that the socially just world critical educators strive for "is connected to the *material* dimension of reality that inhabits the present one. Hope is not merely a projection of reason, a 'mental creation' of human thought, *but an expression of what is really possible*" (p. 38, emphasis in original). The fundamental hope of *Teaching Anti-Fascism* is to open new possibilities for a civic pedagogy that finds resonance with community-based anti-fascist social justice movements and to bring that knowledge into educational research and practice.

A CRITICAL CIVIC EDUCATION

The comprehensive report "Educating for Civic Reasoning & Discourse" represents both intersectionality and critical theory (Lee et al., 2021a). The monograph provides detailed analyses and recommendations that are transferable to an anti-fascist multicultural civic education. Among the many valuable practical recommendations that contribute to civic engagement for young people is the role of formal associations: "Professional organizations of educators and discipline-based educational organizations should engage in dialogue both within and across organizations to consider how they could contribute to civic learning, reasoning, and discourse across the curriculum and lifespan" (Lee et al., 2021b, p. 8). For teacher preparation and teacher professional development, the report urges researchers to "focus on investigating the opposition to discussing controversial topics . . . [which include] factors that contribute to deep oppositions and underlying principles that can facilitate stakeholders' abilities to engage in reasoning around these points of contestation" (p. 10). The conceptual framework of *Teaching Anti-Fascism* offers professional organizations, policymakers, teachers, and teacher educators a means to expand civic education to counter a discourse fixated on silencing content that far-right bullhorns declare as unacceptably controversial and divisive.

CONTESTED TERMINOLOGY

As an advance organizer, what follows are terms that I often find are contested and/or misunderstood as related to themes in this book.

Ideology

An *ideology* is a viewpoint that alone does not make political change. An ideology contributes to strategies to create a worldview in the interests of a particular governing order with specific social, political, and economic practices. An ideology exists in tension with other ideologies, although when put into practice they may overlap. Within contestations over civic education, children and adolescents become subjects of ideological conflicts. Importantly, all of us hold ideological views of the world in regard to what is just and fair.

Proto-Fascism, Fascist Politics, and the Far Right

Proto-fascism generally refers to political movements and programs that are historical predecessors to mid-20th-century fascism. I use the phrase *fascist politics* to signal the advocacy and application of one or more traits of fascism that may or may not necessarily lead to a *fascist regime*. The concept of fascist politics is similar to Ross's (2017) "fascist creep" as a "process" (p. 3) that seeps through "the porous borders between fascism and the radical right" (p. 14). The phrases *the far right* and *far-right extremism* are used as interchangeable ideological positions in this book. The far right, conservatives, and liberals each use forms of fascist politics in liberal democracies. In Part II, further differentiations are made among historical fascism, contemporary far-right extremism, and anti-fascism.

Nation and State

For our purpose, it is important to differentiate between *state* and *nation*. A nation theoretically consists of a homogeneous group of people with common origins, ethnicity, or common characteristics such as similar language, religion, and cultural practices. To become a "nation," it must strive to politically self-determine itself as a nation through common goals. *Nationalism* is generally expressed in favor of a particular group, such as what is implied with the phrase *White nationalism*. (For a more detailed analytic summary of the competing definitions of *nation* and *nationalism*, see Miscevic, 2020.)

In the literature of political theory, a state—unlike a nation—is a bounded territory that serves the aspirations and management of a nation. A multinational (or multicultural) state exists when two or more different nations (or ethnically diverse groups) exist within the state. The state, not the nation, holds legal policing power to enforce adherence for the defense and unity of its territory. Hence, a nation is not necessarily restricted to territorial boundaries as is the state and its governing institutions. Indigenous groups in North America, for example, are discrete nations, even when their respective populations find themselves divided and living in two different states due to artificial colonial borders that were created between Mexico and the United States and Canada and the United States.

In theory a *nation-state* is when a homogeneous population or nation lives within the territory of a state. Although the designation of nation-state is broadly applied around the world, rarely does a modern state consist of only one culturally homogenous population. More often, nation-states are a combination of groups representing various cultural groups or nations in what more accurately should be identified as *multicultural* or *multinational-states*. Most nation-states, however, are reluctant to officially embrace in positive and equitable actions the lived reality of diverse cultural groups within their boundaries in regard to the exercise of full citizenship rights (Banks, 2020; Vavrus, 2015).

Authoritarianism and Populism

The political concept of *authoritarianism* refers to governance that favors obedience. In this definition, support for a nation-state under authoritarian leadership eclipses individual freedom. Far-right extremism and conservatism bend toward authoritarianism under the assumption that individual liberty for their preferred group will remain secure. Central to authoritarian control is the leader's "claim that he and his agents are above the law, above judgment, and not beholden to the truth" (Ben-Ghiat, 2020a, p. 253). Authoritarianism stands in opposition to an inclusionary recognition of diversity and to equitable political participation and redistribution of material resources and opportunities. Authoritarianism taken to its most extreme form is a trait of fascism. Just as not all authoritarian governances end up becoming dictatorships, not all dictatorships are synonymous with fascism.

After WWII and the reign of fascist regimes, political space opened for *populism*. Finchelstein (2017) explains, "Populism is *an authoritarian form of democracy* that emerged originally as a postwar reformulation of fascism" (p. 98, emphasis added). Whereas the goal of fascism was elimination of the rule of law and separation of the powers of the branches of government, populists weaken and destabilize existing laws and state institutions without eradicating them. In its practices, populism of the far right selectively uses traits of fascist politics. A "*populist plutocracy*," or governance by the rich under the direct or indirect leadership of wealthy capitalists, "might more accurately describe American politics today," according to Paxton (2017, para. 17, emphasis in original). Such is the case with billionaires who fund far-right extremists, including one who has asserted that he "no longer believes that freedom and democracy are compatible" (P. Thiel, as cited in Mac & Lerer, 2022, p. A. 13; Mayer, 2016).

Prior to his political dominance, eventual fascist dictator Adolph Hitler (1927/1999) recognized how when traditions and customs merge with authoritarianism and populism, a path to power opens: "The first foundation for the creation of authority is always provided by popularity. . . . *If popularity, force, and tradition combine, an authority may be regarded as unshakeable* (p. 518, emphasis in original). Ben-Ghiat (2020a) explains that the authoritarian populist's "trick is to seem exceptional and yet to embody the national everyman, with all his endearing flaws" (p. 252).

Terrorism

In an authoritarian manner, President George W. Bush (2001–2009) framed the U.S. unilateral invasions and occupations of Afghanistan and Iraq, along with other foreign military engagements, as part of a "global war on terrorism." The standard legal response to *terrorism*, however, is to treat the perpetuators as criminals, not as military combatants waging war. U.S. law defines both domestic and international terrorism as a criminal acts that are "dangerous to human life," not as grounds to declare war (Legal Information Institute, n.d.a., para. 1a).

A key characteristic of terrorism is "the use of violence or the threat of violence by an organized group to attain political objectives" (Lutz & Lutz, 2007, p. 2). Terrorism has a very specific goal: "The victims of terrorist violence are important as a means of influencing a wider target audience" (p. 2). As retired Lieutenant General William Odom (2007) argues, "The United States has a long record of supporting terrorists and using terrorist tactics" (p. 410). Nongovernmental actors such as paramilitaries also engage in terrorism. Critics of terrorism laws, such as the U.S. 2001 PATRIOT Act and Canada's 2015 Anti-Terrorism Act, argue that these laws provide unchecked power that domestically restrict civil liberties (American Civil Liberties Union, 2021b; Canadian Civil Liberties Union, 2020). In effect, terrorism is a social construct that serves as "an interpretation of events and their presumed causes . . . [that] are not unbiased" (Turk, 2004, p. 271). Or, as an old saying goes, one person's terrorist is another person's freedom fighter (cf. Ganor, 2002).

Freedom

Freedom is one of the most fiercely contested political concepts. Depending on one's ideological orientation, the concept of *freedom* varies in meaning. The far right and conservatives believe democratic majorities threaten their freedom and property rights. This threat historically stems from a fear of democracy's potential "of the poor over the rich," the redistribution of material goods, and an expansion of political participation (A. de Dijn, as cited in Steinmetz-Jenkins, 2020, para. 15). Political historian Annelien de Dijn explains that "the idea that freedom depends on the limitation of state power was *invented by conservatives* to defend elite interests against the rise of democracy" (as cited in Steinmetz-Jenkins, 2020, para. 17, emphasis added). In other words, arguments to reduce the size of government and its state institutions in the name of freedom are essentially anti-democracy tropes.

In her comprehensive *Freedom: An Unruly History*, de Dijn (2020) further explains that this dominant historical construction of negative freedom placed an "emphasis on law rather than popular power" (p. 276). Positive freedom exists in tension with negative freedom in this "unruly history." Positive freedom or *freedom to* can necessitate public interventions for the freedom to lead a particular way of life. A relatively mild form of positive freedom is affirmative action programs or positive discrimination as reform measures that acknowledge group-based racial, gender, and ability discrimination, especially in occupational employment.

The foundations of both negative freedom and positive freedom stem from an ideology of individualism. Barring isolated exceptions, both types of freedoms or liberties commonly ignore that individuals have group identities that are part of the larger society. Berlin (1958/1969) theorized that "it is not with individual liberty, in either the 'negative' or in the 'positive' senses of the word, that desire for status and recognition can easily be identified" (p. 158). Recognition with full citizenship status as a basic freedom, for example, has historically privileged White populations over marginalized racial groups. A common shortcoming of hierarchical conceptions of freedom is found when far right, conservative, and liberal ideologies frame "the rights of groups as detrimental to the rights of the individual" (Banks, 2020, p. 129).

Instead, Berlin (1958/1969) explains that freedom is "a desire for something different: for union, closer understanding, integration of interests, *a life of common dependence* and common sacrifice" (p. 158, emphasis added). Rather than serving as a static term, freedom traverses a continuum in "the transitional space between unfreedom and freedom" through the agency of subjugated groups (Roberts, 2015, p. 15). In other words, individuals from politically subordinated groups actively pursuing their freedom are reframed as part of a vibrant, interactive whole that is rarely fixed and stationary. Freedom from this viewpoint opens the way for a plurality of interests and ways of being. Consequently, a conception of liberty that recognizes our collective dependence on one another is recast from an ideology of individualism toward an inclusive civic conception of freedom.

What follows are some common contested forms of freedom. Included are freedom of speech, hate speech, and what the far-right describes as cancel culture.

Freedom of Speech. Whereas in one setting freedom of speech may be benign, in another it may result in imprisonment. The 1791 First Amendment protects freedom of speech: "Congress shall make no law . . . abridging the freedom of speech." Supreme Court rulings make clear, however, that freedom of speech is not absolute but conditional on certain factors. The contingencies that the Court defined, clarified, and nuanced in relation to freedom of speech include settings or forums, libel and slander that defame an individual, imminent lawless action, commercial speech, obscenity, and speech advocating a crime (Legal Information Institute, n.d.b.). As Supreme Court decisions suggest, absolute First Amendment freedom of speech is not legally protected.

Nevertheless, the far right, conservatives, and liberals contend that there is a free speech crisis that impinges on their desire for absolute speech while decrying speech coming from the critical left. From the latter part of the 20th century to the present, billionaires and well-funded think tanks sounded an alarm about a perceived decline in free speech (Moskowitz, 2019). Mishra and Nguyen (2020) explain that during recent decades this manufactured crisis is an outcome of those long-silenced now speaking and writing with less mainstream censorship. Clearly, political hegemony affects the exercise of free speech: "Who can speak, who gets heard, and who makes the rules about what one can say is always about power, as much as about judgments of harm and danger" (Dabhoiwala, 2020, para. 1).

Hate Speech. As an aspect of the rise of hate crimes, *hate speech*, as defined by the American Library Association (ALA, 2021), consists of

> any form of expression through which speakers intend to vilify, humiliate, or incite hatred against a group or a class of persons on the basis of race, religion, skin color, sexual identity, gender identity, ethnicity, disability, or national origin. (para. 1)

Although the "class of persons" listed by the ALA includes those who critical multicultural educators incorporate into curricula, no legal definition of hate speech exists. Hate speech, nevertheless, can become an illegal act "when it directly incites imminent criminal activity or consists of specific threats of violence targeted against a person or group" (para. 2).

Although the far right, conservatives, and centrist liberals claim freedom of speech that may be hateful is a constitutional right, that liberty is not absolute. Unresolved, however, is where the line should be drawn between free speech and hate speech when it comes to policing. Through an in-depth investigation that documented widespread infiltration of White supremacists in police departments, law professor Vida Johnson (2019) observes that "when communities of color hear local stories of hate group affiliations or explicitly racists beliefs being shared in their local police departments, or on social media, this will also cause them to distrust police" (p. 216). The topic of racist policing and the far-right chilling effects on freedom of assembly and speech by social justice movements is further taken up in Chapter 8.

Cancel Culture. Although the concept of cancel culture has a long history, the first known use of the phrase *cancel culture* was in 2017 (Merriam-Webster, 2021). The *Merriam-Webster* (2021) dictionary defines cancel culture as "the practice or tendency of engaging in mass canceling as a way of expressing disapproval and exerting social pressure" (para. 1). In effect, cancel culture is a negative term that implies an act of public shaming. Cancel culture, however, lacks direction and in practice is "a series of spontaneous disruptions with no sequential logic, lacking any official apparatus to enact or enforce a policy or creed" (Mishan, 2020, para. 16). Cries of cancel culture attempt to deflect and minimize claims of injustices of whomever is being challenged while scapegoating and demonizing those who draw attention to histories and contemporary practices of discrimination.

When cancel culture is aimed at the powerful, they are less affected than groups seeking to overcome centuries of discrimination (Mishan, 2020). Nevertheless, former President Trump (2020) in an Independence Day speech at the iconic Mount Rushmore presidential memorial implied that cancel culture threatened the nation. He contended that the United States was "witnessing *a merciless campaign* to wipe out our history, defame our heroes, erase our values, and *indoctrinate our children*" (07:48) and that the "*political weapon is cancel culture*," comparable to "totalitarianism" and a "new far-left fascism" (09:17, 10:24, emphasis added). Despite the fact that fascism developed out of proto-fascist far-right sentiments, a common tactic of the far right and neo-fascists is to name their own ideological desires—totalitarianism and fascism—but to ascribe them to their opponents (Vials, 2014).

As often happens in attacks on multicultural education by conservatives and the far right, Trump contended that cancel culture was an attempt to silence dissent because "our children are taught in school to hate their own country" (13:54). Critiques of a master narrative of American exceptionalism should not be allowed in the public school curriculum because, according to Trump, the United States is "the most just and exceptional nation ever to exist on earth" (27:17). To this end, far-right legislators seek to cancel critical race theory based on the claim of divisiveness (Goldberg, 2021). An economic analysis finds "that the same states enacting bills under the banner of stopping critical race theory are the same states that have historically disempowered workers and today exhibit the worse racial economic disparities" (Banjerjee & Sawo, 2021, para. 5).

Far-right discourse tries to delegitimize any hint of multicultural antifascist actions in and out of schools. By engaging in a form of moral panic that singles out cancel culture, Trump and his allies divert attention "from structural injustice toward a specific ostracized group as an embodiment of evil" (Mishan, 2020, para. 20). Far-right Republicans then construct themselves as victims of cancel culture. Like Trump at Mount Rushmore, the contention is that those who advocate social justice are somehow "creating a climate of fear, preventing opponents of cancel culture from speaking out from concerns that their cancellation will surely follow" (Shephard, 2021, para. 9). During Trump's second impeachment trial, Republican Jim Jordan asserted that drawing attention to Trump's actions on the day of the 2021 far-right attack on the U.S. Capitol was a desire "to cancel the president" (House Congressional Record, 2021, "Mr. Jordan," para. 5). Somehow, the effect of cancel culture did not stop far-right Republican legislators joining Trump in trying to cancel the verified results of the 2020 presidential election.

Deep State

One narrative element of Trump's populist support among the far right was the belief that he faced a battle against a corrupt deep state. The deep state in this construction consists of business leaders and political and celebrity elites who attempt to undermine Trump's effectiveness. The deep state for the far right is part of a conspiracy that, after the Capitol riot, led to such false claims as "martial law being invoked, a mass arrest of members of Congress and the president, COVID-19 being engineered by other countries and a military takeover of the media" (Sadeghi, 2021, "Our rating," para. 1).

Underlying deep state conspiracy theories of the far right is a religious conviction that demons are infecting the body politic. President Trump's own personal spiritual advisor regularly presided over prayers in the name of Jesus Christ as a defense against demonic networks supposedly threatening Trump (Cornejo, 2019). For far-right conspiratorial Christian evangelicals, the deep state operates territorially under demonic control within the borders of the United States. Overcoming deep state evil spirits in this telling is part of far-right efforts to restrict "reproductive, queer, and trans rights, to further dismantling of protections for racial and ethnic minorities and environmental regulations, to greater dehumanisation of refugees and undocumented migrants" (O'Donnell, 2020, p. 713), all of which are significant civic issues for an anti-fascist multicultural education. For the evangelical far right, the aim of the deep state is to disempower selected identities in a pluralistic society that block authoritatively enforcing social norms compatible with a politicized Christianity.

Nevertheless, a deep state does exist, but not as constructed by far-right extremists. The deep state is not synonymous with all of government but is represented in certain state institutions. According to historian Ryan Gingeras (2010), the phrase *deep state* is a translation of the Turkish *derin develet* that described political scandals in that country in the latter part of the 20th century. Gingeras explains that the concept of a deep state "generally refers to a kind of shadow government in which unofficial or publicly unacknowledged individuals play important roles in defining and implementing state policy" (p. 152). One only needs to ponder the behind-the-scenes unchecked power of the U.S. Central Intelligence Agency to grasp one aspect of the deep state (e.g. Savage, 2022). Broadly speaking, then, the anti-democracy structures of the deep state are "a hybrid association of *key elements of government* and parts of *top level finance and industry* that is effectively able to *govern the United States with only limited reference to the consent of the governed* as normally expressed through elections" (Lofgren, 2016, p. 5, emphasis added). The behavior of U.S. border agencies detaining immigrant children is a prime example of the deep state in which unaccountable governmental entities have few restraints and public funds are privatized for profiteering corporations with multimillion-dollar contracts (Dayen, 2018).

The deep state is real and is composed of real governmental representatives in shadowy financial exchanges with private corporations. Most certainly the existence of the deep state is contrary to the ideals of a democracy. Anti-fascist movements and pedagogical exposure of opaque deep state practices can contribute to the deliberative transparency expected of a democracy.

The deep state is not a conspiracy theory. No biblical demonic source guides the deep state. The far-right version of a deep state is not about the effects on democracy. Instead, far-right rhetoric of a deep state is an anti-democracy distraction. Taken further, the far-right construction of a deep state conspiracy opens the door to attacks on judicial and legislative branches—along with educational systems—in an authoritarian effort to vest all power into a single leader in the executive branch.

OVERVIEW OF ORGANIZATION AND CONTENT OF CHAPTERS

My urgency to complete the writing of *Teaching Anti-Fascism* was accentuated by political events during 2020–2022. These developments included

- the public video of the police murder of African American George Floyd in May 2020, subsequent international protests, and a far-right backlash;
- Trump's denial of his presidential defeat in November 2020;
- the continuing effort of Trump and his Republican allies to suppress access to electoral voting and to overturn legitimate election results by nearly any means necessary;
- the January 2021 far-right attack on the U.S. Capitol;
- the far right's politically discursive wedge virulently opposing public health safety measures in the midst of a deadly pandemic; and
- a growing far-right discourse of falsehoods designed to undermine any validity of a critical civic education, a position likely to extend throughout the 2020s and beyond.

Incorporating aspects of the political turmoil of 2020–2022 into this book heightened the importance to bring to the forefront the conceptualization of a robust anti-fascist civic education.

Four parts conceptually divide this book. Part I, "Good Trouble," consists of the first two chapters. The bold actions of anti-fascist teachers from the 1940s and the false security that fascism cannot happen in the United States focuses on the interwar years (1919–1939) between World War I and World War II and contemporary fascist politics that include the 2021 far-right siege on the nation's Capitol (Chapter 2). Part II, "Unpacking Ideological Orientations," includes a qualitative typology of ideal characteristics of historical fascism (Chapter 3), contemporary far-right extremism (Chapter 4), and anti-fascism (Chapter 5). Historical and contemporary accounts complement each of the three typologies.

Part III, "Indicators of Colonial Proto-Fascism and U.S. Fascist Politics," attends to practices of colonial America and the United States. Each chapter in Part III incorporates aspects of the United Nations' (1948) internationally recognized elements of genocide. Analyzed are racist and nativist fascist politics, especially as related to the forced separation of children from their families (Chapter 6); the political economy of proto-fascist and fascist practices of land and property confiscation, with particular attention to the effects of segregation on Indigenous and Black educational and life opportunities (Chapter 7); and the fascistic violence of police and the military as fictitious guardians of public safety and how policing and militarism seeps into public schools (Chapter 8).

In Part IV, "An Anti-Fascist 'Reading the World,'" the final two chapters are organized around Paulo Freire's (1970, 1985) critical consciousness for an anti-fascist civic education. Provided in this Freirean civic context of reading the world are anti-fascist multicultural assessment rubrics for teacher education programs (Chapter 9), along with recommended introductory readings correlated with each of the previous nine chapters for further exploration (Chapter 10). A primary purpose of Part IV is to emphasize that the space and time that we currently inhabit provides critical conditions for a transition toward a more hopeful and engaged transformative civic education.

BRIDGING THE GAP BETWEEN COMMUNITY-BASED ANTI-FASCISTS AND SCHOOLS

The separation between community-based anti-fascists and educational institutions can be closed by policymakers, educators, and students. A knowledge base in anti-fascism can help educators conceptually incorporate this countermovement into curricular efforts that seek to resist far-right political oppression in and out of schools. This research is appropriate for policymakers and educators given that after the police killing of George Floyd and far-right siege on the Capitol, teachers wondered how to talk to their students, if at all, about the significance of these politically volatile events (e.g., Ferlazzo, 2020; Nierenberg, 2021a, 2021b). Both occurrences were in the context of publicly raised questions throughout Trump's presidency as to what constitutes fascism in our current historical era, along with what would be appropriate responses (e.g., Gawthorpe, 2019).

The social context of schooling is not insulated from undemocratic forces and too often is reflective of those influences. To counter repression of civic reasoning, educators can incorporate an anti-fascist multicultural pedagogy across the curriculum. *Teaching Anti-Fascism* offers a "curriculum of insurgency [that] aims to provide learners the opportunity and space to engage in concepts related to oppression and liberation and make sense of them relative to their own lives" (Au, 2021, p. 118). Collectively, critically minded educators can serve as a bridge between community-based anti-fascists and the design of curricular approaches as what it means to be everyday anti-fascists inside the educational establishment. Going forward, the anti-fascist background introduced throughout this book offers an emergent conceptual framework for educational practitioners and scholars to use, modify, and build on that will not be soft on fascism.

CHAPTER 2

"It Can't Happen Here"
Fascist Politics in America

His behavior during imprisonment convinced the authorities that, like his political organization…[Hitler] was no longer to be feared. It is believed he will retire to private life and to Austria, the country of his birth.

—"Hitler Tamed by Prison," *New York Times*, 1924

Although the descriptors *fascism* and *fascist* generally evoke the specter of 20th-century Nazi Germany and fascist Italy of the 1930s and 1940s, the United States was not immune from pro-fascist advocacy and practices during those years. In the midst of the Great Depression and sensing the political winds of fascist sympathies in the United States, Sinclair Lewis (1935/1970) captured the threatening zeitgeist of his day. Lewis's novel presented a dystopian nation that had slipped into a homegrown version of fascism. Lewis's liberal journalist character finds himself self-censoring for fear of far-right reprisals and consoled his readers in the belief that after the election of a fascistic president "[t]he hysteria can't last" (p. 132). Despite the outcome of ensuing fascist politics, the journalist remained in disbelief about the new president: "The one thing that most perplexed him was that there could be a dictator seemingly so different from the fervent Hitlers and gesticulating Fascists . . .; a dictator with something of the earthy American sense of humor" (p. 132). The novel's journalist continued to privately express his belief, "*It can't happen here*" (p. 132, emphasis in original).

In 1939 New York City's Madison Square Garden hosted a rally of over 22,000 pro-Nazi supporters (Bernard, 2018). The year before that event, President Franklin Roosevelt expressed alarm over the disproportionate political power of monopoly capitalism by stating

that the liberty of a democracy is not safe if the people tolerate the growth of private power to a point where it becomes stronger than their democratic state. *That, in essence, is Fascism*—ownership of the Government by an individual, by a group, or by any other controlling private power. (as cited in Roberto, 2018, p. 347, emphasis added)

Roosevelt was not only disturbed over fascist politics on display in public gatherings and street violence of Nazi sympathizers; his administration also warned of fascist support coming from big business.

Nevertheless, in the midst of WWII Roosevelt issued his infamous 1942 executive order to detain 120,000 innocent U.S. residents of Japanese descent in inhospitable internment camps. This racially identified population experienced dispossession of nearly all of their personal property and constitutional rights despite the Fifth Amendment promise that no one will be "deprived of life, liberty or property without due process of law" (Frail, 2017; Takami, 1998). Six years earlier in 1936, a racially encapsulated Roosevelt had already foreshadowed the fascist notion that any Japanese individual who presented a perceived security threat should "be placed on a special list of those who would be the first to be placed in a *concentration camp* in the event of trouble" (as cited in Office of Naval Intelligence, 2020, para. 1, emphasis added). Supreme Court decisions during that era did not overturn Roosevelt's order that led to prison terms for Japanese Americans who resisted internment orders. The Court ominously let stand the possibility of future group detentions without the constitutional right of due process despite the fact that no Japanese Americans were ever found guilty of treason or sedition.

During this contested politically unstable time, a new progressive civic education developed in an anti-racist fight against fascism.

ANTI-FASCIST INTERCULTURAL CIVIC EDUCATION

Civic education during the rise of fascism in the 1930s was reconstructed to prominently highlight anti-racism "to bolster and protect democratic norms" (Beadie & Burkholder, 2021, p. 133). Anti-racism was now more widely acknowledged as a curricular necessity in the anti-fascist battle. During this politically volatile era and in the midst of World War II, the New York City Teachers Union expressed support for a principal's decision to deny a high school diploma to any student participating in racist activities. The Teachers Union (TU) explained that racism was "a *fascist weapon* with which the enemy planned to conquer the world" (as cited in Taylor, 2011, p. 17, emphasis added). Black teachers in racially segregated schools were already teaching "Negro history" but boldly expanded their pedagogy "[b]y contextualizing the *American battle against White supremacy as part of the global struggle against fascism*" (Beadie & Burkholder, 2021, p. 133, emphasis added).

During the height of fascism, the New York City TU did not hesitate to name fascism as encompassing both racism and anti-Semitism. The new intercultural education movement of the 1930s and 1940s found resonance with the TU. Intercultural education was "grounded in the value of cooperation, respect, and acceptance of others" and reflected an educational commitment in and out of schools to reduce "intergroup tensions, prejudice, and discrimination directed toward immigrant and racial and ethnic minorities" (C.A.M. Banks, 2012, p. 2239). In 1938 *The New York Times* praised the positive contribution of 7 years of intercultural education in 40 communities that reached an estimated 25,000 high school students. Intercultural education "proved a potent force in removing many of the popular misconceptions" of negativity and inhospitality toward racial and cultural differences (Fine, 1938). Teacher educators now had access to new curricular materials from the burgeoning intercultural movement (Beadie & Burkholder, 2021). Intercultural education provided the TU with a conceptual basis to create curriculum and instruction focused on "bigotry in the schools and community" (Taylor, 2011, p. 20). Along with other educators across the United States following the call of intercultural education, the TU framed its new curricular approach as a means to unify the nation's racial and ethnic diversity. A common thread in intercultural education was "the centrality of democratic values" (C.A.M. Banks, 2012, p. 2244). The TU aspired to broaden formal and popular education by incorporating global awareness or "world mindedness" (as cited in Taylor, 2011, p. 23), a contemporary citizenship and civic education position of multicultural education (Banks, 2020).

In contrast to the TU, the pro-fascist curricular pedagogy of the American Education Association (AEA) and individual educators within the city's public schools engaged in anti-Black and anti-Jewish discourse (Taylor, 2011). The sentiments of the AEA were prevalent across a significant swath of White-dominated towns whose populations in early decades of the 20th century had participated in extralegal violent "waves of ethnic cleansing across the United States" (Loewen, 2005, p. 23). For Black teachers in the segregated Jim Crow South who employed an anti-racist pedagogy, according to a college professor in 1938, an anti-fascist stance based on existing racism was "like sitting on a ton of dynamite" (M. Eppse, as cited in Beadie & Burkholder, 2021, p. 134).

The TU understood that fascist politics were inherently opposed to democracy. Comprised of politically left educators, the TU in its capacity as the largest teacher union in New York City framed racism and anti-Semitism as unpatriotic and anti-American. The TU explained, "It is against our own national interests, against our own safety to permit acts of violence against any minority group to pass unnoticed and unpunished" (as cited in Taylor, 2011, p. 17).

NEO-FASCISM AND FAR-RIGHT EXTREMISM

After WWII and the military defeat of fascist regimes, international condemnation to overt support of fascism diminished. Although the far right distanced itself from widespread public negativity associated with fascism, forms of neo-fascism arose after 1945. Neo-fascists generally dropped references to fascism as they sought to attain public support that had dwindled in war-torn Europe.

The term *neo-fascism* emerged in Europe. Technically it applies to the sentiments of those who aligned themselves with fascism during the interwar years between WWI and WWII. They resented defeat at the hands of the

Allied forces, refused to lay down arms at the end of WWII, and participated in clandestine terrorism. The anti-communism stance of neo-fascists provided mainstream tacit acceptance of their presence. In the United States "military and secret services shielded numerous Nazi and fascist criminals after the war, and enrolled them as soldiers and spies in the war against communism" (Cento Bull, 2009, p. 592). Neo-fascists downplayed or simply denied that mass exterminations had taken place by fascist regimes while continuing to spew anti-Semitism as the root cause of social problems.

Fascist activists surfaced in relatively small groups in Europe and in the United States in the 1950s and 1960s (Chin, 2017; Simonelli, 1995; Thompson, 2010). Unknown to the general public, however, was that the United States began covertly recruiting and handsomely paying "former Nazis and right-wing terrorists" for service in the Central Intelligence Agency during its nascency in the early 1950s (Ganser, 2005 p. 70; see also Kinzer, 2013). From the late 1970s through the 1990s White nationalists with attitudes of anti-Jewishness visibly engaged in fascist politics, often in the form of "domestic terrorism" (Kelley, 2020, p. 20; Moore & Tracy, 2020). Europe and the United States witnessed a more visible rise in far-right and fascist politics during the presidency of Barack Obama (2008–2016), the first U.S. president identified as Black (Finchelstein, 2017; Vavrus, 2015).

Post-WWII Mainstreaming of Fascist Politics in the United States

Post-WWII expressions of fascist politics by the far right clarify the centrality of fascistic elements that regularly surface in the United States. Examples of the mainstreaming of fascist politics include the late 1940s repression of progressive labor unions; Congressional hearings in the 1950s purging and ostracizing of political leftists as "un-American"; the 1960s–1970s rise of the conspiratorial anti-communism and anti-Jewish John Birch Society; the Republican's 1964 presidential nominee of far-right Senator Barry Goldwater whom future presidents Richard Nixon (1969–1974) and Ronald Reagan (1981–1989) actively supported; and the 1968 third-party presidential candidate George Wallace's anti-intellectualism and dog-whistling racism through virulent "law and order" themes—all presaging the growing rise of the far right in the 21st century. Unabated throughout the post-WWII era and into our current historical moment, the far right continues (a) to align with White supremacists against civil rights activists and Jewish communities; (b) to find allies in evangelical Christian-orchestrated patriarchal aggression toward sexual minorities; (c) to harass and physically attack women and their medical providers for accessing reproductive services; and (d) to denigrate and harm educators who incorporate multicultural and ethnic studies in their schools (Hanebrink, 2018; Huntington, 2004; Lepore, 2018; Lyons, 2018; Moore & Tracy, 2020; National Education Association, 1975/1991; Ripley, 1967; Robin, 2011; Schwartz, 2021).

Is This Fascism?

In the midst of public displays of fascist symbols, violent militias, and far-right political enactment of intolerant policies, questions arose as to the extent such actions represented a 21st-century form of fascism. During the 2020 protests over the widespread lack of accountability for police brutality, a *New York Times* headline observed "Use of 'Fascism' Takes a New Turn" with a subheading explaining "A shift is afoot as word thought to be alarmist gains popularity" (Szalai, 2020, p. C1). Ambiguity about fascism is particularly evident in efforts to differentiate among various ideological orientations and their respective political and cultural goals (Gawthorpe, 2019; Renton, 2019). Decades earlier Payne (1983) speculated as to why misunderstandings exist around the term *fascism*:

> Much of the confusion and ambiguity surrounding the interpretation of fascist movements stems from the fact that only in a few instances did they succeed in passing to the stage of governmental participation, and only in the case of Germany were the full implications of a fascist doctrine—in the form of its most radical variant—carried out by a regime in power. (p. 9)

Today the concept of fascism remains as a source of "confusion and ambiguity" with conflicting interpretations, most certainly for young people, the public, and many educators.

FAR-RIGHT BACKLASH AGAINST PROTESTS AND LOSS OF THE PRESIDENCY

In 2020 millions of people representative of all racial identities, ethnicities, genders, and social classes in the United States and much of the world took to the streets for weeks of protests after a video circulated globally of the blatant killing of a defenseless Black man by a police officer. Much like the New York City Teachers Union warning three quarters of a century earlier about acts of violence that historically go unpunished, protesters collectively pressed for radical reform of police departments and prosecution of police who use excessive force. President Donald Trump responded to these calls from protestors by encouraging federal law enforcement to use tear gas, pepper spray capsules, rubber bullets, and flash bombs to disperse those assembled outside the White House in the nation's capital and by declaring that he was "your president of law and order" (as cited in Liptak & Westwood, 2020, para 1).

Trump's rhetorical dog whistles and actions that the U.S. Attorney General supported all served to condone segments of police forces and White nationalists intimidating, disrupting, and harming peaceful protesters and journalists (Noor, 2020; Shortell, 2020; Wilson, 2020; cf. Reporters Without Borders, 2021). During Trump's 2015 electoral campaign and throughout his presidency, *fascism* and *fascist* were descriptors that commentators and activists had already ascribed to the president and his political supporters (Stanley, 2018; West, 2016). With the sustained protests of the mid-2020s against police violence and racism, many questioned whether *fascist* was a valid way to describe Trump and his domestic allies (Tharoor, 2020).

Denial of Election Outcome and the Capitol Siege

Lame-duck President Trump insisted that election results were fraudulent and continued to falsely repeat that he had won the 2020 election (Pape & Ruby, 2021; Trump, 2021; Palmer, 2022). On January 6, 2021, in Washington, DC, Trump (2020) roused a far-right gathering with the declaration that *"if you don't fight like hell, you're not going to have a country anymore"* (para. 251, emphasis added). President Trump addressed in person an estimated 8,000 of his loyalists in attendance for a rally to emulate "a boxer" to "fight much harder" (para. 51). While continuing to profess unsubstantiated claims of voter fraud, Trump added, "When you catch somebody in a fraud, *you are allowed to go by very different rules*" (para. 200, emphasis added). In his closing remarks to the crowd staged near the White House, Trump told the crowd that, despite no permit to do so at the time, "we're going to the Capitol. . . . So let's walk down Pennsylvania Avenue" (para. 254). Trump assured the gathering that he would be joining them in their march to the Capitol. Moments later on the day the U.S. Congress was scheduled to confirm the election of Joe Biden as U.S. president, both armed and unarmed rightwing extremists broke into the U.S. Capitol and terrorized legislators and staff, hereafter referred to as the *Capitol siege*. Trump in fact did not join his true believers but watched the chaos unfold from the comfort of his White House office (Rucker et al., 2021).

Second Presidential Impeachment

For a second time, Trump was impeached. The grounds for an unprecedented second impeachment of a president was "incitement of insurrection" (House Congressional Record, 2021). The U.S. Senate ended up voting not to impeach for a second time. Senator Susan Collins, considered a moderate Republican, was among those who voted for acquittal. Like the naïve liberalism of Lewis's 1935 cowered journalist, Collins avoided offending Trump and claimed, "I believe that he will be much more cautious in the future" (as cited in Bowden, 2021, para. 4). Six months after his impeachment trial the presidentially defeated Trump apparently had not learned "a pretty big lesson" that Senator Collins predicted (para. 3). On national television Trump lied about the violent far-right Capitol rioters: "These were peaceful people, these were great people . . . the love in the air, I've never seen anything like it" (as cited in Cohen, 2021, para. 2, 7). During the same broadcast he reinforced the ludicrous narrative circulated among his Republican and far-right media supporters that falsely claimed that the Democrats "are the ones that were responsible" for the Capitol siege, not Trump and his fascistic incitement of the crowd (para. 14).

The takeover of the U.S. Capitol by violent far-right extremists that resulted in shutting down Congress was telling by the support of 60% of the 249 Congressional Republicans. They augmented Trump's claim of voter fraud and both directly and indirectly gave paramilitary groups justification for terrorism and vigilantism (Bump, 2021). The scenes of the ineffectiveness of the security forces in stopping a coup d'état—commonly defined as the removal of an existing government from power, usually through violent, illegal, and unconstitutional means—were also revealing (see Cochrane, 2021). Observers have pointedly questioned whether preparation and support of the Capitol security forces would have been so passive if the terrorists had instead been predominately Brown and Black rather than White—unlikely, based on a reading of U.S. history and our current historical moment of police violence against the Black Lives Matter social justice movement (Capps, 2021). Meanwhile, one Congressional Democrat who directly experienced the Capitol onslaught stated, "What I saw in front of me was basically *homegrown fascism*, out of control" (J. McGovern, as cited in Reeves et al., 2021, para. 7, emphasis added).

The demographics of the participants in the Capitol siege did not fully align with far-right extremists identified for most of the 2010s. In fact, the base of far-right extremists' willingness to engage in violence had increased. Robert Pape and Kevin Ruby (2021), lead researchers for the Chicago Project on Security & Threats, analyzed over 1,500 documents to determine the demographics on the first 377 individuals criminally charged as part of the Capitol siege. Pape and Ruby emphasized, "*Storming the US Capitol was an act of political violence,* not merely vandalism or trespassing for other purposes" (p. 29, emphasis added).

Of those arrested within the first 2 months after the Capitol siege, 87% had no affiliation with far-right groups. Business owners and professionals in white-color jobs such as health care and law constituted 43% of those arrested (Frankel, 2021; Pape & Ruby, 2021). White people represented 94% of the rioters and females 16%, the latter an increase over the previous decade of far-right women arrested. For individuals facing charges from the Capitol siege, approximately 60% had some sort of financial difficulties, "including bankruptcies, notices of eviction or foreclosure, bad debts, or unpaid taxes over the past two decades" (Frankel, 2021, para. 4). Defendants had a bankruptcy rate of 18%, nearly double that of the general public, although just 9% were unemployed (Frankel, 2021; Pape & Ruby, 2021).

By the time of the Capitol siege, Pape and Ruby's (2021) analysis indicated, "'Normal' pro-Trump activists joined with the far right to form *a new kind of violent mass movement*" (p. 13, emphasis added). Trump's far-right "grievance politics" of Whites as "undeserving victims" resonated with his followers, especially in the belief that Trump would rescue them from their plights (Frankel, 2021, para. 7–8). Those arrested made clear they were acting because Trump as their trusted charismatic leader encouraged his base to come to Washington, DC, for a "Save America" rally in response to their grievances, like an arrested woman who defended herself by explaining that she was simply "answering the call of my president" (as cited in Pape & Ruby, 2021, p. 30). Overall, nearly 15% of the defendants of the Capitol siege were current and former law enforcement officers as well as military veterans and active service members (NPR Staff, 2021). Equally telling were the 147 Congressional Republicans who joined Trump's far-right conspiratorial bandwagon and *still voted after the Capitol siege to overturn the certified election results* of Joe Biden as the newly elected U.S. president (Yourish et al., 2021).

Only 27% of all Republicans polled shortly after the Capitol siege considered the violence a threat to democracy; 93% of Democrats did. In regard to the storming of the Capitol, 45% of Republicans supported the actions of the far-right rioters (Smith et al., 2021). These percentages reveal a common pattern. When significant numbers of Congressional Republicans and their voters demonstrate support for far-right extremism and have followers commit to undemocratic and violent methods to skew politics toward their direction, the far right no longer just consists of fringe groups and individuals from previous decades. Instead, the far right is positioned as a potent force in electoral politics in the decade of the 2020s and beyond. Indicative of this fascistic trend are far-right legislative candidates and incumbents groveling at the financial trough of more than $100 million, which Trump already had on hand in just 6 months after leaving the White House (Stanley-Becker & Narayanswamy, 2021). And 1 year after the Capitol siege by Trump supporters, the Republican National Committee chairwomen contended that the far-right rioters simply engaged in "legitimate political discourse" (as cited in Dawsey & Sonmez, 2022, para. 3).

EDUCATIONAL DISCONNECT FROM CONTEMPORARY ANTI-FASCISM

As noted in Chapter 1, a review of professional educational journals and books points to a general absence of research on the civic effects of fascist politics on curriculum and instruction policies and practices and the alternative of anti-fascism. A primary aim of *Teaching Anti-Fascism* is to reclaim the anti-fascist curricular orientation that the New York City Teachers Union and segregated Black educators incorporated into intercultural education in the 1940s. Critical multicultural education in the 21st century is positioned to expand on that earlier work of courageous educators by broadening civic reasoning to incorporate anti-fascist actions that informed students can take.

The interdisciplinary foundations of critical multicultural education are appropriate for inclusion of scholarly studies of fascism and anti-fascism. An anti-fascist conceptual framework extends to multicultural education across the curriculum—much in the same way the TU encouraged all academic disciplines to develop subject matter–specific lessons because the "spirit of democracy should permeate every classroom at all times" (as cited in Taylor, 2011, p. 24). Studies of fascist politics and anti-fascist responses hold the potential to function as a basis for civic education. An anti-fascist pedagogy can help young people understand their social, economic, and cultural landscape of policies and practices that both promote and harm the well-being of marginalized groups.

Fundamentally, the anti-racism of multicultural education is inseparable from overall goals of anti-fascism. As I have found in my own teaching experience, an anti-fascist civic education contributes to student recognition of racism and other types of discrimination that are fostered under the goals of fascism. During the past 40 years, the anti-racism foundation of multicultural education has broadened its scope to attend to such biases as those based on gender, sexuality, religion, language, national origins, and ability (J. A. Banks, 2012), all of which are subject to the prejudicial discourse of fascist politics. Multicultural educators can assist teachers in providing a conceptual foundation for a civic pedagogy that differentiates among fascist, far-right, and anti-fascist ideologies. Teaching anti-fascism extrapolates the effects that ideological differences have on aspirations for a fully realized democracy.

Hesitancy in applying the terms *fascism* and *fascist* to any individual or group is the legacy of liberal democracies. They did not produce a totalizing fascist dictatorship as witnessed from the 1920s through World War II in Italy and Germany. Despite *The New York Times*'s 1924 prediction in this chapter's epigraph that Hitler would simply disappear from politics, Lewis's 1935 liberal journalist's belief that the fascism could not take root in the United States, and Senator Collins's misplaced assumption that Trump would no longer incite far-right extremism, prominent proponents of fascist politics do not easily fade away if at all. Instead, a far-right ideology is deeply inscribed in the body politic of governments professing to carry the mantle of liberal democracy.

Multicultural educators draw on a point made by a spokeswoman in the 1930s for anti-fascist intercultural education: "Although the school cannot solve the problem alone, it might well take the lead because it is the only institution which is the common meeting ground of all our varieties of cultures" (R. Davis-Dubois, as cited in Fine, 1938, "To Give Factual Information," para. 4). Schools can be reclaimed as anti-fascist zones to advance teaching and learning for civic engagement and stem the tide of fascistic educational absolutism. Today is not the time to necessarily imagine that the fascist politics of the far right are going to miraculously disappear. We live in a 21st-century historical moment where educators and policymakers have an opportunity to incorporate anti-fascism into a critical multicultural pedagogy for civic engagement.

Part II

UNPACKING IDEOLOGICAL ORIENTATIONS

This section provides conceptual foundations for three key ideologies and their practices: historical fascism, contemporary far-right extremism, and anti-fascism. Presented for each of the three viewpoints is a qualitative typology of ideal or common traits and characteristics that support the design of a critical multicultural pedagogy for civic engagement. Chapters include origins, histories, politics, and economics of each of the ideologies in their cultural contexts.

CHAPTER 3

Historical Foundations of Fascist Politics

In no case was an actual revolution against constituted authority launched; fascist tactics were invariably those of a sham rebellion arranged with the tacit approval of the authorities who pretended to be overwhelmed by force.

—Karl Polanyi, *The Great Transformation,* 1944/2001

The dominant political ideology of the late 19th century was a belief in an unregulated economy guided not by humans but by capitalism's misappropriation of Adam Smith's (1776/2001) "invisible hand" of the market (p. 593). Classical economic interpretations of Smith's metaphysical "invisible hand" assumed that capitalism served the best interests of a society. Under a capitalistic market economy, however, economic inequality ballooned. Political disenchantment with conditions of governance became the norm for the vast majority of people. Liberal democracies failed to respond to a rising desperation among groups seeking solutions. In his now classic work of historical sociology, Karl Polanyi (1944/2001) noted that during the relative economic boom of the 1920s, "capitalism was proclaimed restored" (p. 251). Nevertheless, most of Europe was still reeling from WWI and its economic and political aftershocks—conditions that already by 1919 "made possible the invention of fascism" (Paxton, 2004, p. 550). During this relatively chaotic period, the exuberance of an unregulated market economy was short lived with the 1929 stock market crash and the onset of the Great Depression of the 1930s. Although Mussolini had already coined the term *fascismo* by 1919 for his small band of disillusioned former WWI soldiers, the collapse of economies globally and the inability of liberal democracies to provide concrete solutions was what opened the door for fascism to emerge as a competitive solution for the ills of society (Payne, 1995; Polanyi, 1944/2001).

Concurrently, the Bolshevik Revolution in Russia labeled itself as a communist alternative to capitalist production and inequality, creating alarms within the dominant political classes across Europe and the United States. Mass mobilization had previously come from the left but not until after WWI did the proto-fascism of the far right find political space to operate. Paxton (2009) explains that "the war revealed the incapacity of liberal solutions (elections, the market, the school) no less than the classical conservative solutions (paternalism, religion, deference [to authority], a passive citizenry) to the problems posed by total war and its aftermath" (p. 550). Leaders wedded to capitalism were more concerned with the spread of a communist ideology of equality and equitable distribution of a society's material resources than with the rise of fascism.

But what is fascism? As noted in the opening chapters, contemporary debates surround terminology associated with fascism. Payne (1995) calls attention to how a familiarity of the term *fascism* is problematic: "Everyone is sure they know what fascism is" (p. 9). Over time, Payne continues, popular culture came to associate fascism with newsreels of the past:

> The most self-consciously visual of all political forms, fascism presents itself to us in vivid primary images: a chauvinist demagogue haranguing an ecstatic crowd; disciplined ranks of marching youths; colored-shirted militants beating up members of some demonized minority; surprise invasions at dawn; and fit soldiers parading through a captured city. (p. 9)

This description, however, does not capture the composite of traits that comprise fascism: "Beyond these familiar images, on closer inspection, fascist reality becomes more complicated" (p. 9). Morris (2016), for example, observes a "gaping hole" in curriculum studies because "discussions of fascism—in education—do not take into account the historicity of the term [fascism], nor do critical theorists cite historians who work in what is called fascist studies" (p. 268). For the field of curriculum studies Morris cautions that a reductionist search for *the* core of fascism can lose the complexity of this ideology and can obliterate differences among fascist regimes.

No consensus exists for precise characteristics of fascism, let alone a common definition. Scholars offer detailed descriptions while resisting efforts to simplify fascism down to a single key trait or characteristic. If, for instance, we consider for a moment what constitutes "democracy," we may find a succinct dictionary definition but with a deeper investigation discover contention on what exactly constitutes a democracy (cf. Christiano, 2018). Because the same applies to fascism, this chapter does not attempt to minimize nor simplify the complexities of fascism.

Prominent researcher of fascism Roger Griffin (2018), who claims to have identified *the* most important characteristic of fascism, realizes, "There can be no objective, purely empirical, uncontentious definition of 'fascism'" (p. 127). Instead, identification of characteristic types that constitute fascism is most commonly used by scholars, even Griffin. Still, "very short" introductions to studies of fascism can be 150 pages or more of text (e.g., Griffin, 2018; Passmore, 2002) whereas full explorations of fascism can run from 300 pages to over 500 (e.g., Payne, 1995; Paxton, 2004). The aim of this chapter, therefore, is not to cover fascism in all its manifestations. Instead, based on a synthesis of research by scholars who extensively analyze the nature and substance of fascism, the chapter provides traits found most significant as a basic grounding in historical fascism. Identified common characteristics of historical fascism are foundational to multicultural educational studies of anti-fascism in contemporary politics and citizenship education.

Payne (1995) humbly points to the near impossibility to find a definitive definition of fascism's ideal traits: "Any definition of common characteristics of fascist movements must be used with great care, for fascist movements differed from each other as significantly as they held notable new features in common" (p. 4). It is the "features in common" that this chapter identifies while acknowledging that what follows is "an indication of the chief characteristics that [fascist regimes] shared which distinguish them (in most respects but not absolutely) from other kinds of political forces" (p. 4).

Scholars such as Renton (2019) differentiate a *fascist regime* from *fascist politics* of the contemporary far right, the latter defined by an advocacy and application of one or more traits of fascism. The most prominent historical examples of fascist regimes are Italy and Germany during the 1920s and into the 1940s. From those two cases, studies of fascism extract specific descriptive characteristics of the politics of fascism. A false equivalency is created, however, if we equate a singular characteristic of fascist politics with a fascist regime. The term *fascism* is equivalent to a fascist regime and represents an ideological movement that underlies particular governing systems. In other words, liberalism, conservativism, and the far right can employ fascist politics without necessarily being representative of the totality of fascism or a fascist regime.

To study fascism requires us to consider prominent characteristics of fascist politics as *ideal types* that, taken together, compose fascism. Payne (1995) adds the caveat that identifying ideal characteristic types of fascism helps to "underscore the historical uniqueness of fascism" (p. 465). A *typology* of fascism or any other phenomenon in search of common traits serves methodologically as a "way of describing groups of respondents displaying different clusters of behaviours, attitudes or views of the world" (Association of Qualitative Research, 2013, para. 1). The ideological characteristics in typologies signal interpretations about human nature, society, justice, fairness, and the common good. A typology of fascist characteristics that follows next provides an accessible way to grasp the scope of historical fascism in practice.

COMPOSITE OF HISTORICAL CHARACTERISTICS OF FASCISM

Conceptualizing fascism as a relational web of characteristics is a first step in addressing the complexities of fascist ideology. In such a network we begin to see discourse indicative of fascist politics. Ideologies across the political spectrum—most prominently far-right extremism and authoritarian

Figure 3.1. Composite of Key Historical Traits of Fascism

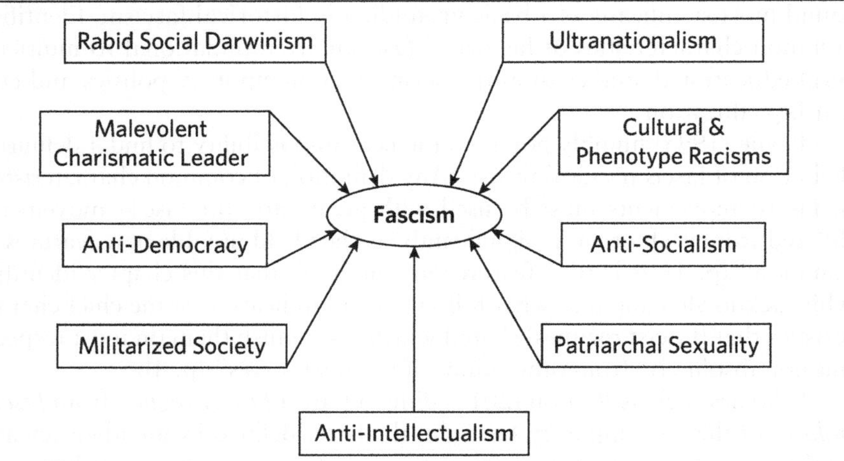

conservatism—that have advocated forms of fascist politics have only in a few instances led to a full-scale fascist regime (Passmore, 2002). Efforts to design a critical anti-fascist civic education fall short without a familiarity with the interlocking traits of fascism.

To explore the concept of historical fascism, nine key characteristics are identified and described based on a synthesis of representative studies of the ideology and practices of historical fascism. These traits include (a) a rabid form of social Darwinism; (b) an extreme form of nationalism or ultranationalism; (c) the malevolent charismatic leader as the embodiment of "truth"; (d) anti-democracy; (e) patriarchal sexuality and its attendant anti-feminism and intolerance of sexual minorities; (f) anti-intellectualism and educational absolutism; (g) centrality of phenotype and cultural racist scapegoating; (h) anti-socialism and pro-capitalism; (i) and a militarized society.

With arrows pointing to "Fascism," Figure 3.1 is an array of fascist characteristics that, *taken together*, compose fascism. Each of these traits contained seeds of structural and physical violence.

The following sections provide overviews of each of these traits. The purpose is to provide policymakers, educators, and students foundational descriptions of ideal fascist characteristics to incorporate into a critical multicultural pedagogy for civic reasoning and discourse.

RABID SOCIAL DARWINISM

During the 19th century, conservatives borrowed Darwin's *biological* theory of evolution and applied it *socially* to diverse cultures of the world. The Englishman Herbert Spencer (1864) appropriated Darwin's notion of natural selection or "the survival of the fittest" and applied it to racialized human populations as evidence that a difference in physiological structures of "the civilized races, as contrasted with the savage races" determined competence, ability, and cultural attainment (p. 455). Passmore (2009) helps us comprehend this ideological phenomena:

> The novelty of late nineteenth-century racism lay less in the notion of race as a scientific fact than in its marriage with Darwin's theory of natural selection, and in the development of racial *policies*. . . . As liberalism and nationalism shifted to the right and as conservatives overcame . . . their religious objections to evolution, social Darwinism developed a right-wing version. (p. 19, emphasis in original)

The invention of social Darwinism provided an explanation, although clearly unscientific, as to why some people are rich and others are poor as well as why some people are "fit" to govern and others are not.

For the extent of fascism's embrace of social Darwinism, the descriptor *rabid* applies. A basic definition of rabid is "furious, raging; wildly aggressive or violent . . . extreme, fanatical" (Oxford English Dictionary, 2021). Rabid social Darwinism permeated all aspects of fascist discourse and was extremely inhumane. Nazi Germany, for example, presented social Darwinism as "the Right of the Stronger" and as a "scientific given . . . in relation to human individuals and collectivities (races, people)" (Winau, 1997, p. 879). Although proto-fascist German scientists popularized social Darwinism, the Nazis took social Darwinism to its extreme through a fanatical program of eugenics or "'culling out' bad hereditary material" through "forced sterilization . . . , the murder of the mentally ill . . . , and the murder, during the course of the Final Solution, of Jews and other groups perceived as racially inferior" (p. 879).

Under social Darwinism, society's outsiders were lazy. In contrast, privileged groups were said to be hard workers. Ideologically, rabid social Darwinism of fascism framed citizenship as the duty to work, not for one's own personal gain but for a mythic nation-building project. In other words, the message to the working class was that the nation was superior to any of their economic interests. In *How Fascism Works* Jason Stanley (2018) explains, "It is the social Darwinist conception of individual worth that gives structure to fascist hierarchy and explains the charge of laziness. Groups are ordered, in fascism, by their capacity to achieve, to rise above others, in labor and wars" (p. 178). In their methodical suppression of independent labor organizations, the Nazi Party went so far as to claim that they were actually the workers' party (Paxton, 2004). Above the entrance way of two concentration camps for forced laborers, the Germans posted signs that ironically read "*Arbeit macht frei*," translated as "work shall make you free." The ultimate outcome of rabid social Darwinism's version of "work" in the camps was genocide that eventually numbered in the millions of victims—all justified by the siren call of ultranationalism.

ULTRANATIONALISM

One of the most common characteristics that most scholars generally agree on is the type of nationalistic sentiments promoted by fascists: *ultranationalism*. Ultranationalism represents an extreme form of nationalism entailing a glorified *mythic history* of the nation (Griffin, 2018; Passmore, 2002; Stanley, 2018). For fascists, myth is "held to be true not as existing empirical fact" but as a benchmark corrective of a perceived decline in the moral fiber of the essence of the nation (Payne, 1995, p. 215). To regain what is imagined lost requires, according to fascist ideology, a rebirthing of the nation anew and purified.

During the interwar years fascists repeatedly pointed out that a source of the problems of the nation was the weakness of existing state institutions that block the aspirations of ultranationalism. In the process of seeking the mythic nation, the existing state must be removed by revolutionary means and replaced with a state apparatus supportive of the new nation, the fascist nation. An aim of the revolutionary state is reversing the humiliation of a victimized nation, the majority population (Paxton, 2004; Stanley, 2018). A detailed political platform is absent as to what fascism might look like in practice beyond the cultural glorification of a dominant racialized group and militarized territorial security and expansion. Fascist supporters accept that the goals of fascism will be "realized in the future" (Payne, 1995, p. 215). In its resistance to a redistribution of wealth to help alleviate economic inequality, "the transformation which fascism offers its supporters is no more than cultural or spiritual" (Renton, 2019, p. 17).

This extreme form of nationalism places limitations on which population groups constitute the renewed nation. Idealized is a folk image of fictitious wholesome representatives of the nation expressed as "rural nostalgia" despite fascism's modernist use of advanced technology and the eventual neglect of priorities of struggling rural residents (Payne, 1995, p. 12). The romanticized rural purity trope contrasts with perceived urban decadence and genetically tainted populations associated with cosmopolitanism. For fascists, certain ethnic and racial groups, sexual minorities, and people with mental or physical limitations contaminated the purity of the nation and were, therefore, undeserving of basic civil rights of a civilian.

MALEVOLENT CHARISMATIC LEADER

Fascism required an alluring, charismatic leader who represented an ultranationalist vision as the savior of the nation. The fascist leader successfully appealed emotionally to his supporters while disregarding reasoning and credible logic while presenting himself as the valid source of "truth." Under a narrative of crisis, the fascist leader took actions in the name of all the impurities that hindered the nation, including the removal of certain racialized and "inferior" populations. The charismatic leader appealed to a resentful population as their defender to exercise malevolent outcomes upon scapegoated groups, a malevolence that appeared justifiable to aggrieved individuals who felt forgotten. The grandiose rhetoric of the leader alone was insufficient to build a fascist nation-state. In other words, fascist leaders could not proceed successfully without the support of elites, state institutions, and a mass following that included the middle class (Ben-Ghiat, 2020a; Lipset, 1959/2003; Paxton, 2004).

Fascist leaders preferred a "personal style of command" (Payne, 1995, p. 7). Historically, Nazi leader Adolph Hitler, the eventual chancellor of the German Reich (1933–1945), represented the personal command style of a fascist leader, a trait that he wrote about while in prison in the 1920s for his participation in a failed coup attempt in a region of Germany. In the second volume of *Mein Kampf* (*My Struggle*), Hitler (1927/1999) spoke of the need for a strong leader: "*One* man must step forward" (p. 381, emphasis in original). This person must be able to act with undisputed "force" to "form granite principles from the wavering idea-world of the broad masses and take up the struggle for their sole correctness" (p. 381). Diversity of opinion was unnecessary. Only one clearly established leader with absolute power could break away from "the shifting waves of a free-thought world" (p. 381). By shutting down free expression and reasoned debate, Hitler contended that "there will arise a brazen cliff of solid unity in faith and will . . . based on necessity" (p. 381). What was required was a leader with sole dictatorial powers to direct the nation. Under such a leadership model, a "*political creed*" forms that requires "*the strict organizational integration of large human masses*" to make "*possible*" the creation of "*preconditions for the victorious struggle of this world view*," that is, a fascist ideology led by one undisputed individual with the populace in tow (p. 385, emphasis in original).

Under fascism, the nation's dominant population accepted that their leader personified truth. An indoctrinated public came to trust their leader who they believed "incarnates the national destiny" (Paxton, 2004, p. 559). The fascist leader became the embodiment of the people as expressed through the party. Lies that were believed and told by the leader and his followers were repackaged as the only source of accurate information. As a result, anti-democratic fascism required the silencing of independent journalism, removal of an impartial judiciary, and the gutting of the expertise in the state's civil service that contradicted proclamations from the leader.

ANTI-DEMOCRACY

Fascism opposed democracy. In the mind of the fascist, no need existed for electoral politics because the leader already knew what was best for the nation and should never be contradicted by elected officials. As a result, police actions and public shaming strove to severely censor opposing opinions in books and newspapers—and in nearly any public setting. Fascist attacks on democracy entailed weakening any sense of an independent judiciary and included efforts to eliminate due process for those detained under fascism, especially "the claims of victims of fascist violence" (Paxton, 2004, p. 558). Besides reconceptualizing the judiciary as an arm of the fascist state, fascists purged the civil service of expertise and replaced the state's bureaucracy with civil servants loyal to their leader and party (Paxton, 2004). In *Mein Kampf* Hitler (1927/1999) denounced parliamentary democracy for failing the nation by not having one unified voice to address Germany's social and economic problems after WWI and to counter the rise of what he perceived as a menace from "the organizational power of Marxism" (p. 376), a scapegoat Hitler conflated with widespread European anti-Semitism. He further critiqued as ineffective representative governing through legislative bodies and the allowance of liberal individualism.

Strategically, fascist leaders used the electoral system to their advantage to publicize and legitimize their ideology that did not necessarily depend on actually winning elections. For example, Italy's fascist Prime Minister Benito Mussolini (1922–1943) and Hitler in the interwar years attained their dictatorial powers through votes of their respective legislative bodies despite never receiving a majority of general election votes. In other words, neither Mussolini nor Hitler came to power through the violent seizure of power of a coup d'état but rather through coalitions with conservatives who ceded absolute governmental control.

PATRIARCHAL SEXUALITY

Fascist discourse on sexuality is nothing less than contradictory. Sexuality under fascism is often assumed as repressive, rigid, and uniform, but in practice functioned along a broad spectrum of sexual behaviors and differently across nations with fascist politics (Paxton, 2004). Under fascist regimes, "the public and private spheres of fascist life became inexorably intertwined . . . where the *lines between individual sexuality and collective politics became indistinguishable*" (Merjian, 2001, p. 4, emphasis added).

Germany, like Italy, during the interwar years and WWII sought to rid the nation of those identified as genetically undesirable criminals of the state through a discourse of purification. For example, Germany prioritized efforts to control, sterilize, and exterminate the racialized Other who could potentially "pollute" the gene pool of a mythic race of Aryan Germans through offspring conceived between one parent's German "blood" and an ethnically different parent. Publications further emphasized the sexualized beauty of the German body over what was presented as the ugliness of the Other. Dagmar Herzog (2002) explains:

> Without question, Nazis were conflicted among themselves over sexual mores; some did indeed want a return to more conservative values and behaviors, but some others worked to detach emancipatory impulses from their association with "Marxism" and "Jewishness" and to redefine sexual liberation as a "Germanic," "Aryan" prerogative. (p. 6)

Sexual liberation, however, necessitated fascist state intervention into private sexual lives so that the highly prized males were sexually satisfied, especially for military service.

Illustrative of the paradoxes and overall cruelty of fascist sexuality toward the Other was prominent German psychotherapist Dr. Johannes H. Schultz. Publicly, Schultz was an advisor on the importance of a fulfilling sexual life that mimicked liberalism. In private, Schultz "choreographed torture" by endorsing "extermination" for those considered unredeemable (Herzog, 2002, p. 14). The primary populations Schultz determined could never fit the purity of ultranationalistic aspirations consisted of homosexuals and the physically and mentally less able.

To more fully grasp the patriarchal sexuality of fascism, the following sections highlight hypermasculinity, female accommodation with fascism, and the persecution of homosexuals.

Hypermasculine Dominance

Fascist politics are unequivocally patriarchal and hypermasculine. Hypermasculinity amplifies traditional masculinity and ignores differences among men by advancing an essentialized, one-dimensional conception of masculinity. Heterosexual men who reflect a hypermasculine discourse resent and loathe men who fall outside the parameters of this intense form of masculinity and consider such men as effeminate and a danger to society.

Within this extreme form of patriarchy, research finds that hypermasculine men are misogynistic and seek authority over women. Such men demonstrate a willingness to engage in dangerous behavior that readily accepts the use of violence. Men who display traits of hypermasculinity abhor constructive or negative feedback on their actions, are comparatively less empathetic than other males, and resist practicing positive social behavior such as altruism and humanitarian kindness (Vass & Gold, 1995). Expressions of hypermasculine attitudes are not, however, wholly the domain of men; women, too, are capable of hypermasculine discourse (Aez et al., 2009; Karp, 2010). Such was the case of U.S. anti-feminist women who supported fascism and far-right extremism during the 20th century (Jeansonne, 1996).

Fascist leaders reflected a hypermasculine orientation. The leader exclusively sought males for his advisors, heads of state agencies, and the core of his pivotal supporters. In the early 1920s a well-known Italian jurist waxed ideologically about masculine fascism in contrast to the female:

> *Fascism is male.* It loves danger, dislikes gossip, scorns courting because of its natural tendency to roughness, strikes when necessary. It is made of hard stone, not of the sweet consistency of candied fruits which hide inside—like the female—a hard pit that can break your teeth. That is all that is needed to determine its gender. . . . Fascism, in a word, *evokes virility against any effeminacy* and

> weakness of spirit. But it is also *against . . . the democratization and the liberalism of politics . . . and freehandedness in education.* Can one be more masculine than this? (G. Maggiore, as cited in Benadusi, 2004, p. 175, emphasis added)

The Italian judge's endorsement of fascist ideology captured the inherent violence and anti-democratic stance of patriarchal virility structured around an essentialized female body and mind. Particular groups in this social construction were identified as too feeble and soft for the hardness of fascism.

Hypermasculinity was promoted for the violence required to build a new ultranationalistic society. The Nazi view on the importance of the vitality of their favored male population further required the institutionalization of brothels to create a fit force ready for war. Ideologically, satisfaction of male sexual desires became a military necessity. Despite fascism's contradictory stance toward female prostitutes as asocial, German brothels were available to both soldiers and workers under the rationalization that male sexual fulfillment contributed to an ultranationalistic future. Women who were prostitutes were registered and literally imprisoned in state-run brothels. For nearly any scurrilous reason, prostitutes were moved to concentration camps to be accessible for any sexual needs of enslaved laborers (Timm, 2002).

Hypermasculine fascism stanchly opposed advocacy for women's equal political and civil rights with men in and out of the home. Fascists valued a certain kind of woman who was subservient to men, caretaker of the home and children, and willing to organize other women into fascist support organizations. Paradoxically and often unrecognized in studies of fascism and gender is what can be described as a *fascist matriarchy*: "As an idealized link between nature and culture, between familial and political law, the mother at once legitimates and [unites] an ostensibly masculine form of dominance" (Merjian, 2001, p. 8). For the racialized purity of the nation, roles for women were instrumentally legitimatized.

The body of woman ultimately belonged to the state for the enhancement of the fascist welfare state in the absence of individual civil rights for women (Griffin, 2018). For those women judged as undesirable based on fascist assessments of ethnicity and physical and mental health, sterilization and the possibility of death awaited them. As Renton (2005) summarizes, "The involvement of women was not in planning but rather in the maintenance of fascist rule" (p. 395). Within this context, however, it is an overstatement to assume that women completely lacked agency to act in what they considered their best interests.

Female Accommodation With Fascism

Women during the interwar years "occupied positions of relative, not absolute, weakness in movements that were gendered as masculine" (Passmore, 2008, p. 644). In other words, anti-feminist conservative and far-right women accommodated themselves to fascist regimes. That segment of women believed that fascist governance would improve their situation while maintaining their traditional roles in the home. For young females, fascist politics offered them opportunities to participate in traditional male domains such as joining para-militaries (and wearing uniforms) and, as adults, participating in auxiliaries to support the military (Griffin, 2018).

Fascism attracted a variety of women's groups that covered a range of political ideologies from authoritarian conservativism to even socialism. Their commonality was two-fold: a hostility to leftist movements such as communism and a belief that existing political parties did not serve their interests (Passmore, 2002). The complex choices made by anti-feminist women produced both intended and unforeseen outcomes—such as a "final solution" for mass extermination of Jews and Others deemed "undesirable."

In summarizing the intricacies of women's decisions under fascism, Passmore (2008) explains, "Women used a range of discourses and practices, differentially invested with power, and exploited contradictions in fascist ideologies, to influence their own futures, and indeed those of the movements and regimes in which they participated" (p. 644). Over time, anti-feminist women became loyal to fascist ideology rather than to the interests of gender equality.

Persecution of Homosexual Males

Male homosexuality contradicted the one-dimensional construct of hyper-masculinity. A historical perspective helps clarify the position of homosexuality under fascism—with Nazi Germany a primary example. Germany made homosexuality illegal in 1871. Homosexual men, not women, were the subjects of German criminalization laws that were rarely enforced. By 1933 a committee of the parliament had drafted a revised law that would have decriminalized homosexuality. Germany's liberalism toward a range of sexual behaviors ended, however, with the rise of fascism (Beachy, 2010).

The concept of the revolutionary "new man" was common in fascist Europe and was used against non-fascists (Ledeen, 1969). Gay men violated and threatened fascism's ideological image of the revolutionary new man of action destined to rebirth a purified nation. Instead of a liberal-democratic stance toward sexuality, Nazis intervened and strengthened anti-homosexuality laws as preventive measures to a perceived threat to the nation. A new law, for example, revised the infamous Paragraph 175 from the Reich Penal Code and stated, "A male who commits a sex offense with another male or allows himself to be used by another male for a sex offense shall be punished with imprisonment" (Internet History Sourcebooks Project, 2021, para. 3). Convicted men were required by law to wear an inverted pink triangle for ease of identification.

Additional laws permitted judicial orders of castration of convicted homosexuals (Internet History Sourcebooks Project, 2021). Under Paragraph 175, Nazi police arrested an estimated 100,000 men of whom 50,000 were imprisoned. An estimated 5,000–15,000 of the men arrested ended up in concentration camps where many died after being subjected to invasive medical experiments to "cure" homosexuality. Paramilitaries eventually raided Berlin's liberal Institute for Sexual Science and confiscated nearly 12,000 books that they publicly burned (U.S. Holocaust Memorial Museum, n.d.a.).

In concentration camps, medical doctors arranged for homosexual men to have sex with interned women to determine to what extent these men were actually a weak link in the mobilization of men to serve the nation. Those who achieved sexual intercourse could be released from incarceration while those who could not were among those murdered (Timm, 2002). This practice paradoxically and hypocritically illustrates how a fascist regime could tolerate and accept a particular type of gay man, including some placed in high leadership positions (Paxton, 2004).

ANTI-INTELLECTUALISM

Anti-intellectualism was a key trait of fascism. Anti-intellectualism is the opposite of analytic reasoning and the consideration of evidence-based positions. To say, "That's what I believe and therefore it is true—end of discussion" represents banal anti-intellectualism. Derided under fascism was reasoned discourse that sought to reduce uncertainty through cycles of external investigations into the reliability of validity claims. Hence, expertise lacked standing in fascist anti-intellectualism where mythic ultranationalistic propaganda was the primary source of information. Expertise allowed for a debate of ideas, a situation that was intolerable under fascist absolutist claims on reality. Public debate endangered fascism as the only legitimate belief system. Suppressed were distinctions between mere propagandistic opinion and the exploration of knowledge claims.

The following sections consider elements of the trait of anti-intellectualism by focusing on the political socialization of children and youth, learning in an environment of educational absolutism, and the militaristic indoctrination of young people.

Political Socialization of the Young

Political socialization in public schools through some form of citizenship education is universal and not necessarily unique to fascism (Jennings, 2015). An extreme form of anti-intellectual civic education was a common socialization thread and priority under fascism. Suffused with indoctrination and absolutism, fascist anti-intellectualism during the interwar years spread throughout the school curriculum and extracurricular activities. All aspects of schooling were critical for fascists to control. Under fascism "the function of the education system is to glorify the mythic past, elevating the achievements of members of the nation and obscuring the perspectives and histories of those who do not belong" (Stanley, 2018, p. 47). In this fascist construction of the role of the citizen, politically socialized children were prized to become part of a vanguard for ultranationalistic expectations (Goutam & Gautam, 2014).

School-age children were subject to the patriarchal expectations of fascism. The fascist hypermasculine imagining of the "new man" was projected on youthful vigor. Emphasizing the budding energy of the young, a patriotic anthem of Italian fascists was "Youth, Spring of Beauty" (as cited in Laqueur, 2012, p. 16). Rather than framing the paternalistic home as the source of authority, cultural fascism portrayed the vitality of young people as a fascist symbol of strength that "came to reconcile Italian Fascism's many contradictory principles" (Merjian, 2001, p. 7). The spirit of youth would lead the transformation away from non-fascist forms of governance. It would be young people, especially males, supplanting the patriarchal father in the home to usher in fascism to recover the presumed lost heritage of the nation as guided by an uncontested forceful male leader. The family in turn was subordinated ideologically to the absolutism of the fascist political party.

Fascists sought the active involvement of young people who would internalize the patriotic project of mythic renewal of a nation embedded with cultural racism. To this end, fascist cultural artifacts portrayed children as the way forward to restore the virility of the nation and to break free from the subjugation of domestic and foreign enemies. What was needed, however, were institutional structures of the state to ensure that children unquestionably embraced the ideology of fascism. The totality of the lives of young people should not be left to chance in eliminating any doubts about asserted merits of fascism. Therefore, education in schools, clubs, and magazines that were aligned with fascist party politics became the primary means of instilling anti-intellectual expectations to patriotically serve the nation in any capacity without hesitancy (Fallace, 2017; Merjian, 2001). Education and extracurricular opportunities for young people were by no means intended to be democratic. Instead, conspiratorial theories replaced truth with loyalty by discrediting the liberal exchange of ideas of associated with universities and independent journalism (Stanley, 2018).

Hinged on cultural racism, fascist educational opportunities were set aside for privileged youth. Mussolini made his inequalitarian position clear in a 1933 article in the U.S. publication *High School Journal* in which he proudly proclaimed that he was placing "on the scrap heap the Democratic conception which considered a state school as an institution for everyone—a basket into which treasure and waste were piled together" (as cited in Fallace, 2017, p. 47). Mussolini confirmed that equity and a democratic organization of schooling were never goals under fascism because education was conceived for those who matched fascist idealization.

Educational Absolutism

The philosophy of education in Italy impressed U.S. educators such as John Dewey during the rise of fascism in the 1920s. Dewey and other progressive educators initially assumed Italian education in particular was implementing the principles of pragmatic education. These educators misunderstood, however, how fascists construed the relativity of truth claims in education. Whereas pragmatists encourage problem solving that requires the testing of ideas and evidence, uncertainty of this sort had no place in fascist education. Fallace (2017) explains that fascist regimes "embraced the relativity of knowledge while simultaneously, and paradoxically, demanding absolute acceptance of this relativistic knowledge" (p. 46). In contrast to the anti-intellectual fascist "outlawing deliberations and revisions," pragmatists were receptive to uncertainty and revision of their claims (p. 48). The absolutist position on information presented in fascist schools did, nevertheless, appeal to Italian and U.S. Catholics, especially when Mussolini required the incorporation of religious studies in the curriculum (Fallace, 2017).

Fascist regimes did not necessarily implement similar blueprints for education. Using the most prominent examples of fascism, historical differences in scale existed. In Italy, for example, some older students resented the schooling they were experiencing and considered it a flawed form of fascism. Contrary to the absolutism of fascist ideology toward education, dissent arose among adolescents and adults at the national level in Italy on what was the proper course of education, an issue never fully resolved in that country (Ledeen, 1969).

In contrast, Nazi Germany held a tight and secretive grip for outsiders on the substance of education and youth associations (Fallace, 2017). More so than Italy, the German school curriculum and youth associations were steeped in the cultural racism of anti-Semitism. Every imaginable school subject, activity, and publication adhered to a fascist ideology. Girls, for example, at one stage of their schooling studied such topics as "Racial Policies in the Third Reich," "Law for the Preservation and Assistance of Families with Many Children," and "Opponents to Racial Thinking" (Goutam & Gautam, 2014, p. 1019). Germany's racist education built on the populace's proto-fascist cultural hatred of the Other from the 19th century. This racial animus found a home in the curricular mainstream by the mid-20th century, an indoctrination that was internalized by generations raised in the 1920s and 1930s and documented lasting with that particular demographic of Germans decades later, well into the 1990s and 2000s (Voigtländer & Voth, 2015).

Militaristic Indoctrination of Youth

After the end of WWI in 1919, disillusioned Italian war veterans created paramilitaries, a process known as *squadrism* or squads of action. The young men who comprised these violent squads were intent on defending the valor of war and opposing the pacifism of socialists. The search by Italian paramilitary "Blackshirts" was first for internal enemies who were perceived as a threat to national unity and greatness (Franzinelli, 2009). The Blackshirts' longing for action and a youthful desire to follow the example of the squads was "accompanied by a profound crisis of family bonds and adult authority . . . [that] pushed adolescents into squadrism" (Dogliani, 2009, p. 186). Hitler came to admire how the squads appealed to young people. Italian squadrism provided an impetus in the development of the *Hiterjudgen* or Hitler Youth and his Brownshirt paramilitaries.

Separate clubs were established by the Nazi party for boys and girls as young as 6. These organizations had millions of young members even before the Nazis mandated enrollment in 1939. Gender construction and divisions existed in monthly magazines for young people. In these gender-specific publications, exciting adventures were promoted for boys while girls were told their role was to "take quiet hikes, care for wounded soldiers, prepare for raising children, and work hard in factories" (Goutam & Gautam, 2014, p. 1022).

The importance of a militarily prepared nation against those the state identified as domestic and foreign enemies to fascism permeated the activities of youth organizations and textbooks for young children and adolescents. For instance, a Nazi mathematics textbook posed a problem that asked students to determine "how much fuel a bomber would need to attack enemy cities" (Goutam & Gautam, 2014, p. 1020). A middle school geography text under the heading "Building the New Germany" claimed that because Germany was located in central Europe and supposedly surrounded by enemies of nationhood, Germany needed to imperialistically expand its territorial boundaries of control for the safety of the German people (p. 1023). For Italian young people, the early experience of youth-oriented clubs mirroring squadrism aided in the recruitment for the eventual 1935 invasion of Ethiopia, a militaristic act of imperialism to avenge Italy's humiliating defeat in 1896 at Adwa at the hands of a people considered by fascists as racially inferior and subhuman (Dogliani, 2009; Paxton, 2004). Young Italians mobilized under the motto "Believe, Obey, Fight" (Dogliani, 2009, p. 191).

In summary, all educational activities under fascism infused anti-intellectualism for the sole purpose to provide structures for the promulgation of disingenuous ultranationalist dreams rather than for the self-development of children and youth for their own personal enlightenment and intellectual growth.

CULTURAL AND PHENOTYPE RACISMS

Racism based on ethnic cultural differences and phenotypes or physical features were essential characteristics under fascist regimes. Racism was directed toward both internal and external populations—regardless of their citizenship status—who fascists declared diluted the purity of the nation. While racism is not uncommon under nationalism, fascist ultranationalism intensified the hostilities to racial and ethnic groups, including immigrants and refugees considered undesirable. To create an idealized nation, fascists believed a program of eugenics was a good "scientific" solution. Among those who fascists considered enemies of the state, Jews were prominently singled out. Up to WWII, dominant populations internationally considered Jews a biological race rather than an ethnic group centered around distinct religious and cultural practices (Brodkin, 1998). Taking advantage of anti-Jewish resentment and illusions, Christian fascists channeled problems of the nation-state through a discourse scapegoating all Jews as not just a threat to the nation; they were also constructed as a danger to Western civilization (Hanebrink, 2018). The seriousness of the singling out of Jews cannot be understated in light of the devastating outcome of the fascist holocaust.

Chapter 6 extends an analysis of racism's effects as promoted by proto-fascists and the contemporary far right.

ANTI-SOCIALISM

Despite the often-contradictory anti-capitalistic rhetoric of fascist politics—especially when tied to the damning trope of the greedy Jewish capitalist financier—fascism as well as far-right and conservative policies and practices consistently protected capitalism (Roberto, 2018; Robinson, 2014). Fascists were not critical of the exploitive side of capital–labor relations. Instead, they objected to the individualistic side of capitalism that was indifferent to the needs of a nation. Fascist regimes sought "to defeat for all time any possibility of capitalism's replacement by a more egalitarian order" (Renton, 2019, pp. 16–17). Once in power fascists did not follow through on anti-capitalistic intimidation and sought to restructure and align the economy with ultranationalistic priorities (Paxton, 2004; Payne, 1995).

Fascist governance was not necessarily the first choice of capitalists during the interwar years, which included the economically devastating Great Depression. The capitalist class made some objections but did not stand in the way of the expansion of fascist politics. With few exceptions, capitalists were more concerned with the spread of socialist and communist ideologies of equality and equitable distribution of a society's material resources than with the rise of fascism. In fact, many prominent figures lauded fascism as a necessary response to socialistic inroads. Fascism both demonized and defined itself as the opposite of the communism of the Russian Bolsheviks, but in many regards fascists "mimicked its organization and its tactics" (Markwich, 2009, p. 340).

More often, international and domestic leaders of industrial and finance capitalism praised the direction in which fascists were taking their political economies. For example, in 1926 the U.S.-based J. P. Morgan Corporation supported fascist Italy by lending more than $100 million to Italy as part of a post-WWI revival of commerce with the United States (Robinson & Gilmore, 2019). U.S. corporations also participated directly in supporting the Nazi regime (E. Black, 2003). Fascist leaders, though, were most interested in gaining absolute political control in the belief that they could direct the course of a nation's economy by their willpower.

To control a potent source of progressive opposition, fascism corresponding-ly opposed and suppressed independent worker-controlled labor unions. Because labor unions can extend solidarity to other social justice movements, the capitalist class did not object to the suppression of labor unions. As with socialism, organized workers prioritized attention to the inequities of socioeconomic class relations rather than fascism's foremost priority, the renewal of the mythic nation (Passmore, 2002). Advocates of a different model of a nation's political economy such as socialism faced the hostility and inherent violence of fascists and the capitalist class (Markwich, 2009; Paxton, 2004). In Italy, for example, Franzinelli (2009) notes, "Industrialists and land owners proffered their financial backing to the [paramilitary] squads in large part out of pleasure at seeing the pro-socialist political and union network demolished" (p. 95). Under fascist arrangements with businesses, wages of workers declined while industrialists producing armaments received substantial financial support.

Despite fascism's anti-socialist/anti-communist stance, fascist regimes took some actions that resembled socialism. Fascist socialism funded public welfare but just for racialized privileged populations and not for the demonized Other. Infrastructure development such as highways is an example where fascists socialized public resources. Economists Voigtländer and Voth (2014) explain that "infrastructure spending can indeed create electoral support for a nascent dictatorship—it can win the 'hearts and minds' of the populace" (p. 32). For example, in an effort to secure support from rural Germans, Hitler created an extensive highway system, the Autobahn. For Nazi propaganda, "the 'Führer's highways' became the seemingly incontrovertible, concrete proof of the regime's claim that it had the organizational ability to overcome" the inability of democratic processes to meet the needs of the public (p. 33).

In summary, fascist regimes supported the property rights of capitalists who produced goods for the nation by advocating a mild version of economic autarky, which in the extreme creates a political economy with no external trade. Despite an anti-internationalist discourse that included some international trade, fascists publicly praised domestically based businesses as a critical component in the revitalization of the nation. The opposition to international trade under fascist regimes did negatively affect their national economies when a shortage of goods existed that the state was unable to secure and produce domestically (Paxton, 2004).

Chapter 7 follows up this discussion with an examination of the political economy impact of proto-fascism and fascism in the formation of monopoly capitalism as experienced by vulnerable populations since the European invasion of the Americas.

MILITARIZED SOCIETY

Fascist regimes were uninterested in peace but instead obsessed with the supremacy of the military, national security, and crime and punishment (Pilisuk & Rountree, 2015). Renton (2019) succinctly explains, "*Fascism is a form of politics saturated in violence*" (p. 23, emphasis added). Fascist violence was revolutionary in manifesting aspirations for an eventual ultranationalistic triumph of a rebirthed nation-state. Fascist leaders justified the use of "redemptive violence" because established state institutions failed to carry out ultranationalistic liberation (Paxton, 2004, p. 549).

Fascism represented an extreme form of state-sanctioned violence and terrorism, basic elements for a modern police state. Fascists took pride in the use of violence over words to discipline those groups judged to be a threat to the racialized integrity of the nation. In the process of securing total power over the state, fascists created their own forces to patrol mass gatherings sponsored by the party and to engage in street battles against anti-fascists. To meet this goal, fascism depended on disciplined cadres of paramilitaries, police, and military to enforce uniformity and adherence to its ideological mission. Military might alone was insufficient under fascism: *a zealous and unified populace evident in supportive mass rallies was a necessary element of fascism*. Of these militarized groups, private paramilitaries loyal to fascist ideology were essential in carrying out domestic attacks (Markwhich, 2009; Paxton, 2004; Renton, 2019).

Once in power, fascists elevated the status of police as a leading state authority in a new revolutionary state that enabled spreading terrorism without restraint or accountability. Under a fascist regime, "the police takes on itself the responsibility for acting as the mobilizing agent of society, one of the principal functions of the ideological party" (Chapman, 1968, p. 439). In a police state, the police see themselves as the only reliable protector of the state and view other state institutions with suspicion. The police become a law upon themselves. In a police state, Chapman (1968) clarified, "The permanent professional skepticism of all policemen in pathological form becomes elevated to the theory of the state" in which "all is suspect, everyone a potential traitor" (pp. 439–440).

In addition to those named as domestic enemies, fascists sought security through imperialistic military attacks on foreign nation-states perceived as both (a) hostile enemies to the fascist state and (b) the legitimate territorial expansion of the nation-state. Gandesha (2020) notes that "the application of colonial techniques of violence" in turn was eventually used on the nation's out-group population (p. 7). Under fascism, the dominant population was relatively unconcerned and unsympathetic to the application of violence as long as the racialized Other would be the victims (Paxton, 2004). The most prominent outcome of mainstream populace indifference to fascist violence was unleashing what became WWII and the loss of tens of million civilian and military lives.

It is worth recapturing historical memory to consider the estimated number of the millions murdered by category as a result of German fascist violence alone, as presented in Table 3.1. In light of far-right neo-Nazi denials of a WWII Holocaust, a purpose of this itemization is to underscore the full impact that the free hand of a fascist regime had and could have in the future on vulnerable populations.

Table 3.1. Deaths by German Fascists, 1930s–1940s

Targeted Group	Number Killed
Jews	6 million
Soviet Union civilians	7 million, including 1.3 million Soviet Jews
Soviet Union prisoners of war	3 million, including 500,000 Jewish soldiers
Non-Jewish Polish civilians	1.8 million
Serbian civilians	312,000
People with disabilities living in institutions	250,000
Roma people	250,000
Jehovah's Witnesses	1,900
Repeat "criminal" offenders	70,000
Homosexuals (possibly repeat "criminals")	unknown
German political opponents and resistance activists	unknown

Source: Data from U.S. Holocaust Memorial Museum (2020).

Chapter 8 continues this discussion with an emphasis on how this trait of fascist politics emerged in U.S. history and continues with far-right policing and militarization in our current era and its effects on youth and schooling.

A background in the traits of fascism presented here helps to clarify what anti-fascism historically has opposed and what should be taken into account when designing an anti-fascist civic curriculum. Aspects of certain discrete traits of historical fascism are manifest in contemporary far-right movements, the topic of the next chapter.

CHAPTER 4

Contemporary Far-Right Extremism

The right can always go still further right and will.

—Harvard sociologist David Reisman, 1964/1993

The public's collective understanding of far-right extremism rapidly changed after the January 6, 2021, attack on the U.S. Capitol. From K–12 to higher education, teachers who attempted to explain to their students the significance of the Capitol siege struggled to find an appropriate tone and historical perspective as a headline in *The New York Times* observed: "After the Capitol Was Stormed, Teachers Try Explaining History in Real Time" (Nierenberg, 2021a). Beneficial for policymakers, educators, and students learning about and teaching anti-fascism is a civic foundation infused with a knowledge base in the historical roots of the manifestation of the far right and its growth during the first 3 decades of the 21st century. Lacking such a context places limitations on the pedagogical effectiveness of teachers grappling with how to explain the Capitol siege to their students. For example, educators may erroneously equate the Capitol siege by 800 individuals as equivalent to paramilitaries of the fascist regimes, such as the more than 200,000 regimented SS (*Schutzstaffeln* or Defense/Protection Squads) paramilitary members who were responsible for Germany's internal security under the control of Hitler and the Nazi party (Wegner, 1997). The Capitol siege was very different than well-disciplined street militias terrorizing specified populations in a coordinated effort condoned and encouraged by a fascist dictatorship. Nevertheless, certain characteristics that are aspects of an amalgamation of a fascist regime exist among contemporary far-right traits. In other words, far-right extremism contains elements of fascist politics rather than the totality of fascism as witnessed in the 20th century.

The magnitude of the Capitol siege elevated public attention to the potency of the far right. Relatively smaller daily acts of far-right extremism rather than a mass movement, however, are often overlooked or minimized. These small acts resemble fascist politics or "micro-fascism" (Genosko, 2020, p. 164). Fascist politics from the 20th century did not die out; instead they continue to filter into the body politic to erode the already shaky foundations of liberal democracies. Today far-right incursions represent a shift in tactics to electoral politics that are cause for additional alarm in the multicultural struggle against fascist tendencies. As Miller-Idriss (2020) in *Hate in the Homeland* observes, "Historically, the far right has worked actively against mainstream governments, but in recent years, there has been a tactical shift toward undermining governance from within," as evident by the rise of outspoken far-right sympathizers legislating at all levels of governance in the United States (p. 5).

Historical analyses of the far right finds shifting characteristics and strategies that differentiate it from the record of fascist regimes in the 20th century. In many regards, far-right extremism and neo-fascism express similar ideological stances that oppose a pluralism represented in the cosmopolitanism of multicultural nation-states. *Teaching Anti-Fascism* asks educators to "refuse to allow any fascist formula to slip by on whatever scale it may manifest itself" (F. Guattari, as cited in Genosko, 2020, p. 168). By being alert to daily politics that reflect far-right applications of fascist politics, anti-fascism provides policymakers, educators, and students insights that clarify and make accessible comparisons between current events and historically full-blown fascism. A cursory knowledge base of far-right extremism and factors that contribute to micro-fascism can, however, stymy our collective response to designing robust anti-fascist curricula for civic engagement.

What follows are brief overviews of ideological shifts since 2001 and the decentralized nature of the far right. After this are sections outlining key ideal or common characteristics in a typology of far-right extremism, including the normalization of political violence. The chapter concludes with brief comparisons between the ideologies of the far right and conservatism.

IDEOLOGICAL SHIFT IN POLITICAL DISCOURSE AFTER SEPTEMBER 11, 2001

For the far right and conservatism, the September 11, 2001 (9/11), criminal destruction of the World Trade Center in New York provided a significant authoritarian turn (Bouie, 2021; Morgan & Shanahan, 2018). Actual fascism in the interwar years and WWII "diminished in our collective memory" and was replaced by the "legacy" of 9/11 (Renton, 2019, p. 19), especially for anyone born since 2000. The aftermath of 9/11 changed "the tone of right-wing politics, from a register of nostalgia into *a new language of confident aggression and assumed public approval*" (pp. 36–37, emphasis added). Far-right discourse from 2001 to our present moment serves as the primary baseline to isolate common characteristics of this ideological orientation.

While generally distancing political discourse from overt references to fascism, far-right extremism displays links to the politics of fascism. The purpose here is to identify traits and emphases that emerged more clearly since 9/11—and more recently from the Capitol siege and its aftermath. This contemporary typology of far-right characteristics is not intended to lessen any possibility of a 21st-century fascism regime in the United States because "*the far right's rejection of fascism may not continue indefinitely*" (Renton, 2019, p. 22, emphasis added).

DECENTRALIZED LEADERSHIP OF THE FAR RIGHT

Stephen Miller, who served as a senior policy and speechwriting advisor to Trump throughout his term of office, sought to elevate Trump to the status of an unquestioned supreme leader within the first month of Trump's presidency. In response to a judge's objections to Trump's national security authority to ban Muslims entering the United States from selected nations, Miller proceeded with a verbal rant that claimed "our opponents, the media and the whole world will soon see as we begin to take further actions, that *the powers of the president* to protect our country are very substantial and *will not be questioned*" (as cited in Blake, 2017, para. 6, emphasis added). Miller's absolutism echoed Nazi Germany's elevation of the "Führer's Will" as "the basis for all governmental activity" (Zentner, & Bedurftig, 1997, p. 308). Miller held unequivocal fascistic hopes as revealed in an investigation of his 900 pre-election private emails that exposed a deep affinity and connection with White nationalist fringe organizations, rightwing media, and immigration laws from the 1930s eugenics era in the United States and Germany (Hayden, 2019). However much the far right demonstratively gravitated to Trump in their hope for an uncontested leader, the far right in the United States has no central leadership organization. Instead, the far right has been characterized by a variety of decentralized organizations and lone provocateurs (Renton, 2019). Nevertheless, recent efforts by the Republican National Committee and their wealthy backers constitute an attempt to consolidate and centralize far-right leadership through electoral politics (e.g., Mac & Lerer, 2022; Rappeport et al., 2022).

Although Lyons (2018), in his impressive survey of the U.S. far right, does not consider far-right extremism a separate ideology, I follow Renton's (2019) and Miller-Idriss's (2020) categorization of the far right as a distinct ideology despite all its seemingly disparate groups and discursive practices. What follows is a way to help us envision the far right more holistically.

IDEAL TRAITS OF U.S. FAR-RIGHT EXTREMISM

Outlined is a typology of key far right characteristics, some of which draw from the legacy of historical fascism. The ideal or common traits in this typology include (a) White supremacist nationalism, (b) anti-government insurgency, (c) misogynistic postfeminism, and (d) evangelical Christian absolutism. These characteristics are less a holistic composite than found about fascism in Chapter 3. Although the traits present discrete categories, adherents often blend characteristics from each category. White nationalism, however, is the dominant trait, as emphasized in Figure 4.1.

Figure 4.1. Centrality of White Nationalism Among Ideal Traits of U.S. Far-Right Extremism

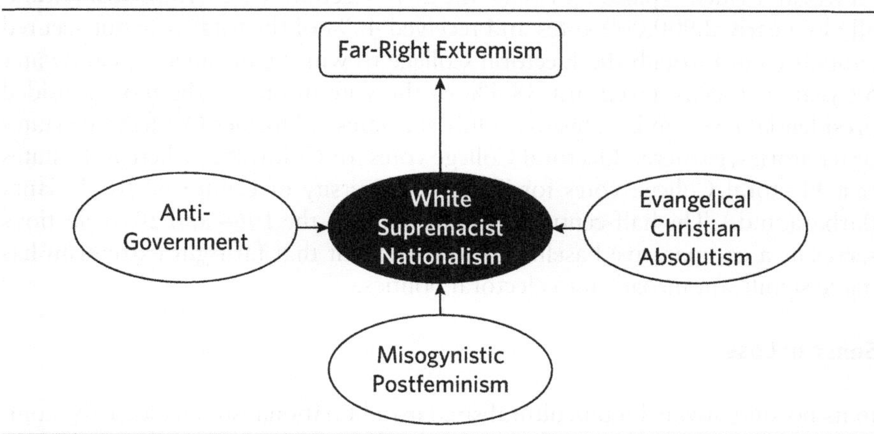

WHITE SUPREMACIST NATIONALISM

The far right in our current era racializes nationalism and imagines a separation of "nations" or people according to ethnic identities. This viewpoint reduces diversity to "a series of multiple regional and national apartheid states" (Renton, 2019, p. 148). The main thrust of far-right extremism voiced in electoral politics advances a racially defined democracy. Anything less, however, than an election outcome reflective of a White nationalistic form of democracy is framed as illegitimate and must be questioned. Such was the claim after the 2008 election of President Barack Obama as the first Black person to hold that office.

Throughout Obama's presidency the far right sought to discredit his legal right to hold office by conspiratorially claiming he was born in Kenya, not in the United States. Beginning in 2011 Donald Trump was among those far-right voices questioning the citizenship of Obama. After Trump was Republican nominee for president in 2016, he then passively acknowledged for political expediency that Obama was born in the United States as required under the Constitution (Barbaro, 2016). During his campaign for re-election in 2020, Trump once again questioned the origins of the birth of a political opponent of mixed ethnicities, in this case eventual Vice-President Kamala Harris who was born in the United States and, therefore, eligible for that office. What spurred Trump's racist inquiry was the fact that biracial Harris was not White and her parents were immigrants—her father was a Black Jamaican and her mother was from Chennai, India (Rogers, 2020).

Today far-right White nationalists would likely affirm and see nothing unusual about Goldwater's (1964/1998) acceptance speech as the Republican Party's presidential nominee in which he stated "extremism in the defense of liberty is no vice," to which he followed up to "remind" his audience "that moderation in the pursuit of justice is no virtue" (para. 42). Like today, Goldwater claimed that the nation was paralyzed by ineffective politicians in the face of "a world divided" (para. 7). Unlike the 2016 election when Trump lost nationally by nearly 2,900,000 votes and received 46% of the total vote but secured enough votes through the Electoral College to win the presidency, Goldwater 52 years earlier received just 38.5% of the vote in one of the most lopsided presidential losses in U.S. history. Only six states, all former Confederate states or territories, garnered Electoral College votes for Goldwater, whereas 30 states cast Electoral College votes for Trump (University of California [UC], Santa Barbara, n.d.). The half-century contrast between the 1964 and 2016 elections serves as a comparative baseline as to the extent that far-right extremism has made significant inroads into electoral politics.

Sense of Loss

In its hostility toward multiculturalism, far-right nationalism ideologically combines scientific racism, social Darwinism, and a romanticized lost history, much like fascism in the last century. For example, after Obama was reelected in 2012, popular Fox television commentator and best-selling author Bill O'Reilly bemoaned, *"It's not a traditional America anymore"* (as cited in Weinger, 2012, para.1, emphasis added). O'Reilly's lament sprang from the reelection of a person identified as Black; hence, something was lost, a "traditional America" without a White president. This sense of a loss of a White identity found further resonance in the presidential 2016 election of Donald Trump and his campaign slogan "Make America Great Again," plagiarized from the campaign slogan of President Reagan who the Ku Klux Klan publicly endorsed (Moore & Tracy, 2020; Speipel, 2019). In effect, Trump signaled to racists that the nation was in decline and needed to return to some mythical era when the United States was "great" for certain socioeconomic classes of racially privileged Whites.

Contemporary White nationalists' sense of loss can be traced to a long cultural and political backlash against the defeat of the Confederacy in the Civil War (1861–1865) coupled with the aim of the Reconstruction era (1865–1877) to racially integrate formerly enslaved people into the political establishment of the South. In response White racists created a mythic history—the "Lost Cause"—that nostalgically claimed the actions of the Confederacy were noble, moral, and fair. The Lost Cause served in popular culture as a master narrative justification for segregation, for public displays of Confederate symbols, for a distorted education for young people, and for "White supremacist terrorist organizations . . . who lynched, beat, burned, and raped African Americans throughout Reconstruction" (Lineberry, 2019, p. 1190).

"The People" Racialized

The far right forwards a racialized demo as "the people" who are viewed as the true representatives of democracy and who should hold ultimate power to rule the nation. For example, while campaigning in 2016, Trump signaled his nationalistic historical alliance to a White-dominated political culture when he stated, "I am 'America First,'" a catchphrase harkening back to far-right xenophobia and racism from the 1930s (Churchwell, 2018). After Trump's defeat for a consecutive term as president, far-right congressional Republicans began to form an "America First Caucus" to promote "uniquely Anglo-Saxon political traditions" (Wang & Itkowitz, 2021, para. 5). From the far right's perspective, only those who they designate as rightful citizens should be allowed to vote and run for public offices; the designated Other should have limited or no access to the ballot box and no involvement in the affairs of government.

White nationalists continue to throw obstacles in the path of the fulfillment of the 1870 15th Amendment to the Constitution, which states, "The right of citizens of the United States to vote shall not be denied or abridged by the United States or by any state on account of race, color, or previous condition of servitude." Nearly a century later, the overriding purpose of the 1965 Voting Rights Act, according to U.S. Department of Justice (2017), was "to break the grip of state disfranchisement" (para. 1) by giving the federal government "special enforcement provisions targeted at those areas of the country where Congress believed the potential for discrimination to be the greatest" (para. 3). Despite the 15th Amendment and the Voting Rights Act, voter intimidation during balloting in the 2020 election was visibly conducted by far-right groups along with their political allies who controlled a significant number of state legislatures (Phillips, 2020). Within 2 months after Trump's presidential defeat for a consecutive term, Republican legislators proposed more than 250 laws in 43 states to limit access to voting (Gardner et al., 2021).

Far-right efforts at voter suppression of historically marginalized individuals represent attempts to skew the electoral process to gain disproportionate political power (DeRienzo, 2020). When the results of elections are conspiratorial denied if far-right candidates are not declared victorious, the far right can go as far as using violence to make their point. The Trump-encouraged Capitol siege is a vivid indicator of this long history of political violence by the far right that has now spilled into local school board meetings (Bryant, 2021; Hochschild, 2021; Rutenberg et al., 2021).

"The Great Replacement"

The concept of "The Great Replacement" resonates with the sense of loss White nationalists perceive. The phrase originated from the French aristocrat Renaud Camus who lives in a medieval castle. Camus's writings expressed fear of a "replacement of a people" by Muslims and migrants from former French colonies in Africa (as cited in Onishi, 2019). By "a people" Camus is clear that he was referring just to those French citizens who are White. By 2022 the racist conspiracy theory of "replacement" had entered French presidential campaigning (Onishi, 2022). Camus's far-right anxiety encapsulated a perceived threat to France from a *loss of its cultural identity through multiculturalism*" (as cited in Onishi, 2019, para. 18, emphasis added). In

2019 far-right vigilantes in their respective manifestos cited Camus's racialized "replacement" theory as justification for mass murders: killing 51 at two mosques in Christchurch, New Zealand, and the mass shooting of 23 Latinx individuals at a Walmart store in El Paso, Texas (Onishi, 2019). The same rationalization contributed to the anti-government death and destruction from the Capitol siege (Bennhold & Schwartz, 2021).

ANTI-GOVERNMENT INSURGENCY

White nationalistic discourse singles out "elites" as a problem for the full realization of democracy. Far-right anti-government insurgents believe that the interests of Whites "are being ill served by a timid and pacifist ruling elite" (Renton, 2019, p. 44). During his 2016 presidential campaign Trump tapped into right-wing conspiratorial sentiments against elites by claiming that, if elected, he would "drain the swamp," a phrase popularized by Reagan in the 1980s.[1] The phrase referred to downsizing and limiting the reach and oversight of state institutions within the federal government while negatively implicating "elites" inside and outside the federal government. In this far-right anti-government narrative, journalistic elites spread "fake news" of reality and must be stopped by nearly any means necessary, including denigrating, silencing, and harming reporters (Sullivan, 2020). The far right views state institutions that provide any relief to populations of color as a problem related to their White sense of loss and, like conservatives, calls for reductions in the size of the government.

The Trump administration did its part trying to dismantle the role of the state by stripping the clout of key governmental agencies such as the Environmental Protection Agency (EPA), State Department, and Department of Justice. In contrast to what his anti-elite "drain the swamp" supporters may have hoped, numerous civil servants and their staff of knowledgeable specialists were replaced by wealthy elites who were financial supporters of Trump with little or no background consistent with their appointed positions. After winning the 2016 election, Trump foreshadowed his intentions when he told a crowd of supporters, "*I want people who have made a fortune. You watch what's going to happen*" (as cited in Alexander et al., 2019, para. 3, emphasis added). According to the financial publication *Forbes*, Trump's cabinet appointees alone included 17 millionaires, two centimillionaires whose wealth is $100,000,000 or more, and one billionaire (Alexander et al., 2019).

Most telling of reductions in state action for public safety were appointees who contradicted and belittled scientific recommendations from the EPA and Centers for Disease Control and Prevention (CDC). The Trump administration undermined the science related to the climate crisis through a massive series of rollbacks of EPA rules to increase the profitability of capitalistic industries while externalizing the cost of a suffering ecosystem to a tax-paying public. The reversal of more than 100 EPA rules from previous presidential administrations included severely limiting assessments of potential effects of infrastructure projects on the natural environment as well as rescinding regulations designed to protect the environment against air pollution and emissions, drilling and extraction, water pollution, and toxic substances (Popovich et al., 2021).

The most extreme example of dismissing the CDC's scientific advice for public safety and health was the Trump administration's response to the COVID-19 pandemic. The result was an absence of a federal government plan to coordinate a distribution program of protective gear and vaccines during the COVID-19 health crisis. By the time Trump left office in early 2021, in just the 1 year from when cases were first detected in the United States, more than 400,000 people in the United States had died among the estimated 26,000,000 who had been infected. One month after Trump's departure the official death count climbed to half a million, and during 2022, with an average of 2,300 reported daily deaths, the figure was likely to approach 1 million confirmed COVID-19 deaths (Lee, 2021; The New York Times, 2022; Tompkins et al., 2021).

The experiences of state institutions such as the EPA and CDC limited governmental interventions to reduce harm to humans and the environment. Taking an anti-government ideology to its logical end can result in an increasingly violent and stateless nation.

Violent Alternative to Electoral Politics

A somewhat contradictory element within the far right is between groups attempting to gain power through the electoral system and those intent on a violent coup to overthrow the existing government, the latter often expressed through attempts to incite a racialized civil war. For the far right, the anti-statist "drain the swamp" promises of the Trump administration fell disappointingly short of expectations. When electoral politics do not match far-right expectations, far-right adherents view as reasonable turning to violent intimidation and terrorism.

With Trump's 2020 defeat and Joe Biden as president, this faction within the far right finds their hopes diminished for the advancement of White supremacy through normal political channels. The decentralized far right instead turns to an anti-politics, anti-government strategy of "*accelerationism*" to bring about the necessity of a "'system collapse' through acts of violence . . . to prepare for *the apocalyptic end* that they assume is *inevitable in a multicultural, democratic society*" (Miller, 2021, para. 5, emphasis added). Accelerationism necessitates "a 'cleansing fire' of violence" (para. 2). In this terroristic scenario, accelerationism takes cultural racisms to its own internal logic of genocide as the final solution.

Ecofascists who have infiltrated progressive environmental groups support the violence of acceleration. In an investigative report Amend (2020) emphasizes that the "climate crisis, which promises to scramble *all* politics, provides ecofascists an opening" (para. 10, emphasis in original). In addition to fears of White replacement by immigrants marked as undesirables as well as an increasing population growth in ethnic diversity, ecofascists call for population control through eugenic culling and, if necessary, outright genocide of the Other. For example, the 2019 perpetuator of the mass murder in El Paso fed on ecofascist logic and previous mass murders as evidenced in a manifesto attributed to him titled "The Inconvenient Truth." In this case the killer cites a "Hispanic invasion" into Texas that can lead to the White supremacist dread of miscegenation or "race mixing" (P. Crusius, as cited in Alltucker, 2019, "What the Manifesto Said," para. 3). "Because the environment is getting worse by the year," the killer further explained that he targeted "invaders" to "get rid of enough people . . . [so that] *our way of life* can become more sustainable" (as cited in Amend, 2020, "The Killers," para. 10, emphasis added). In other words, genocide becomes a strategy to avoid the feared replacement of a White population. Ecofascists explain that their viewpoint on ecology "follows an organic, hierarchical view of society [and] the rejection of equalitarianism" and blame Jews for capitalism's anti-environmentalism (G. Johnson, as cited in Amend, 2020, "The Intellectuals," para. 5). Ecofascist logic further leads to a defense for the creation of racialized ethnostates on the basis of human biodiversity.

Ethnonationalism

Far-right anti-government insurgents consist of multiethnic adherents who do not necessarily subscribe to White nationalism. This multicultural contingent is not directly associated with White supremacy and often includes individuals who adopted an anti-government ideology while in the military despite regularly drawing a check from the government (Thompson, 2021). Nevertheless, the vast majority of anti-government advocates support an exclusive White nation-state. Miller-Idriss (2020) explains,

> The desire to establish a separate white territory or to restore a white homeland is at the root of far right and white supremacist extremists' calls to end immigration, re-migrate ethnic minorities, and accelerate a race war in order to achieve rebirth and restoration of the white civilization. (p. 39)

With a White ethnostate in mind, the ultranationalistic far right appropriates the concepts of diversity and difference and replaces them with "ethnopluralism" to propose the creation of separate, racially homogeneous nations with a regional territorial enclave for Whites only. Ethnopluralism rationalizes ethnonationalism through a perversion of "human biodiversity" and the "right to difference" (Amend, 2020, "The Intellectuals," para. 7). The far right's notions of diversity and difference appears as a 21st-century version of an 1896 Supreme Court decision that declared separating people on the basis of skin color produced equality, not discrimination, a White supremacist decision that was U.S. law for more than half a century.

One similarity between far-right extremism and fascism is their respective emphasis on international cooperation with those who share similar ideological orientations (e.g., Graham-Harrison & Lindeman, 2022). Despite the centrality of mythic ultranationalism, 20th-century fascism sought international allies, as do 21st-century far-right extremist movements. Indicative of the internationalism of far-right extremism is Trump's outreach to governing autocrats during his presidency and the 2015 Russian-initiated World National-Conservative Movement conference that attracted 58 far-right political parties, organizations, and groups (Rachman, 2018; Ross, 2015). Far-right extremists from the United States use international contacts to share strategies. They have traveled to military training camps in Europe and reciprocated by hosting members of the terrorist organization Russian Imperial Movement in the United States (Bennhold & Schwirtz, 2021).

Using Hungary as a scenic backdrop to support the erosion of free and fair elections in the United States, among other topics, popular Fox network commentator Tucker Carlson (2021) hosted his show in a country whose political leadership embraces far-right authoritarian nationalism. With Hungary's iron-fisted prime minister in the audience, Carlson was scheduled to speak at a far-right conference. Hungary had paid a U.S. lobbying firm $265,000 to arrange an interview for the prime minister on Fox (Ecarma, 2021a). A few months before his week-long trip to Hungary, Carlson affirmatively agreed with a far-right guest who confidently predicted that the United States will "pick a fascist [leader] within 10 to 20 years" (J. Kelly, as cited in Ecarma, 2021b, para. 2). In a tacit nod to European far-right movements, toward the end of 2021 Fox News released Carlson's "documentary" *Patriot Purge*. Carlson's film claims to present the "true story" of the Capitol siege while conspiratorially and ludicrously forwarding the false claim that "the left is hunting the right and sticking them in Guantanamo Bay" (as cited in Corn, 2021, para. 2, 3). The distorted narrative juxtaposed with imagery taken out of context is "embracing the hallmarks of fascism. Any reluctance to call it that only assist the fascists" (Corn, 2021, para. 8).

Despite identifying with international fascistic movements, the far right is opposed to globalization for its implied limitations on nation-state sovereignty by international and regional institutions such as the United Nations and the European Union (Worth, 2015). Globally, the far right stands against the focus of international organizations on "human rights and democratic safeguards" (Raj, 2017, para. 5). After the 2016 election of Trump, a member of a terrorist militia group proclaimed that "the leftist/Globalist cabal lost the election. People are waking up to what Globalism is all about, and they are rejecting it" (S. Dawkins, as cited in Lyons, 2018, p. 210).

MISOGYNISTIC POSTFEMINISM

Like 20th-century fascism, 21st-century far-right extremism remains unequivocally patriarchal. To clarify, patriarchy is

> a social system in which *men disproportionately occupy positions of power and authority*, central norms and values are associated with *manhood and masculinity*

(which in turn are defined in terms of dominance and control), and *men are the primary focus* of attention in most cultural spaces. (Whisnant, 2013, para. 5, emphasis added)

Restrictions on patriarchal dominance remains abhorrent to the far right and fuels its resentment toward feminism.

The far right's *postfeminism* is a politically motivated counterattack against the goals of feminism through a narrative of fear that men, especially White men, are victims of any feminist gains for equality in the home and public square. Faludi (1991) clarifies that "the antifeminist backlash has been set off not by women's achievement of full equality but by the increased possibilities that they might win it" (p. xx). Postfeminism embraced by the far right "virtually omits even a brief consideration of the possible benefits of feminism" (M. D. Vavrus, 2002, p. 10). Like postracialism's claim that people of color now have the same opportunities as Whites to achieve the meritorious American Dream of success, postfeminism shifts the gaze away from expanding the social and political participation of females in the public sphere. Instead, postfeminism highlights and encourages a femininity expressed in subservience to men and in "women's private, consumer lifestyles" (p. 2).

Backlash Against Feminist Movements

Efforts to break through a patriarchal wall resulted in the 1920 passage of the 19th Amendment that technically gave all women the right to vote. The decades of feminist mobilization and protests leading up to women winning suffrage is historically referred to as first-wave feminism. Feminism lost steam during the 1930s as women overall continued to lack equal opportunity on par with men in employment and political participation as well as in the patriarchal structure of the home. Women in mainstream political leadership roles were rare or nonexistent. Although first-wave feminism was a significant social justice movement, it did not make as significant in-roads into a broad array of gender-defined social relations as second-wave feminism did 50 years later.

As the civil rights and feminist movements of the 1960s and into the early 1970s gradually expanded formerly closed opportunities for people of color and women, a conservative backlash ensued. By the 2020s the far right was the primary ideological orientation to carry the banner of vehement opposition to the gains of women and those not considered White. Patriarchy in the 2020s remains entrenched in the far right's opposition to equality and equity for women. Ideologically, the far right represents more than a half century of counterattacks against second-wave feminism and its 21st-century inclusivity of a spectrum of sexualities and nonbinary gender identities. Far-right adherents view feminism as a threat to a White patriarchal social order reinforced by a politicized strain of evangelical Christianity (Vavrus, 2015).

By the latter part of the 20th century, feminism included an intersectional analysis that "considers differentially allocated material and symbolic wealth and how they are related to the nexus of gender-race-class" (M. D. Vavrus, 2002, p. 13). Whereas the far right wants to naturalize a subordinate female identity, feminism emphasizes transparency as to how distribution of material resources and status recognition are significantly skewed toward White males by patriarchal institutions and governance. For example, labor disparities in 2020 reveal persistent inequality of opportunity and earnings: women disproportionately lived in poverty and composed 63% of all workers earning the national minimum wage of $7.25; represented just 5% of chief executive officers of the 500 top corporations; and held only between 23–31% of all local, state, and national elective positions by 2021 (Center for American Women and Politics, 2022). Adopting a feminist perspective pulls back the cultural veil of "everyday life practices [that] reproduce patriarchal domination" (M. D. Vavrus, 2002, p. 13).

The exposure of "everyday life practices" of gendered social relations produced a shift in public attitudes and policy that recast the private sphere of the home as no longer the unrestricted domain of male dominance and expectations for female subordination. The second-wave feminist slogan "the personal is the political" took hold as physical violence against children and women in the home moved out of the shadows of a private or personal matter behind closed doors; domestic violence became a public health issue that merited legal intervention. Rape and child abuse were no longer the legally protected right of patriarchal males. By 1994 Congress passed the Violence Against Women Act, but during the Trump-controlled Congress the act was allowed to lapse in 2018. After Biden's election, efforts were underway to expand the act to bar the purchase of a gun by anyone convicted of domestic abuse or stalking, a revision opposed by far-right congressional members (Davis, 2021).

Expectations for Far-Right Women

Online analyses of social media forums reveal an increasing overlap between those who hold postfeminist views and those who visit far-right sites (Stokel-Walker, 2021). In other words, the far right provides a welcoming community for anti-feminists. Far-right postfeminism prefers women who assume traditional feminine roles that are constructed as a "natural" difference between men and women. The patriarchal far right in Europe and North America emphasizes that the primary role of women should be mothers whose reproduction helps stem the "replacement" of Whites by an increasingly ethnically diverse population. Far-right women understand that their main role is to serve as caretakers and supporters of men to perpetuate misogyny "under the guise of protecting 'traditional' gender roles" (Anti-Defamation League, 2021, p. 11). As an aspect of a White supremacist future, far-right discourse constructs "Western civilization as a gift from white men to white women" and "becomes a racial position as a reclamation of white heritage, culture, traditions, and identity" (Campion, 2020, pp. 5, 12).

The participation of females in far-right movements is statistically insignificant in comparison to males. Nevertheless, women associated with the far right support a postfeminist ideology and are not passive participants. As observed in Chapter 3, anti-feminist conservative and far-right women accommodated themselves to 20th-century fascist regimes. The state of Indiana during the 1920s, for example, had the largest Ku Klux Klan (KKK) membership that included an estimated one third of all White Protestant women living in the state. According to historian Linda Gordon, it was these women who "organized Klan rites of passage, baptisms, graduations, marriages and funerals [and] supported vigilantism" (as cited in Provost & Whyte, 2018, para. 6). Far-right women actively opposed the Equal Rights Amendment and contributed to its demise in the 1970s. Since 9/11 and the rise of the U.S. security state, women increasingly became involved in the far right as protectors and sanctioners of macho militarization.

"Security Mom" Propaganda

In *Postfeminist War: Women in the Media-Military-Industrial Complex*, research by communications studies scholar Mary Douglas Vavrus (2019) points to how after 9/11 attention shifted from the liberal construction of the "soccer mom" to a popular culture imaginary of a "security mom." A security mom is a "woman with children who believes the most important issue of the day is national security, particularly the fight against terrorism" (p. 201). During the 2004 presidential campaign between George W. Bush and his Democratic opponent John Kerry, mainstream media and far-right politicians reconstructed peaceful soccer moms into militarized security moms to the beat of war drums supportive of U.S. invasions into Afghanistan and Iraq. This renegotiation of womanhood to security moms by media and politicians helped to "justify patriarchal masculinity, sanctioning it as acceptable—even necessary—to make home and homeland safe from external threats" (p. 71). Whereas women historically were resistant to sending young people to war zones, mothers after 9/11 were reimagined as militarized cheerleaders championing involvement in the vagaries of a global war on terrorism and its implicit imperialism. The media construction of the security mom replaced feminism with a desire for a patriarchal strong*man* to lead the nation.

The discourse of the "security mom" fits well with women involved in contemporary far-right actions, including participation in the Capitol siege and disrupting school board meetings as self-described "moms for liberty" (see Craig, 2021). Such groups reflect a rise in educational absolutism that eventually took hold under German fascism. Far-right women acting in the name of personal and national security and "liberty" demonstrate a willingness to condone incivility and the use of physical violence as a valid means to protect their homeland against ideologically constructed domestic enemies such as migrant refugees, Muslims, Black Lives Matter protesters, and, in some instances, public school board members, administrators, and classroom teachers. Campion's (2020) detailed international ethnographic research found that far-right women assume a variety of roles that include those who (a) participate directly in terrorism, (b) promote and participate in far-right actions online or in public rallies, and (c) play a support role such as providing safe houses from legal authorities. Weaving together findings by Campion and M. D. Vavrus (2002, 2019), we find far-right women's embracement of postfeminism and patriarchy in tandem with White superiority over their racialized "enemies." In summary, women in the contemporary far right represent an anxiety that must be acted on if America expects to fend off attacks on the righteousness of White nationalism.

Misogynistic Violence

Misogynistic postfeminism ranges from a prejudice and dislike of women, especially feminists, to structural and physical violence and overt expressions of hate. Misogyny is sanctioned structurally, for instance, through job discrimination, verbal slights, and expectations for domestic deference to males. The popular far-right radio commentator Rush Limbaugh regularly amplified postfeminism from the 1990s until his death in 2021. A favorite of far-right politicians, including Trump who awarded Limbaugh the Presidential Medal of Freedom in 2020, Limbaugh invented the term *feminazi* to disparage any women asserting their rights in the public sphere. By attaching the label "Nazi" to feminism, Limbaugh used a common tactic of neo-fascism by shifting attention from far-right fascistic discourse and misapplying fascism to the left. Limbaugh's widely repeated assertion of the "feminazi" helped "to short-circuit any real discussion of feminism in millions of American households" (Hesse, 2021, para. 3).

Despite the revelation 1 month before the 2016 election of Trump caught on tape contending that all a man had to do to a woman was to "[g]rab 'em by the pussy. You can do anything" (Trump, 2005/2016, para. 19), he nevertheless won the presidency. Regularly on public display was Trump's misogynic denigration and violent contempt for women, especially those who were feminists (Lange, 2018). Trump's publicly documented objectification of women existing in service of male sexual drives emboldened a segment of the far right. As one prominent far-right misogynistic commentator clarified, "As men, it is our responsibility to bring girls back to their proper place. . . . We reward [females] for their willingness to please us and make us happy, and in doing so make themselves happy" (M. Forney, as cited in Anti-Defamation League, 2021, p. 9).

The first documented modern mass murder in the name of misogynistic anti-feminism was in Montreal in 1989 when a 25-year-old male murdered 14 women and injured 10 more. The killer believed that he was "fighting feminism" because feminists apparently, he contended, "have always ruined my life" (M. Lépine, as cited in DiBranco, 2019, para. 1). As an outgrowth of the so-called "men's movement," the postfeminist ideology of *masculinism* emerged more visibly in the 1980s. In their study of social movements, Blais and Dupuis-Déri (2012) explain, "Masculinism asserts that since men are in crisis and suffering because of women in general and feminists in particular, the solution to their problems involves curbing the influence of feminism and revalorizing masculinity" (p. 22). Composed mainly of White heterosexual men, masculinism morphed in the 21st century to "incels," short for "involuntarily celibates." Incels express their misogyny as revenge on women for having "thwarted male sexual entitlement" (DiBranco, 2020, "Terrorist Intent," para. 2). In her research into the horrendous outcome of incel misogyny, DiBranco (2020) observed how the connection between male domestic abusers and publicly visible incels are overlooked by law enforcement. She explained that "intimate partner violence is in of itself a manifestation of aggrieved entitlement, a process to terrorize victims, and the leading cause of female homicides in the U.S." ("Ignoring Red Flags," para. 2).

Postfeminism offers a zero-sum equation of gender equality as males perceive they are losing out on opportunities from any equity gains by women. Violent misogynistic postfeminism continues to grow primarily through online forums. Feminist activists who are active on social media regularly face online misogyny, including death threats. The increasing level of life-threatening harassment harms women who seek to address feminism online (Barker & Jurasz, 2019). Violent misogynistic anti-feminism intersection with hypermasculinity endures as a dominant element of the far right and "acts as a bridge to white supremacist and anti-Semitic ideology" (Anti-Defamation League, 2021, p. 5).

EVANGELICAL CHRISTIAN ABSOLUTISM

Evangelical Christians believe in "traditional" values based on their interpretation of the Bible. Evangelical Christianity as a movement is "revivalistic, interested in maintaining the faith's cultural relevance, and *demanding political relevance*" (Griffis, 2017, p. 150, emphasis added). By the 1970s far-right powerbrokers began creating organizations to enable the politicization of evangelical Christianity. Starting with elections on school boards and exploding violently in efforts to ban multicultural curricula in schools, significant numbers of evangelical Christians found their calling in far-right politics, a strategy that reemerged nationally in 2021 (Benner, 2021; National Education Association, 1975/1991).

By the beginning of the 21st century there was a dramatic shift among political leaders from expressing personal religious convictions to exploiting a politicized religious absolutism in policy decisions. Using religious absolutism, President George W. Bush in 2003 justified the U.S. preemptive attack on Iraq and the war that ensued because *"God is on our side"* (as cited in Gaddy, 2005, p. 48, emphasis added). Bush used his Christian absolutism to inform a foreign policy in a dichotomous *us-versus-them* construction: "The course of the conflict is not known, yet its outcome is certain. Freedom and fear, justice and cruelty have always been at war, and we know that God is not neutral between them" (p. 48). Bush further contributed to creating a 21st-century political context for religion to frame the United States as representatives of "civilization" and those who oppose U.S. foreign invasions as godless barbarians—similar to the defense of settler colonialism warring on Indigenous populations, a topic examined in Chapter 7.

Divine Apocalyptic Rationale

Far-right evangelicals were disproportionately influential both inside and outside of the Trump administration, including Trump's original cabinet appointments. Rick Perry (2019), former Texas governor and Trump cabinet member, enthused about weekly Bible studies conducted for Trump's cabinet. The day before the Capitol siege, a right-wing minister and Trump supporter proclaimed at a Washington, DC, rally that God now had "an army of patriots" who exemplified the founding of the nation: "The church of the Lord Jesus Christ started America. *We're going to take our nation back!*" (B. Gibson, as cited in Stewart, 2021, p. 6sr, emphasis added). Although they contend that they are supporting the Constitution, far-right evangelical Christians overlook the Establishment Clause of the First Amendment, which states, "Congress shall pass no law respecting an establishment of religion."

Religious absolutism powered by political operatives normalized "more and more candidates for public office . . . [to] engage in rhetoric that establish them as 'chosen by God,' 'divinely ordained,' 'God's man for this hour in history,' or a 'blessed candidate'" (Gaddy, 2005, p. 53). Representing nearly 20% of the U.S. electorate, far-right evangelical Christians overwhelmingly came to the voting booth to support such candidates. Nearly 80% of evangelicals who planned to vote for Trump in 2020 did so because they saw him as a biblical savior for the nation (Gabbatt, 2020; Newport, 2020; Sherwood, 2020). By favoring evangelical Christians, Trump "confers privilege in exchange for constant loyalty at the ballot box, no matter what he does" (R. Laser, as cited in Gabbatt, 2020, para. 6).

Far-right politically elected legislators position themselves as opponents of a "ruling elite" while being faithful to Protestantism in drawing a sharp line between an asserted superiority of Christianity and all else as "pagan secularism" (Stewart, 2021, p. 6sr). The divisive language of far-right evangelicals denigrates multiculturalism, according to religious scholar Katherine Stewart (2021): "It says that human existence in an inevitable pluralistic, modern society committed to equality is inherently worthless" (p. 6sr). Using an apocalyptic rationale, politically motivated Christian extremism

> comes with the idea that *a right-minded elite* of religiously pure individuals should aim to capture the levers of government, then use that power to *rescue society* from eternal darkness and *reshape it* in accord *with a divinely approved view of righteousness.* (p. 6sr, emphasis added)

Like fascist anti-intellectualism discussed in Chapter 3, religious absolutism in its opposition to multiculturalism's religious diversity eliminates rational debate necessary for a healthy democracy and a critical civic education for young people.

KKK's Violent Religious Legacy

Kelly Baker, a researcher of the KKK, sees parallels and differences between the far-right Protestantism of the KKK in 1920s to contemporary far-right discourse. Like the KKK a century ago, today's far-right religious extremists are ideologically White supremacists. Whereas the KKK opposed immigrants who were Catholic or Jewish, today far-right evangelicals direct their animus toward those who follow the religion of Islam. Nevertheless, their religious intolerance originates from the same deep well of racism. In this regard, Baker notes that KKK men and women "were nervous about the enfranchisement of Black people as well, but so much of their effort was directed toward other religious groups" (as cited in Dias, 2021, p. A11).

One difference between the KKK and far-right evangelicals is that formerly KKK members publicly concealed their identities, whereas today's White supremacist Christians are quite open about their political beliefs and alliances. Although some far-right evangelicals may have opposed the violence during the Capitol siege, their support of exclusionary policies represents less visible forms of structural violence on individuals from historically marginalized groups. "*Cultural violence leads to structural violence* when it is incorporated into the formalized legal and economic exchanges of the society*," explain Pilisuk and Rountree (2015, p. 81, emphasis added). Whereas direct violence by an individual is more visible, structural violence can be more difficult to recognize: "The invisibility of the structure of violence is frequently the result of our inability—or refusal—to see below the surface" (p. 82). In regard to the far right's resort to violence during the Capitol siege, Baker warned, "It's a mistake to assume that this is some sort of anomaly that we can just move past" (as cited in Dias, 2021, p. A11).

Undermining Democracy

The use of religious absolutism by the far right as a political tool not only undermines any theological integrity of Christianity, but *"threatens the vitality of democracy"* in shutting down opposition and debate on nearly any issue opposed to theirs (Gaddy, 2005, p. 56, emphasis in original). More than a half century ago Reisman (1964/1993), as suggested in the epigraph to this chapter, warned that liberals compromising with far-right extremists and conservatives is "an illusionary operation" (p. 95). In the absence of compromise, incivility is uncritically heightened and opens space for zealous religious fanaticism in political discourse. Propelled by evangelical Christians, far-right extremism in electoral politics served to move conservatism further to the right.

Figure 4.2. Summary of Elements Within Far-Right Ideal Traits

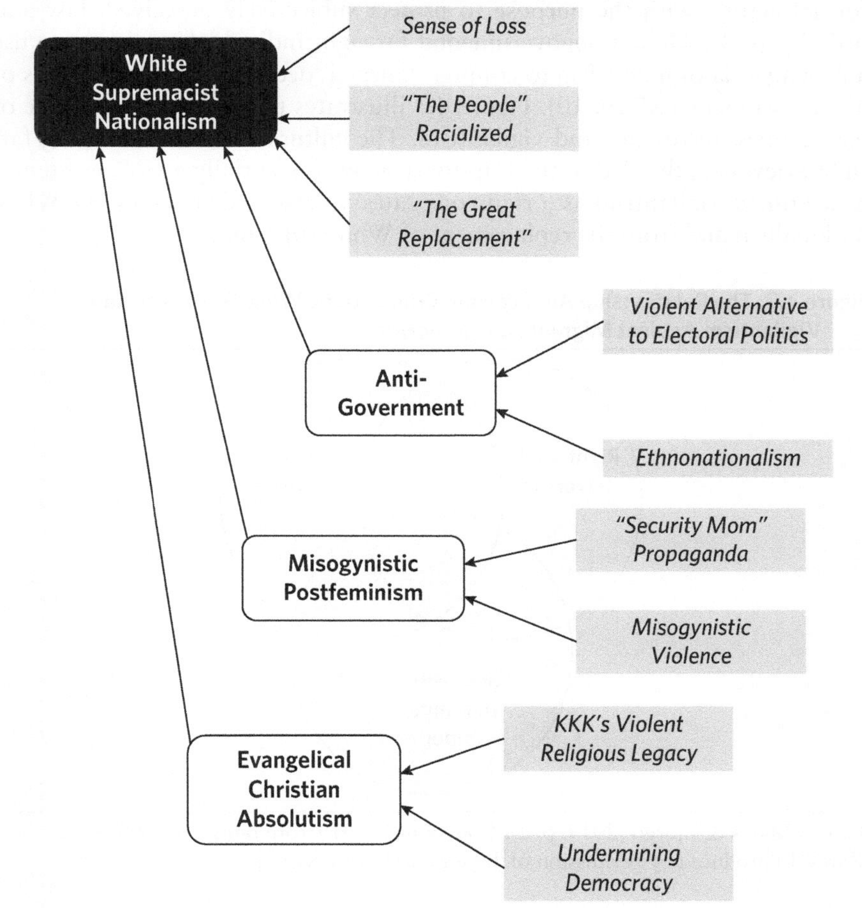

Figure 4.2 offers a visual outline of the individual features within each discrete common characteristic of far-right extremism as described.

FAR-RIGHT NORMALIZATION OF POLITICAL VIOLENCE

Whether a lone actor or part of militia group, the threat of vigilante terrorism is a primary tool for the far right. Governmental policing agencies historically offer tacit support for vigilantes acting alone or part of organized paramilitaries militias in support of anti-immigration actions. Vigilantes come to believe that they are protectors of public safety when they conclude a lack of governmental action is inadequate against refugees and immigrants of color. International researchers Tore Mareš and Miroslav Bjørgo (2019) define *vigilantism* as "the use of extra-legal enforcement of a particular conception of justice or a threat or intention to use such enforcement, carried out by informal actors, with the purpose to protect subjectively perceived 'law and order'" (p. 4). These nongovernmental far-right individuals and groups use a propaganda of militarism to counter "alleged 'decadency' and weakness of liberal democracies" (p. 10). Figure 4.3 illustrates the overlapping nature of hate crimes, terrorism, and vigilantism. The cultural racism underlying far-right grievances that led to the Capitol siege was essentially a violent attempt to legitimize vigilantism as a righteous cause to rescue democracy for White nationalism and from the replacement of White supremacy.

Figure 4.3. The Relationship Among Hate Crime, Right-Wing Terrorism, and Vigilantism Against Migrants and Minorities

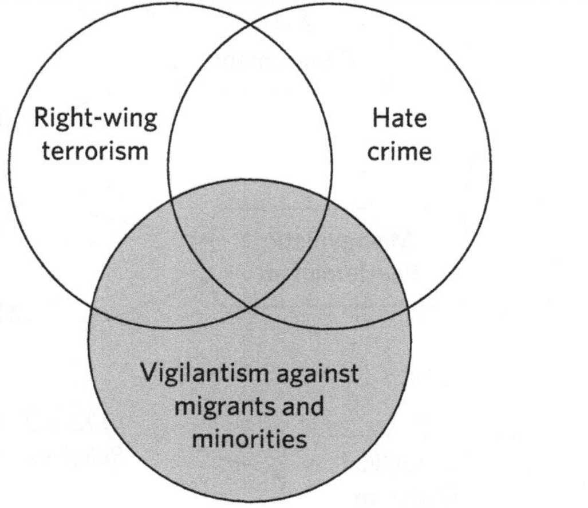

Source: Mareš & Bjørgo (2019, p. 2). Copyright © 2019 Tore Bjørgo and Miroslav Mareš. Reproduced by permission of Taylor and Francis Group, LLC.

COMPARISONS BETWEEN FAR-RIGHT EXTREMISM AND CONSERVATIVISM

Far-right extremism and the authoritarian streak of conservativism display ideological similarities and differences. A global study of varieties of democracies and their respective political parties over the past 50 years indicates a dramatic rightward shift in the United States of both the Republican and Democratic parties. Based on their data analysis, Lühmann and Medzihorsky (2020) found that the Republican Party "has retreated from upholding democratic norms in recent years" (para. 2) of liberalism's promise of equality and is internationally "far more illiberal than almost all other governing parties in democracies" (para. 6). The elements of far-right illiberalism of the Republican Party include an asserted religious cultural superiority in its opposition to multiculturalism, racial minority voting rights, and LGBTQ+ equality; a disrespect of political opponents; the encouragement of violence; citizen-centric anti-immigration;

and advocacy of harsh economic austerity policies that reduce and privatize formerly public goods that in effect hold negative effects for the well-being of vulnerable populations (Lühmann & Medzihorsky, 2020). In another international study, The Economist Intelligence Unit (2021) reported a significant decline globally in people living under democracy, including the United States, and a rise in authoritarian governments.

Similarities

Both the ideologies of the far right and conservatism conceptualize a racialized democracy that primarily privileges White populations in a patriarchal gendered hierarchy. Both minimize or simply ignore social and economic class status as a relevant factor for public policy. Instead, both emphasize individualistic merit as the basis of economic well-being. With an emphasis on meritocracy, these two ideologies oppose public intervention to ameliorate disparities in wealth and income, especially when perceived as assisting populations of color.

The ideologies of far-right extremism and conservatism result in a form of political theater that uses cultural symbols "associated with 'the people'" rather than actually proposing and enacting concrete policies that could be beneficial for the public good (Saull et al., 2015, p. 5). Both ideological positions are *"anchored in fixed or 'natural' hierarchies"* (p. 5, emphasis added) and view contemporary "multiculturalism and immigration" as unnatural and corrupting the White "ethnic distinction of the nation" (Worth, 2015, p. 155). An overriding commonality of the far right and conservativism is a religious absolutism that intersects with a racialized, gendered, and classist anti-equalitarianism (Mareš & Bjørgo, 2019).

Differences

Whereas conservatism seeks to preserve the status quo, the far right is more willing "to commit to a more fundamental transformation of state-society relations that has consequences" domestically and internationally in its circulation of conspiratorial politics (Saull et al., 2015, p. 5). Far-right nativism views both conservative and liberal elites as negligent in restricting the political influence of multiculturalism and prefers to eliminate diversity from political consideration. Enabled by evangelical Christians and a vigilantism of militarized "patriot" movements, far-right extremism stresses "the need to protect American society from big government and from 'a new world order' . . . organized by globalists, liberals and socialists across the world" (Worth, 2015, p. 156). In opposition to international institutions and their advocates, a far-right version of American exceptionalism takes on the mantle of protecting the nation against perceived internal and external threats and enemies.

In "its perverse 'anti-capitalism,'" the far right leans toward fascist politics that blame marginalized ethnic populations for society's economic problems while denying the role of capitalism in shaping social relations of inequality (Saull et al., 2015, p. 8). The far right leans further than conservatism toward a belief in autarky or nationalistic economic protectionism rather than policies that include global trade of goods. Despite recognition through electoral politics, the far right—more so than conservatism—retains an antagonism toward state institutions that support a liberal democracy. Overall, since 9/11 the far right has increasingly become entrenched and central to mainstream political discourse in and out of governmental bodies.

Chapter 3's analysis of historical fascism and this chapter's focus on the far right provide a civic background as to what anti-fascist movements have stood for and against, the topic that we turn to next.

NOTE

1. In her book on fascism, Albright (2018) erred in stating that the far-right political application of the phrase "drain the swamp" came from the Italian fascist leader Mussolini. He was referring to public works to drain actual malaria-ridden swamplands from the physical environment near Rome, not in the politicized way Presidents Reagan and Trump used the phrase (Jacobson, 2018).

CHAPTER 5

Everyday Anti-Fascism and the Struggle for a Multicultural Democracy

> If you oppose racism, white supremacy, homophobia, transphobia, misogyny, Islamophobia, anti-Semitism, and the xenophobic, ultranationalist ideologies of the far right,…you are an EVERYDAY ANTIFASCIST.
>
> —Antifa flyer, Portland, Oregon, 2019

Anti-fascism emerged nearly a century ago during the interwar years leading up to WWII. Anti-fascism then and now is more than simply the opposite of fascism. Anti-fascism in the late 20th and early 21st centuries in the United States and Europe is most recognizable in actions that support anti-racism, decolonization, migrant protection, feminism, and anti-patriarchal policing of sexual and gender boundaries, all of which are bedrocks of critical multicultural education. Anti-fascists are not only opposed to any signs of fascist politics but take actions to disrupt fascistic expressions. Since its origins anti-fascism stands in opposition to cultural racisms along with any fascist impulses to place undemocratic limits on subordinated groups who are in pursuit of equality and equity.

In the United States the emergence of contemporary anti-fascism originated as an anti-racism movement in the 1980s in response to emboldened actions of the KKK that openly supported the dog-whistle racism of Ronald Reagan's presidential campaign. Given the political atmosphere of that decade, the label "fascism" often sounded overly doctrinaire and reduced to a slogan without a grounded meaning. Therefore, anti-fascist national networks such as the John Brown Anti-Klan Committee (JBAKC) and Anti-Racist Action (ARA) pragmatically avoided the term *fascism*. By the end of the 1980s, however, JBAKC changed the name of its newspaper to *No KKK—No Fascist USA!* (Bray, 2017; Moore & Tracy, 2020). Bray (2017) explains that anti-fascism in the 21st century "was not born overnight" and instead today's "anti-fascist movement that grew out of ARA never died" (p. 106). Mullen and Vials (2020) add, "'Antifa' as we know it is largely a post-1980 phenomena and a European import" (p. 15).

Often overlooked in chronologies of groups identifying as anti-fascist is the Black Panther Party for Self Defense, which recognized and named the perpetuators of anti-Black police violence as "fascist pigs." In 1969 the party "called for a United Front Against Fascism" (Descartes et al., 2020, p. 183). A 1970 edition of their newspaper *Black Panther* that accompanied "pictures of 19 dead Panthers" pointed out "evidence and intimidation of fascist crimes in the U.S.A." (Calloway, 1977, p. 62). That same year Black auto worker and public intellectual James Boggs (1970) warned that *"majority rule can easily become for all Americans the fascism that the Negro has known all his life"* (p. 37, emphasis added).

It was during this latter quarter of the 20th century that multicultural education emerged as a counternarrative to a White-washing of the school curriculum. Anti-fascism as part of civic education, however, was not conceptually incorporated within multicultural education that was ostensibly disconnected from the anti-racist roots of anti-fascists active in street confrontations and in popular education outside of formal schooling. Hence, a purpose of this chapter as well as the entirety of *Teaching Anti-Fascism* is to make overt organic linkages among critical multicultural education, citizenship education, and anti-fascism.

Since WWII the attitudes of contemporary mainstream media, politicians, and historians toward anti-fascism range from silence and minimal acknowledgement to displays of open hostility (Bray, 2017; Bray et al., 2020). Nevertheless, not until the televised anti-capitalist protests toward the end of 1999 that shut down a World Trade Organization meeting of finance ministers in Seattle did mainstream media take notice of 21st-century anti-fascism via its newfound discovery of contemporary *Antifa*—a contraction of anti-fascism related to "militant antifascist organizing" (Burley, 2021b, p. 18; Gordon, 2020). Political antagonism and misrepresentation of anti-fascism peaked during the Trump administration (2017–2021). For example, a far-right member of the House of Representatives introduced the "Unmasking Antifa Act" (2018) to criminalize with 15-year prison terms any masked individuals counter protesting far-right gatherings and police use of excessive force.

After major Black Lives Matter protests in 2020, Trump openly attacked Antifa, which had become "a stand in for every cultural trend the right finds frightening" (Burley, 2021b, p. 18). Antifa, according to Trump, would be placed on a terrorist list, a step that never transpired (Haberman & Savage, 2020). So that Antifa might be considered a terrorist group, the Department of Homeland Security tried to connive a connection between foreign powers and Antifa activists protesting anti-Black police violence (Klippenstein, 2020). U.S. Attorney General William Barr (2019–2020) and others on the far right falsely claimed that anti-fascists were actually fascists and supported the idea of naming Antifa as a terrorist organization in part because of their leftist anti-capitalistic stance and inclination toward socialism. In countering the projection of fascist politics onto anti-fascists, Bray (2020) succinctly responds that *"fascists are the real fascists* because they pursue a fascist political agenda" ("Myth No. 5," para. 2, emphasis added). Nevertheless, with no evidence, right-wing media outlets and Republican members of Congress attempted to deflect attention away from far-right extremists who led the Capitol siege by concocting the blatant lie that somehow Antifa was involved (Armus, 2021).

In their introduction to *Rethinking Antifascism: History, Memory and Politics, 1922–Present*, Garcia et al. (2016) note how mainstream scholars during the final decades of the 20th century conflated and misrepresented anti-fascism with the communism of the former Soviet Union: "Perhaps the greatest obstacle to understanding antifascism as a historical phenomenon is the persistent tendency of historians to identify it with communism" (p. 3). Traverso (2016) points out how mainstream historians delegitimize anti-fascism by a use of two different premises that lead to a *false equivalency*: "antifascism = communism and communism = totalitarianism; consequently, antifascism = totalitarianism" (p. 328). Such a distortion through a historical master narrative ignores what anti-fascism actually represents as well as the diversity of backgrounds of individuals who became anti-fascists. During the interwar years and WWII, individuals opposed to the very real threat of fascism represented a range of ideological orientations that included most prominently "socialism, Communism, and anarchism, . . . pacifism, anti-imperialism and feminism" (Garcia et al., 2016, p. 4). During this same era that coexisted with the Great Depression, anti-fascism became "the most ambitious response to the challenge to come up with new relations between liberty, equality and justice, civil rights and social rights, state and market, and political and social representation" (p. 4).

To understand what actually constitutes anti-fascism, we next consider a composite of its ideal traits, all of which help to account for the animosity from far-right extremists and conservatives, and centrist liberals.

FOUNDATIONAL TRAITS OF 21ST-CENTURY ANTI-FASCISM

Anti-fascism ideologically falls under the broad umbrella of the characteristics of *anarchism* with roots that, according to Vysotsky's (2021) research, have "always been an explicitly leftist position" (p. 55). Furthermore, current "militant antifascism within groups that identify as antifa . . . is a largely anarchist phenomenon," drawing on the anarchism of anti-fascist/anti-racist groups from the 1980s (p. 55). Anarchism is most evident in how anti-fascists deliberate and organize themselves.

The term *anarchy* originated from the Greek and literally means a leaderless state. This reflects the *anti-authoritarianism* of anti-fascism's deep distrust of state authority. The *nonhierarchical* nature of anti-fascism forwards an alternative model of decision-making that is participatory and expressed as *direct democracy* through self-management that contributes to developing consensus in deliberations (see Graeber, 2002). The nonhierarchical characteristic of anti-fascism stands in opposition to domination and in support of *emancipation of oppressed populations*. According *To Change Everything: An Anarchist Appeal* (CrimethInc., 2018), "Anarchists oppose all forms of hierarchy—every currency that concentrates power into the hands of the few, every mechanism that puts us at distance from our potential" (p. 44). Anti-fascism, therefore, in congruence with anarchism "offers a critique of anything and everything that smacks of hierarchy, centralization, and unjustified authority" (Fiala, 2018, p. 7; Vysotsky, 2021).

Anti-fascism opposes the antidemocratic dominance of a political economy of capitalism in structuring social relations of inequality that benefit the few. As the *Oxford Dictionary of Economics* explains, it is a relatively small class of capitalists, not ordinary citizens, who politically take "an important role in decision-making" for a society's allocation of resources (J. Black, 2003, p. 46). In its opposition to exploitation and domination, "anarchism is necessarily anti-capitalist" (Chomsky, 2013, p. 9). Anti-fascism instead looks to a socialistic economy to produce and distribute goods and services democratically determined to fulfill human needs for the vast majority of people, not for private profiteering.

Anti-fascism upends liberalism's assertion of a morally just economy that is centered on individual self-interest. Liberalism rests on an unproved assumption that individual pursuit of self-interest by everyone adds up to what is best for individuals and families. The moral economy orientation of anti-fascism, however, considers what is in the best interests of the public good for the whole of society. Based on mutual aid through an equitable sharing of resources, *democratic socialism* is the opposite of capitalism's underlying acceptance of fictitious social Darwinism and the trope of survival of the fittest. Rather than outright neglect or charity, mutual aid represents "a form of solidarity-based support, in which communities unite against a common struggle, rather than leaving individuals to fend for themselves" (Arnold, 2020, para. 2). Mutual aid, for example, was significant in support of anti-fascists who have been detained during protests under arbitrary policing practices (Burley, 2022). The social relations of mutual aid as envisioned by anti-fascism within a democratic socialism that is premised on a participatory economy for economic justice capture how anarchism represents a "positive theory of human flourishing" (Fiala, 2018, p. 1).

Anti-fascism repudiates oppressive ideological foundations of fascism, the far right, and conservatism in their construction of racial and cultural hierarchies in the defense of discrimination of subordinated groups. Anti-fascism in the 21st century critiques how liberal multiculturalism obfuscates and limits equality and equity. Liberal multiculturalism perceives inequality as an exception to an ideology of individualism and meritocracy despite existing socioeconomic stratification that liberal democracies permit. Liberal multiculturalism's recognition of nondominant groups stops with mild reforms as a means to reduce inequality. In contrast, the transnational cosmopolitanism of critical multiculturalism focuses not only on recognition, but also on the necessity of proactive expansion and enforcement of an equitable redistribution of rights and material goods (Vavrus, 2015).

Critical multiculturalism shares anti-fascism and anarchism's trait of *equity*. As suggested by the quote from an Antifa flyer in the epigraph to this chapter, both anti-fascism and critical multiculturalism find congruity in critiquing how the intersectionality of group identities such as race, ethnicity, gender, and sexuality relate to socioeconomic class power and privilege (Bray, 2017; May, 2012).

Figure 5.1 is an array of characteristics representative of anarchism that holistically compose common characteristics of anti-fascism. To summarize, the traits are (a) anti-authoritarianism, (b) nonhierarchical organizing, (c) the goal of emancipation of oppressed populations, (d) direct democracy through self-managed consensus decision-making, (e) a political economy based on democratic socialism, and (f) equity as realized through fairness of opportunities and inclusion.

Figure 5.1. Composite of Key Ideological Traits of Contemporary Anti-Fascism

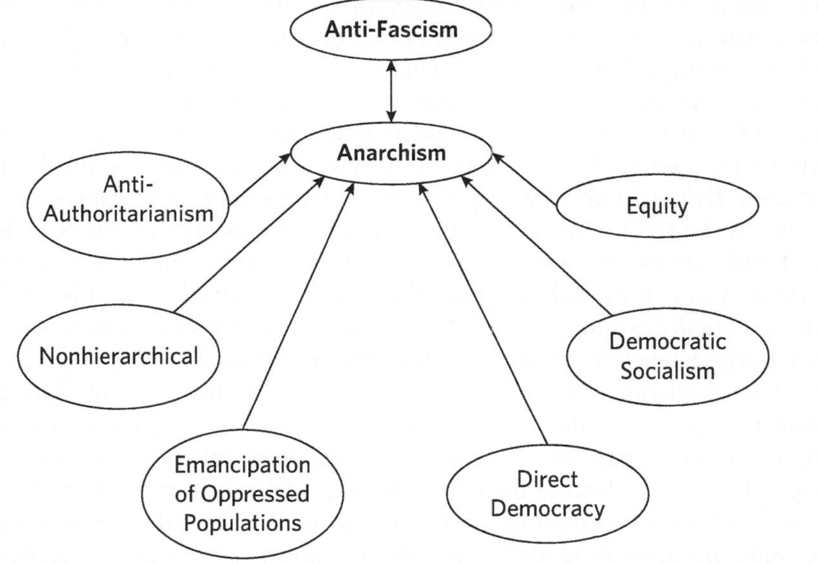

Early forms of socialistic anarchism existed in 18th-century religious communities in Europe and colonial North America, 19th-century utopian communities in the United States, and countercultural communes in the 1960s and 1970s. Efforts to organize communities removed from mainstream society and direct political engagement are commonalities among these types of anarchistic groups. Anti-fascism rooted in anarchism, however, views involvement in the political world as requisite to stop the spread of fascist politics exhibited in word and deed.

To grasp the significance of mainstream animus toward anti-fascism in relation to anarchism necessitates looking back to the late 19th and early

20th centuries in U.S. history. To do otherwise can minimize both the ideological significance of anarchism within anti-fascist groups and the uphill struggle against dominance and repression.

U.S. SUPPRESSION OF WORKING-CLASS ANARCHISTS

Anarchist underpinnings of anti-fascism are consistently a subject of attack by dominant forces. Throughout U.S. history, corporations and governments at all levels used the power of the state and paramilitaries to suppress any political leanings that challenged capitalism. Among the oppressed historically were wage laborers who identified as *anarchists*.

The late 1800s was when the popular imagination reduced anarchism to bomb throwers intent on creating bedlam. This imagery of a destructive ideology emerged from the subsequent chaos in the aftermath of a public gathering of workers to denounce Chicago police shootings of labor activists and to collectively organize for a living wage, an 8-hour workday, and safer working conditions. The 1886 event infamously became known as the "Haymarket Affair." During a labor rally at Haymarket Square, as the police stormed into the crowd during a speech by an anarchist, a bomb exploded, killing police officers and civilians. Arrested were eight anarchist labor organizers, although, except for the speaker that day, none of them were at the event. The pro-business *Chicago Tribune* daily newspaper went so far to offer to pay jurors if they found all eight of the workers guilty. Although the identity of whoever threw the bomb remains unknown to this day, all eight were found guilty; seven of them were sentenced to death, while the other one received a life sentence. Four were eventually executed, one died in his jail cell, and the other three eventually had death sentences commuted to life in prison (Adelman, 1986; Fiala, 2018).

The convictions of the innocent pro-labor anarchists provided the government a pretext to declare martial law, not just in Chicago but across the United States, as part of a violent crackdown on socialists and organized labor. Following the lead of the United States, foreign governments and media used the Haymarket Affair to justify repression of their local labor movements by conflating anarchism with terrorism. Seventeen years after the Haymarket Affair, Congress passed the Immigration Act of 1903, commonly known as the "Anarchist Exclusion Act" (Adelman,1986; Barton, 2015; Colson, 2017). Judicial affirmation of the law "marked the first time that the Supreme Court held exclusion and deportation, *based purely on political conviction and ideology*, to be constitutional" (Barton, 2015, p. 305, emphasis added).

Terrorizing and Racializing Laborers

Following the Russian Revolution of 1917 and the end of WWI in 1918, U.S. anarchist labor activists who were advocating for worker's rights in hostile environments of repression became victims of governmental anti-communism extralegal actions. What became known as the "Red Scare" was a reign of state-sponsored terrorism conducted in opposition to the promises of the Fifth and 14th Amendments to the Constitution that no person should be "deprived of life, liberty, or property, without due process of law." U.S. Attorney General Mitchell Palmer authorized a series of raids in late 1919 and into the 1920s under direction of a new Justice Department appointee, 24-year-old J. Edgar Hoover. Known as the Palmer Raids, in the span of just 1 day "Hoover's agents swept through 33 cities in a spectacular show of force, targeting two Russian labor organizations and arresting more than 3,000 labor activists" (Pusey, 2015, p. 100). Palmer conflated "Bolsheviks" with U.S. labor leaders while racializing their phenotype genetically in a stereotypical manner: "out of the sly and crafty eyes of many of them leap cupidity, cruelty, insanity and crime. From their lopsided faces, sloping brows and misshapen features may be recognized the unmistakable criminal type" (as cited in Powell, 2019, p. 108). One of the most extreme instances of labor suppression during the early 1920s took place in the coal hills of West Virginia when the governor called for support from the U.S. Army to intervene against miners in armed struggles with local authorities. Acting beyond the authority of the law, mine owners hired a private plane that dropped bombs near resistant mine workers while the U.S. Army awaited deployment, if necessary, with 17 planes at a nearby airport (Laurie, 1991).

Using patriotism as a pretext, political and business elites helped stir anti-labor sentiments through a propagandized "campaign of *racializing communism*, drawing on the *rampant nativism* of early twentieth-century Americans . . . to ensure that the ideology and its attendant union collectivism gained no ground" in the United States (Powell, 2019, p. 104, emphasis added). Mainstream media in a xenophobic fervor contributed to this rationalization of racist and violent stereotypes of immigrant labor. Applauded by political, business, and religious leaders, the Palmer Raids also gave a governmental green light to corporate-hired militias and local police to continue the use of fascist techniques of violent suppression of unionizing efforts by workers seeking less deadly working conditions and livable wages. Although by 1921 the oppression directed at miners in West Virginia's coal-laden mountains "closed a chapter involving extraordinary extra-legal procedures in the domestic employment of federal troops" who "closely cooperated with state and local officials and mine owners and operators," governmental authorities continued to allow repressive measures elsewhere (Laurie, 1991, para. 3). Under the pretext of fighting terrorism, the ideology of state-supported capitalism and anti-communism during the 1920s and the early part of the 1930s was a significant factor in the acceptance of fascism as a reasonable response to maintain capitalism's control of labor (Levine, 1988; Markwick, 2009).

Post-WWII Labor Repression and Growth of Inequality

Repression of progressive labor unions continued immediately after WWII and was followed by Congressional hearings in the 1950s purging and ostracizing of political leftists as "un-American." By the end of the 20th-century anti-labor tactics included threats of firings, "electronic surveillance, illegal unilateral changes in wages and benefits, bribes, threats to refer undocumented workers to the INS [Immigration and Naturalization Service], promises of improvement, and promotion of union activists out of the [union organizing] unit" (Bronfenbrenner, 2000, p. vi). Indicative of the success of anti-union propaganda and intimidation for more than a century was the dismal percentage of only 6% of all workers in private-sector unions by the beginning of the 2020s. The significance of the overall decline in both public and private union membership represents a key element in the growth of income inequality. Figure 5.2 chronologically illustrates how when union membership was at its height, the gap between the share of income going to the wealthiest 10% and unionized workers narrowed significantly through WWII. With declines in union membership since the 1950s and 1960s, however, the gap in inequality has continued to grow for the past 50 years. The political economy of fascist politics of inequality is further discussed in Chapter 8.

Figure 5.2. Union Membership and Share of Income Going to the Top 10%, 1917–2019

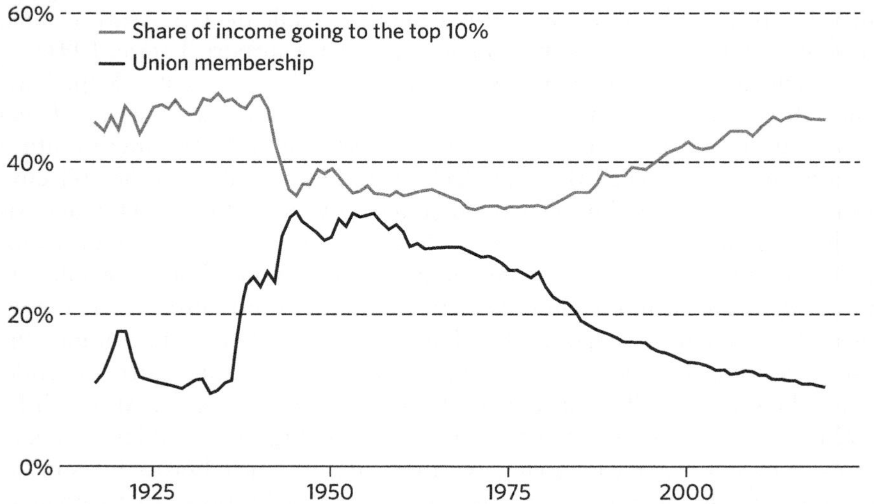

Source: McNicholas et al. (2021, figure B).

U.S. Anti-Fascism Hypocrisy During WWII

Often forgotten in public memory and absent from school textbooks is the anti-fascist impulse within an anarchist-oriented working class that played a key role in the initial civil resistance against fascism into the latter part of the 1930s. U.S. policy during WWII, on the other hand, was not focused on anti-fascism per se but more on securing geopolitical economic interests. Bray (2018) explains, "The Allied hostility to fascism was the result of geostrategic contingency, not ideological animus . . . and was not motivated by opposition to racism or anti-Semitism" (p. 9). Domestic anti-Semitism, civic and military racial segregation, and the internment of 120,000 innocent people of Japanese descent by the U.S. government all fly in the face of any claims that the United States actively opposed European, Latin American, or domestic fascism. Only after the Japanese bombing of a U.S. military base at Pearl Harbor in the colony of Hawaii did anti-fascism become "for the first and last time" the "official logic of the state" (Vials, 2014, p. 59). According to the U.S. Holocaust Memorial Museum (2017), not until 1944, 3 years *after* U.S. entry into WWII, did a hypocritical government begin to actually devise a plan "to rescue and provide relief for Jews and other minorities who were targeted by the Nazis" despite State Department knowledge 2 years earlier of Germany's plan to exterminate Jews (para. 4).

Next, we consider who and what constitutes anti-fascism, finding along the way conceptual differences and nuances depending on interpretations as to what it means to oppose fascism. A major conceptual stumbling block happens when making everyone who is not a fascist into an anti-fascist. To do so places the ideology of anti-fascism "in danger of losing all meaning" (Buchanan, 2016, p. 65).

NONFASCISM

Nonfascism is a contested categorization. From one perspective, nonfascists across the political spectrum often oppose fascism by looking back at fascist regimes of the mid-20th century but may overlook micro-fascist tendencies within contemporary mainstream politics and daily life. Nonfascists may be perceived as neutral bystanders and somewhat passive in their opposition to fascism on practical or ideological grounds in part because they tend to believe that the state will intervene to curb fascistic expressions. However, Bray (2017) notes, "We should be warier of those who are truly neutral toward fascism than those who honestly espouse their opposition to racism, genocide, and tyranny" (p. xxii). "Neutral" nonfascists from this point of view are not among the activists who mobilize against fascist politics and everyday micro fascisms experienced directly by oppressed populations.

Nonfascists may also be ordinary people who are simply trying to escape the psychological and physical brutality of fascist politics as happened in parts of Europe during WWII (Vials, 2014; Vysotsky, 2021). Traverso (2016) notes the dilemma of nonfascists in France when the government accommodated itself to fascism. For this population "the only legitimate resistance was a civil one, the resistance of rescuers, not combatants. Historically understood, nevertheless, the civilians' resistance was deeply connected with both the political and military Resistance" (pp. 332–333).

From yet another vantage point, anti-fascist journalist and activist Natasha Lennard (2019) uses the phrase "Non-Fascist Life" as the subtitle to a collection of her essays. She suggests that the term represents a way of being and living. When interviewed about her book, Lennard explained that she sought a term between actual fascism and anti-fascism that would "speak of the sort of intellectual, affective, communal, and emotional work needed to fight 'micro-fascisms' and everyday fascisms" (Lennard & Miller, 2020, para. 3). Representative of this type of nonfascism is the 2011 Occupy Wall Street movement that drew attention to economic inequality with its identification with the "99 percent" compared to the wealthiest 1% and grew nationally and internationally to 900 Occupy sites (cf. Taylor & Smucker, 2021).

Lennard further noted that she partially drew from French philosopher Michel Foucault's use of the concept of nonfascism. Foucault (1972) proposed that a nonfascist life involves "living counter to all forms of fascism" (p. xiii). Foucault included in his summary of nonfascism an anarchist principle of the freedom of "political action, . . . thought, and desires" not dictated by hierarchical decision-making so as to "not become enamored with power" (pp. xiii–xiv). Foucault stated this with the caution for what he believed was "the fascism in us all, in our heads and in our everyday behavior, the fascism that causes us to love power, to desire the very thing that dominates and exploits us" (p. xiii). Lennard's and Foucault's sense of critically reflective nonfascists captures an ideal trait of the nonhierarchical, anti-authoritarian engagement of 21st-century anti-fascists culturally within their affinity groups.

ANTI-FASCISM

Anti-fascism is manifested informally by individuals spontaneously reacting to immediate fascist provocations or more formally through organized affinity groups focused on disrupting the effectiveness of fascistic organizations such as far-right paramilitaries. Both informal and formal fascism consider it necessary to act in some form, be it "expressions of sympathy for targets of fascist degradation and violence to verbal or physical confrontation with fascists" (Vysotsky, 2021, p. 50). Although no single anti-fascist organization exists, many anti-fascists are active in social justice movements such as labor organizing, anti-racism, gender and sexuality rights, migrant support, and anti-war/anti-militarism. Anti-fascists, therefore, have already demonstrated a critical civic commitment to equity through actions to counter the harm experienced by marginalized groups, often prior to identifying more broadly as anti-fascists. Whereas informal and formal anti-fascist approaches can overlap, anti-fascists are further distinguished between tactics that are either nonviolent or militant. When perceived as a necessary form of self-defense against those who embrace fascistic violence, Antifa engages in direct confrontation with far-right extremists and is willing to use violence only as a last resort (Bray, 2017; Lennard, 2019; Vials, 2014; Vysotsky, 2021). Before addressing Antifa militancy, we first take note of the type of movement anti-fascism represents from a sociological assessment.

Nontraditional Countermovement

Anti-fascism is a countermovement in its response to signs of fascist politics. A countermovement is "an organized response to a social movement, with the purpose of blocking the movement's activities, resisting change, and presenting alternative points of view" (Oxford Reference, 2022). Anti-fascism as a countermovement is "a radical social movement that operates . . . outside of the bounds" of calls for reforms characteristic of typical social movements (Vysotsky, 2021, p. 10). The objective of a countermovement "is to halt or neutralize the goal attainment activities of the movement in question" (Adams & Snow, 2010, p. 6), in this case fascist politics of the far right.

In the 1980s the anti-fascist group John Brown Anti-Klan Committee was a countermovement primarily involved in calling attention to gatherings of neo-Nazis and White supremacists groups. The committee used leafleting, graffiti, and a newsletter, as well as attending city council meetings, not to call for reforms as a traditional social movement might do, but to alert municipalities as a way to publicize and create public opposition to far-right gatherings in their midst (Moore & Tracy, 2020). As a countermovement anti-fascism "exists outside of the realm of policy or state appeals" and, therefore, does not attempt to influence public policy but instead focuses on undermining and disrupting any fascist formations (Vysotsky, 2021, p. 10).

Anti-fascism is not a single organization and instead consists of relatively small, decentralized activists with little or no external funding. Although most visible in street confrontations, most anti-fascist activity today takes place in researching, monitoring, interrupting, and exposing far-right extremists who use a variety of social media platforms to advance their anti-democracy views. Most recently, for example, anti-fascist researchers uncovered a deceitful far-right Alaska assistant attorney general who concealed his identity to advocate anti-Semitic, racist, and homophobic positions. In addition to promoting "vigilante action against political opponents" and denigrating Jewish women, he called for "the summary imprisonment of Black Lives Matter protesters; vigilante violence against leftwing groups; and a punishment of execution for acts including performing gender reassignment surgery" (Wilson, 2021c, para. 9, 39). He was also part of a far-right Mormon "Deseret" nationalistic group that supports the creation of a theocratic state similar to a White supremacist ethno-state imagery embedded with a discourse of misogyny, homophobia, and transphobia (Wilson, 2021b.). In summary, the approaches of U.S. anti-fascists from the 1980s to the present are "rooted in the idea that ignoring fascist and racist formations, no matter how small, does not prevent them from growing" (Moore & Tracy, 2020, p. 211).

Within affinity groups, anti-fascists prefiguratively model an inclusive collective where social relations are self-managed democratically. The anarchist direct democracy trait of anti-fascists represents a self-awareness that they are organizing in the political sphere as "a movement about reinventing democracy" (Graeber, 2002, p. 70). Anti-fascists working in affinity groups generally come from working-class backgrounds that are majority White, although in urban anti-fascist organizations more racial diversity exists. Anti-fascists range in age from their mid-20s to mid-30s, although a small number are older, including some who are over 60. Anti-fascist affinity groups work toward a gender-balanced feminism that is inclusive of those identified as LGBTQ+ who increasingly are targets of fascist violence (Vysotsky, 2021; see Human Rights Campaign, 2022).

Anti-fascists during the Trump presidency realized the need to move from single acts of disruption of far-right extremism to a more popular, mass-based social movement that included increased attention to the economic struggles of people trying to survive from day to day. As an anti-fascist organizer explained to Bray (2017), anti-fascism involvement needs to expand because "[t]here have to be roles for elderly folks, disabled folks who are not going to be able hit the streets" (p. 119). To create a more welcoming environment for everyday anti-fascist activism and "to push back on insurgent far-right groups," Burley (2021b) observed how Portland, Oregon, organizers "built carnival-like protest spaces that exist alongside more militant anti-fascist groups" (p. 149). Educators and policymakers can enable a transition to the expansion of anti-fascism into preservice teacher education and teacher professional development, which is discussed in Chapter 9. To grow as a countermovement, anti-fascism needs broader participation and to create additional strategies to confront the phenomenon of far-right in-roads into cultural spaces and electoral politics in Europe and the United States in the 2020s and beyond. Schools as cultural and political spaces are one site to claim for anti-fascism public deliberations and involvement as an aspect of multicultural civic engagement.

Misrepresentations of Anti-Fascist Militancy

The tactics of anti-fascists have drawn a range of reactions. Until the 2021 Capital siege by violent Trump-supporting far-right extremists, mainstream liberals in particular clung to a false sense of security in the belief that freedom of assembly by any group—fascist or otherwise—was sacrosanct to a democracy. During the mid-1980s after members of the anti-fascist John Brown Anti-Klan Committee were attacked by White supremacist neo-Nazis in Chicago, the committee realized that engaging only in popular education was insufficient to counter fascist politics and accepted the need for militant self-defense. A far-right officer with the same infamous Chicago Police Department that working-class anarchists protested against in Haymarket Square in the 1880s, as described earlier, responded to clashes between neo-Nazis and anti-fascists by claiming that anti-fascists "are trouble, not the Nazis" (D. Eichler, as cited in Moore & Tracy, 2020, p. 171).

Fast-forwarding more than 30 years later, in 2017 liberal Democratic House of Representatives leader Nancy Pelosi, in a manner similar to the Chicago officer, decried the violent property damage and physical attacks against far-right extremists by Antifa. The confrontation between the far right and Antifa she cited was at a "No to Marxism in America" rally that used anti-socialism and free speech propaganda to shield their White supremacist and fascist desires (Swenson, 2017; Weigel, 2017). Three and half years later Pelosi was literally scrambling for her life during fascist violence by those urged on by President Trump on January 6, 2021. Pelosi was on a far-right death list, as evidenced by a woman who sent a video to her children during the Capitol siege, in which she said, "We were looking for Nancy to shoot her in the friggin' brain, but we didn't find her" (D. Bancroft, as cited in Kornfield, 2021).

Flawed "Equalviolence" Thesis. Liberal and conservative educators, politicians, and mainstream media equating the rare use of physical, nonlethal violence by anti-fascist to murders by far-right extremists and fascists creates a false equivalency. The conservative and liberal "value neutral" argument of "equalviolence" between fascists and anti-fascists at the end of WWII helps to account for the contemporary conundrum of this skewed perspective (Traverso, 2016, p. 329; Traverso attributes "the thesis of 'equalviolence' [*equiviolencia*] . . . to the sarcastic definition forged by Spanish historian Ricardo Robledo" [p. 329]). The flawed thesis of "equalviolence" favored neo-fascists who could justify their violence against anti-fascists as an equivalency. Traverso (2016) clarifies that "equalviolence" is basically an "*anti-antifascist history*" (p. 332, emphasis added). Mark Bray (2017), author of *Antifa: The Anti-Fascist Handbook*—recognized as "the first English-language transnational history of Antifa" (Penny, 2017)—was publicly misrepresented by his Dartmouth University president at the time who falsely implied that Bray was "supporting violent protest" (as cited in Gluckman, 2017, para. 3). The Dartmouth president, whose statement was opposed by more than 100 of his faculty, ignored Bray's emphasis on Antifa's rare recourse to violence as a self-defense response against fascistic advances by the far right (Gluckman, 2017). Data supports that anti-fascist violence rarely if ever leads to deaths of others. During the 25-year period from 1994–2019 far-right violence killed 329 people compared to none by anti-fascists (Beckett, 2020a, 2020b). In contrast to Antifa, far-right "movements consistently deploy violence in attempts to achieve their ideological goals" and interpret advocating violence as "a moral good" (Vysotsky, 2021, p. 85).

Traverso (2016) points to a false equivalence within an "equalviolence" thesis of liberalism evident during the latter stages of WWII:

> Led to logical conclusions, the idea of "equalviolence" should not exclude liberalism itself. The allied forces carried out air warfare against the Third Reich as a planned destruction of German civil society, and their systematic bombings of German cities resulted in six hundred thousand dead and several million civilian refugees. The horror of Hiroshima and Nagasaki was not the result of a totalitarian ideology; it was planned by [U.S. President Franklin] Roosevelt and ordered by [President] Truman, not Stalin. (p. 331)

The legacy of "equalviolence" was evident 4 decades after WWII when President Ronald Reagan visited a German cemetery in 1985, despite protests from prominent Jewish groups and 53 senators, and claimed that the WWII fascist soldiers buried there were somehow "victims of Nazism just as surely as the victims of the concentration camps" (as cited in Shannon, 1985, para. 1). President Trump used "equalviolence" after a 2017 "Unite the Right" rally of White supremacists and neo-Nazis in Charlottesville, Virginia, in which one of them deliberately drove a vehicle into a group of Antifa and anti-racist counter protesters, killing one and injuring 19. Trump responded by condemning the violence with the logic of "equalviolence" by claiming that there were "some very fine people on both sides" (as cited in Gray, 2017, para. 6).

"White supremacy is violence." Clergy members who were among the counter protesters in Charlottesville, however, credited Antifa activists for protecting them from harm and viewed the aggressive acts much differently than the president. After the "Unite the Right" rally, a minister from Charlottesville recalled how Antifa "saved [his] life" (S. Wispelwey, as cited in Lithwick, 2017, "Rev. Seth Wispelwey," para. 1). The pastor described how a

> phalanx of neo-Nazis shoved right through our human wall with 3-foot-wide wooden shields, screaming and spitting homophobic slurs and obscenities at us. It was then that *antifa stepped in to thwart them*. They have their tools to achieve their purposes. . . . The white supremacists did not blink at violently plowing right through clergy, all of us dressed in full clerical garb. *White supremacy is violence*. I didn't see any racial justice protesters with weapons; *as for antifa, anything they brought I would only categorize as community defense tools and nothing more*. Pretty much everyone I talk to agrees—including most clergy. My strong stance is that *the weapon is and was white supremacy*, and the white supremacists intentionally brought weapons to instigate violence. (para. 3–4, emphasis added)

Naming White supremacy as inherently a form of violence undercuts the thesis of "equalviolence" that attempts to equate Antifa self-defense actions to the hate-laden aims of far-right extremists. The 2021 Capitol siege confirmed the fallacy of "equalviolence."

Distrust of Police

Anti-fascists do not believe state institutions with their police apparatus can effectively challenge fascist and far-right politics. The reluctance to depend on the state to defend democracy emerges from skepticism about governmental use of power that includes structural and physical violence against vulnerable and subordinated groups considered outside the mainstream of the nation-state. The distrust of police does not stem from a leftist conspiracy theory but results from direct experiences with police and is buttressed by research that "uncovered hundreds of federal, state, and local law enforcement officials participating in racist, nativist, and sexist social media activity" (German, 2020, para. 7). Furthermore, however, "these officers' racist activities are often known within their departments" but were only disciplined or fired *if* their actions "trigger public scandals" (German, 2020, para. 7). In his book subtitled *How the New FBI Damages Democracy*, Mike German (2019), a former FBI undercover agent who infiltrated far-right groups, notes how his former employer rarely took extremists' threats from the right seriously. Instead, he observed that after the September 11, 2001, terrorist attack on the United States is when "the highly secretive FBI predictably turned its sights on those it has always viewed as the most dangerous to the established order: minority communities, immigrants, and those agitating for political, economic, and social change" (p. 10). In this light, anti-fascists have legitimate reasons to distrust law enforcement at all levels of government.

Figure 5.3 summarizes a flow of anti-fascism that starts with support for targets of fascist degradation and violence and leads to actions that

Figure 5.3. Anti-Fascist Approaches Toward Political Action

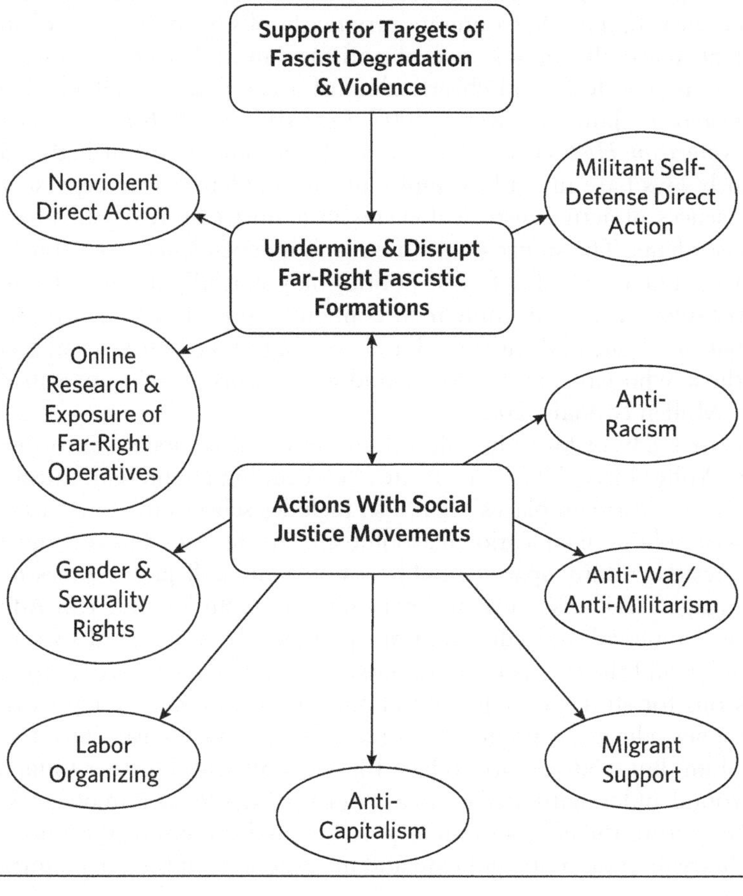

strive to undermine and disrupt far-right fascistic formations that policing regularly fails to confront. Graphically illustrated are community-based anti-fascist actions that involve nonviolent direct action, militant self-defense, and online research and exposure of far-right operatives. Visually outlined is anti-fascist participation with social justice movements that they may have already been active in, such as those focused on gender and sexuality rights, labor organizing, anti-capitalism, migrant support, anti-war/anti-militarism, and anti-racism. The constellation of anti-fascist political actions with other groups seeking equity and a just society is congruent with the best intentions of critical civic reasoning and discourse for an informed citizenship education.

ABSENCE OF ANTI-FASCISM IN THE SCHOOL CURRICULUM

Given the nature of anti-fascism and dominant political regimes long opposed to any challenge to its authority, it is not completely surprising that anti-fascism topics in schools are generally devoted to fights against mid-20th-century fascism, if at all. Contemporary textbooks for public school students are silent about the significance of anti-fascism and instead present a disjunctive, myopic feel-good cheerleading of a claimed triumphant American exceptionalism. James Loewen's (2007) *Lies My Teacher Told Me: Everything Your American History Textbook Got Wrong* uncompromisingly and meticulously lays bare myriad examples of the problems of misrepresentations and absences of actual historical events in mainstream textbooks for public school students. The stance of anti-fascism's independence from state institutions to counter everyday fascist politics may partially account for absence of anti-fascist curricular content in contemporary education. Additionally, information about both historical and contemporary anti-fascism has come from those who have been activists and in most instances from outside academia (Mullen & Vials, 2020).

In her study of far-right cultural and political incursions into the mainstream, Miller-Idriss (2020) advocates "embedding counterextremism into a variety of mainstream places" that also includes schools (p. 174). To counter the fascist politics of educational absolutism, anti-fascist educators must claim the contested cultural space of public schools and colleges as zones for critically engaged civic discourse and reasoning (e.g., Burley, 2021b). Adherents to critical multicultural education are particularly well suited to take anti-fascism beyond the streets into the classroom. In Chapter 9 we return to considerations for strategic multicultural anti-fascist advocacy for policymakers and teacher education programs to incorporate anti-fascism into a school's curriculum. But next we turn to Part III, which provides further foundational background and longitudinal cases of fascist politics located in phenotype and cultural racism, the effects of an imposed capitalistic political economy, and the militarism of domestic policing and interventions in foreign countries.

INDICATORS OF COLONIAL PROTO-FASCISM AND U.S. FASCIST POLITICS

An overriding purpose of Part III is to provide longitudinal historical indicators and examples of multicultural topics that fit under the conceptual umbrella that anti-fascism offers. From the colonial era to the present, the following chapters present material evidence in historical and contemporary contexts of proto-fascism, far-right extremism, and fascist politics and governance in the United States. Among the cases explored for *Teaching Anti-Fascism* are the practices of and resistance to phenotype racism, cultural racisms, nativism, political and economic domination, policing, and militarism. Topics are viewed through the lens of discrete elements of the 1948 United Nations "Convention on the Prevention and Punishment of the Crime of Genocide," a foundational anti-fascist knowledge base for a critical multicultural pedagogy for civic engagement. Part III recalls the importance of *We Charge Genocide,* a petition presented to the United Nations in 1951 by the Civil Rights Congress.

CHAPTER 6

Othering

Genocidal Racist and Nativist Fascist Politics

My maternal grandparents were stolen from their families when they were only 8 years old and were forced to live away from their parents, culture and communities until they were 13. Many children like them never made it back home.

—Deb Haaland (2021), U.S. Secretary of Interior, First Indigenous American to serve as a Cabinet secretary, 2021

Forms of far-right characteristics outlined earlier that comprise an ideology of White supremacist nationalism reach back to the first European invasions of the Americas that eventually manifested in the conservative founding of the United States. By the 2020s far-right extremism continued to produce a toxic intolerance of multiculturalism in schools and society. By further excavating historical fascism and far-right extremism, we recover buried memories and material evidence of genocidal practices. In *By Any Other Name,* a report written for the U.S. Holocaust Memorial Museum on the 70th anniversary of the international recognition of genocide as a crime, Buchwald and Keith (2019) explain,

> The word genocide has power. For groups who have faced eradication, naming their existential harm a "genocide" serves as an important symbolic recognition of the inherent value the group itself brings to the world. It recognizes their human dignity. It is also powerful as a legal matter. (p. v)

As a powerfully relevant concept, the legal tenets of genocide relate directly to what amounts to the genocide of the Other, be they of Indigenous, African, Latinx, or Asian origins and/or culturally Jewish or Muslim. And it is fascism and far-right extremism that disregards the integrity of families that do not fit within a politicized Christian evangelical ideology of White supremacist exclusions by engaging in genocidal discourse.

From the U.S. founders to contemporary far-right politicians, full citizenship rights were never envisioned for non-Whites. As a tactic, genocide attempts to block efforts toward a more inclusive civil society with equal rights for all inhabitants of a multicultural nation. Viewed through the lens of genocide, this chapter attends to proto-fascist, fascist, and far-right extremism that include the forced separation and removal of children from their families. Because the contemporary far-right's anti-multicultural ideology represents efforts to incite and commit genocide, a knowledge base of the legal structure of genocide along with specific examples provides both a theoretical and grounded background for policymakers, educators, and students. To begin, we first review how the concept of genocide entered international law along with what constitutes the specific elements of genocide, a critical knowledge base for an informed anti-fascist citizenship education.

GENOCIDAL ELIMINATION OF THE OTHER

Evident in a long view of history is Eurocentric genocidal brutality inflicted on Indigenous populations, enslaved Africans, and Latinx and Asian populations in efforts to exploit, segregate, and eliminate the Other as any potential barrier to White settler colonialism. The Other appeared to dominant eyes and Eurocentric world views as barbarian strangers who were less than "normal" human creatures without culture, morality, and redemption offered by Christian interpretations of civilization. The genealogy of full-scale 20th-century genocide reaches back to proto-fascist European invasions of the Americas. The seeds of proto-fascist European invasions of the Americas grew roots that eventually branched into industrial, 20th-century genocide by fascist regimes. As Paxton (2004) observes, in comparison to modern industrial technologies available to 20th-century fascist regimes, "old-fashioned pogroms would have taken two hundred years to complete what advanced technology wrought in three years of Holocaust" during WWII (p. 13).

Raphael Lemkin's (1944) use of *genocide* was the first time the term appeared in a publication. Lemkin combined the Greek root *genos* (race or tribe) with the Latin *cide* ("to kill") to find an adequate description to capture the horrors he witnessed in Europe during height of fascism and to name earlier historical events. The United Nations (UN) went on to adopt Lemkin's concept of genocide as a punishable violation of international law. Although some limit the application of genocide to only mass murders of an identified group, the UN definition based on Lemkin's ground-breaking research is much broader and relates to our study of far-right fascist politics in our historical present.

The act of genocide covers massacres of a designated population but also includes additional nefarious practices as spelled out by the UN. Shortly after the end of WWII, members of the UN defined genocide as the *"intent to destroy, in whole or in part, a national, ethnical, racial or religious group"* (UN, 1948, Article II, emphasis added). The UN definition included the term "intent" and the phrase "or in part" to signal that complete annihilation was not required in order to fall within the legal scope of genocide.

Ethnic cleansing is a phrase that surfaced during the violence in the former Yugoslavia in the 1990s but, unlike genocide, international law provides "no precise definition of this concept or the exact acts to be qualified as ethnic cleansing" (UN, n.d., "Definition," para. 1). Nevertheless, a UN Commission of Experts concluded that coercive acts labeled as ethnic cleansing that lead to the partial or total removal of an ethnic group from a particular territory can "constitute crimes against humanity and can be assimilated to specific war crimes. Furthermore, such acts could also fall within the meaning of the Genocide Convention" (UN, n.d., "Definition," para. 3).

The UN (1948) General Assembly negotiated and approved what constituted the crime of genocide:

a. Killing members of the group;
b. Causing serious bodily or mental harm to members of the group;
c. Deliberately inflicting on the group conditions of life calculated to bring about its physical destruction in whole or in part;
d. Imposing measures intended to prevent births within the group;
e. Forcibly transferring children of the group to another group.
   (Article II)

Importantly, the proto-fascist history of White supremacist racial and ethnic segregation and its far-right advocacy today should be understood as representative of what became defined as genocide in accordance with international law.

The Convention on the Prevention and Punishment of the Crime of Genocide was the first human rights treaty adopted by the General Assembly of the UN that awaited approval by individual nation-states. Noted at that time in the pages of the *American Bar Association Journal*, once a treaty is ratified by the two thirds of the Senate and signed by the president, "it would become the supreme law of the land" (Phillips, 1949, p. 624). Due to resistance from congressional opponents of the treaty who contended it infringed on U.S. sovereignty, it was not until 40 years later in 1988 that the Senate ratified the treaty and a president signed it (U.S. Holocaust Memorial Museum, n.d.b.).

Under the Convention's criteria, genocide involves physical and mental harm and outright killing. In its racist and violent discourse, the fascist politics employed by the contemporary far right should be recognized as *"punishable" acts*, according to the definitional elements of genocide, for

a. Genocide;
b. Conspiracy to commit genocide;
c. Direct and public incitement to commit genocide;
d. Attempt to commit genocide;
e. Complicity in genocide. (United Nations, 1948, Article III, emphasis added)

To be clear, *fascism is genocide* and *far-right ideology leans forcefully toward genocide.*

Lemkin's (1944) scholarly research on genocide was not only focused on 20th-century fascism but extended to European colonialism in the Americas and Africa from the late 1400s:

> Genocide has two phases: one, destruction of the national pattern of the oppressed group; the other, the imposition of the national pattern of the oppressor. This imposition, in turn, may be made upon the oppressed population which is allowed to remain, or upon the territory alone, after removal of the population and the colonization by the oppressor's own nationals. (p. 79)

We find in Lemkin's writings on the phases of genocide both the oppressor's territorial "destruction" and "imposition" on a subjugated people who remain under colonialism. By following historical threads and patterns, the following sections take up Lemkin's work and the UN convention's definition of genocide with particular attention to White supremacist contemporary practices of family separation of the Other.

GENOCIDE OF INDIGENOUS PEOPLE

What today we label racism based on phenotype or physical characteristics and cultural attributes was stamped on Indigenous populations from the 15th- and 16th-century arrival in the Americas of Spanish and Portuguese conquistadors in search of riches with their Christian Bibles and overwhelming military power. Bartolomé de Las Casas (1542/1992), the priest who accompanied Columbus in 1492 and participated in other missions in the Americas during the 1500s, wrote *A Short Account of the Destruction of the Indies.* He described the multitude of Indigenous people he encountered as "gentle lambs" (p. 11) who were "without malice" (p. 9) and "pure of mind" and possessed "a lively intellect" (p. 10). Las Casas argued that the conquistadors and settlers were responsible by his "conservative estimate" for "the unjust and totally unwarranted death of more than twelve million souls, women and children among them" (p. 12). Throughout his book Las Casas chronicles in great detail the horrors of torture employed by diabolical soldiers and settlers who he witnessed "laughing and joking . . . as they spared no one" by the most ghoulish means (p. 15). Despite Las Casas's protestations, it was the papal "law" of ethnic cleansing or genocide based on *limpieza de sangre* or purity of blood that provided a religious justification for the racialized mass extermination of the Other (Baum, 2006; Dunbar-Ortiz, 2014).

Genocidal Settler Colonialism

Dunbar-Ortiz (2014) emphasizes that *settler colonialism* in the Americas institutionally "requires violence or the threat of violence to attain its goals"

(p. 8) and *"is inherently genocidal* in terms of the genocide conventions" (p. 9, emphasis added). A U.S. Senate (1989) report in effect acknowledged genocide as evidenced by "brutal oppression and persistent attempts at forced assimilation" of Indigenous populations that had "been decimated by military assaults and fatal disease" as part of a broader design "to rob Indians of their very identity, pushing them to relinquish their language, arts and religion" (p. 23). Kakel (2019) summarizes,

> American settler-colonial policies and practices included exterpative warfare (deliberate, outright killing of Indian noncombatants—irrespective of age or sex—and deliberate destruction of their agricultural resources), forced relocation (removal/cleansing), forced concentration (on reservations), and forced assimilation (at residential boarding schools). (p. 8)

In this genocidal process, Indigenous people, in what is today the United States, "lost 97 percent of their land" (U.S. Senate, 1989, p. 23).

Genocidal Family Separation of Indigenous Children

A 19th- and early 20th-century example of genocidal family separation is located in the placement of Indigenous children in boarding schools under the premise that they would be able to assimilate to a dominant and foreign Euro-American culture. A colonial mindset justified the transfer of children to off-reservation boarding schools rather than day schools because "sustained confinement was . . . deemed to be the key element in the civilization process" of "individualizing" Indian youth away from their culture of communalism (Adams, 1995, pp. 30, 53). Common in government-run boarding schools was forced labor of Indigenous children in the name of vocational training, the onset of malnutrition among students due to inadequate federal subsidies to these schools, corruption among those who were gaining financially through patronage systems extended to boarding schools, and a curriculum designed to socialize Indigenous youth into an alien world. Echoing the imposition of a capitalistic political economy on the Indigenous cultural practices, Commissioner of Indian Affairs Francis Pratt in 1907 considered Native American children learning "what a dollar means to be "the most important part of their education" (as cited in Adams, 1995, p. 155).

Noted in a House of Representatives (1978) report in preparation for the eventual passage of the 1978 Indian Welfare Act was that 17% of all Indigenous children in 1971 still attended government or missionary off-reservation schools. Between 1969–1974 approximately 25–35% of Native American children were *separated from their families* and placed in foster homes, adoptive homes, or institutions" (p. 9). In our current century, the UN (2013) pointed out how public schools continue as "a way of indoctrinating indigenous youth with the dominant culture while denying them access to their indigenous culture" (p. 6; Hopkins, 2020). The UN critiqued the liberal "melting pot" narrative that in effect "ignores cultural differences between groups, and thus strips groups of their cultural heritage" (p. 7).

The Truth and Reconciliation Commission of Canada (2015) acknowledged that residential schools for Indigenous children resulted in *cultural genocide*" (p. 1, emphasis added). While no such admission exists by the United States, a governmental agency recently did offer a summary of the effects of centuries of settler colonialism and neocolonialism: "The oppression of American Indians and Alaska Natives and the resulting *historical trauma and adverse childhood experiences* have contributed to disproportionately high rates of depression, other mental illness, and suicide among Tribal youth" (U.S. Department of Health & Human Services, 2021, para. 1, emphasis added). In his work with Indigenous communities, psychiatrist and Cherokee nation member R. Dale Walker shared, "One of the most difficult things to hear is when the community says, 'We can grieve no more. We're cried out. We just can't respond anymore to the problem'" (as cited in Almendrala, 2016, para. 3). This deplorable mental health condition remains a contemporary manifestation of a historical legacy of proto-fascistic genocidal colonialism.

GENOCIDE OF PEOPLE OF AFRICAN ORIGINS

Within 3 years after the UN (1948) convention on genocide, Black activists petitioned the UN General Assembly with a detailed document of genocidal crimes in a historical context from the colonial era through WWII. At over 200 pages *We Charge Genocide* was subtitled *The Historic Petition to the United Nations for Relief from a Crime of the United States Government against the Negro People* (Patterson & Civil Rights Congress, 1951). Lasting effects on many Black families stem from the genocide convention's criteria of deliberate infliction of "conditions of life calculated to bring about its physical destruction in whole or in part" and the forced removal of "children of the group to another group" (UN, 1948, Article II). The critically transformative Whitney Plantation (n.d.) museum in Louisiana is an example that captures this proto-fascist history in its presentation of slavery from the perspective of the enslaved by inclusion of the memorial "The Field of Angels" dedicated to children who died from the brutality of slavery and were unceremoniously buried.

The horrendous conditions and outcomes for enslaved Africans brought to the Americas is well documented, as summarized by social historian Sylviane Diouf (2015) in her keynote address to the UN General Assembly on the International Day of Remembrance of the Victims of Slavery and the Transatlantic Slave Trade. Diouf emphasized the psychic outcomes on the involuntary migration of Africans: "The *sheer agony at being brutally separated from the family that loved them*, uprooted from their community forever can never be adequately described" (para. 6, emphasis added). Once in the Americas, marriage among enslaved Africans was not recognized and "couples and families could be broken up at any time" by their owners (para. 11). During the 1960s the U.S. Department of Labor (1965), however, portrayed the Black family "in a tangle of pathology" and blamed Black mothers for this condition rather than a long genocidal history of governmental policies and practices that continue to this day (p. 45).

"Whiteness" in Solidarity Against Black "Enemies"

Africans composed 80% of all migrants to the Americas during the 300-year span from the arrival of enslaved Africans up to 1820 (Diouf, 2015). By the mid-1770s when North American colonists were fighting the British for independence, more than 1 million slaves had lived in what would become the United States. By the beginning of the Civil War 80 years later, nearly 9 million slaves had lived in the United States, and by the conclusion of the war the tally was close to 10 million (Hacker, 2020). Hacker (2020) concluded a data analysis of slavery by noting that 40% of enslaved people of African descent who had ever lived in the United States "witnessed or participated in the struggle for freedom" during the Civil War (p. 850).

Being outnumbered, European American slave owners perceived the Africans as a threat and an enemy. Historian Gerald Horne (2014) describes how slave owners in the British colonies in the 1770s expressed alarm when England declared the slave trade illegal. Conservative colonial elites pressed for a break from England and for the creation of a new nation-state that would allow legalized slavery because they feared (a) losing the labor and monetary value of their enslaved property and (b) the increasing insurrections by enslaved Africans. An estimated 2,000 people of African origin were willing to fight on the side of England in order to be freed from civil restrictions and bondage. Throughout this period of slavery, numerous instances exist of African Americans subversively finding creative and strategic ways to resist their status as chattel and marginalized human beings. For this reason, Horne emphasizes, "*Suppressing African resistance became a crucial component of forging settler unity—*and the *solidifying identity that was 'whiteness,'* which cut prodigiously across religious, ethnic, class, and gender lines" (p. 240, emphasis added). Additionally, property-owning reactions of conservatives against the British stemmed from "the fear that the relationship between master and slave could be reversed to their crushing detriment" (pp. 240–241). Resistance by Blacks to White rule made them "enemies" in the minds of their owners, an enemy status that continued into the 1950s and 1960s civil rights movement and the contemporary Black Lives Matter social justice movement.

Genocidal Restrictions on Black Lives

After the Civil War, people of African descent who stayed in the South faced arrests for nearly any reason, were sold to corrupt Whites who caged their subjects when they were not laboring, and buried the dead "inmates" in mass graves, practices that continued into the 1940s, according to Blackmon (2008) in his appropriately titled investigative study *Slavery by Another Name*. Examples of continuing genocidal treatment of people of African descent throughout the 20th century were evident with (a) Nazi-like, macabre medical experiments on Black bodies, including sterilization of women and infecting others with diseases; (b) restrictions on where to live that included genocidal clearing of Black neighborhoods and communities; (c) violence inflicted on those working on behalf of full citizenship rights for Blacks; and (d) the blowing up of a Black church that killed four African American girls—among numerous White supremacist atrocities (Loewen, 2005; Meacham, 2020; Washington, 2007).

In a 17-month period during 1995–1996, 17 predominately Black churches were burned, and anti-racist activists recorded at least 45 such attacks between 1990 and 1995 (Fletcher, 1996). During a 10-day period in 2015 six Black churches were burned. In the days leading up to the 2021 Capitol siege, a far-right militia roaming the streets of Washington, DC, vandalized Black churches as well as those displaying signs supporting Black Lives Matter (Boorstein, 2021; Sakuma, 2015). Overall, victims of anti-Black racism constitute the majority of hate crimes (Southern Poverty Law Center, 2020).

In the 2020s the United States experienced continuing efforts by the far right to restrict Black freedom by limiting their access to voting in light of Donald Trump's defeat for a second presidential term. Eight months after Trump lost the 2020 election, 17 Republican-led state legislatures passed a variety of voter restriction laws (Boschma, 2021). For example, Texas Republicans introduced a voter restriction bill to protect the "purity of the ballot box" (Lindell, 2021, para. 13). The phrase was reminiscent of both the Catholic Church's 15th-century notion of racial blood purity and justifications for segregationist White-only elections and terrorizing efforts to disenfranchise Black and Latinx citizens that continued for 100 years after the Civil War. The bill eventually was amended without "purity" in it, but the racist intention remained as the bill went into law (Lindell, 2021).

GENOCIDE OF MIGRANTS AND CITIZENS AS THE OTHER

White nationalism in effect asserts itself in policy decisions as to which people are worthy or unworthy of admittance to the United States or citizenship. In 2019 President Trump provided a dog whistle of racial hierarchies by singling out Haiti, Nicaragua, El Salvador, and all nations within Africa as "shithole countries" (as cited in Kendi, 2018). In response to Trump's characterization of those particular nations, the head of the Congressional Black Caucus (2018) responded that Trump's far-right "Make America Great Again agenda is really a Make America White Again agenda." Trump's aggressive actions at the U.S.–Mexico border accelerated processes set in motion by President Obama, a legacy that President Biden's administration immediately inherited.

For a critical civic education, history contextualizes a continuing migrant crisis at the border that links to the creation of the U.S. Border Patrol.

Genocidal Border Patrol

Following Supreme Court decisions in the early 1920s that limited citizenship requests by immigrants to just those who visually appeared White, Congress passed the 1924 Immigration Act, which "meant that even Asians not previously prevented from immigrating—the Japanese in particular—would no longer be admitted to the United States" (U.S. Department of State, n.d.). The act closed the circle of anti-Asian immigration that originated in 1882 with the Chinese Exclusion Act. By 1904 horseback-riding immigration inspectors patrolled the U.S. southern border for any undocumented Asians or Europeans trying to entry into the country. Even when Mexicans entered the United States legally, they were subjected under a 1917 immigration act to a literacy test and head tax to restrict and deny their entry. In addition to excluding Asians, the 1924 Immigration Act codified that people from Eastern and Southern Europe were not considered White and, therefore, limited their immigration. The same act authorized the creation of the U.S. Border Patrol in 1924 to enforce the new immigration law ("Some Events in the History of Mexico and the Border," 1999).

In 1931 Harlon Carter killed a 12-year-old Mexican American boy in the chest at close range, was found guilty, served 2 years in prison, had his conviction overturned, joined the National Rifle Association, and eventually was hired in what was to become the U.S. Border Patrol, which by 1937 served as a "refuge for white violence within Mexican-dominated Laredo [Texas]" (Hernádez, 2010, p. 73). The Border Patrol in its formative years possessed a "monopoly on violence" to intimidate Latinx people living within the United States, including shooting up the Laredo Police Department and terrorizing police officers who were Mexican Americans (p. 69). By 1953 Carter was the head of the Border Patrol and in charge of operations along the U.S.–Mexico border. In a 1974 document to celebrate the history of the Border Patrol, no mention was made of Carter's killing on the streets of Laredo nor "the borderland's history of racial violence lived within the Border Patrol" (p. 199).

Under a 1954 governmental program that included in its title "wetback"— a slur on Mexican Americans—Carter illegally took money earned by 11,000 undocumented migrant farmworkers and forced them to pay for their own deportation (*The New York Times*, 1954). By 1965 Carter was now president of the National Rifle Association (NRA) and helped turn the NRA from a gun-safety organization of hunters to a far-right lobbying group intent on expanding the access of lethal weapons to whomever wanted them while opposing any form of gun control. As a transformed political organization, the NRA endorsed presidential candidate Ronald Reagan in 1980 for his anti–gun-control stance—who notably survived an assassination attempt a year later by a gunman who simply purchased his weapon at a pawnshop.

Immigration services is riddled with a history of endemic corruption and impunity synonymous with a "good old boys club" characteristic of far-right masculinism and misogyny (Engelberg & Sontag, 1994, para. 5). Deportations during the 1930s and again in the 1950s, for example, affected over 1 million men, women, and children under "questionable legality" that resulted in "the mass *removal of Latinx citizens* as well as immigrants" (Johnson, 2019, p. 1446, emphasis added)—although U.S. immigration law since the 1920s has been "crystal clear" that citizens cannot be unilaterally deported (p. 1457). While the Border Patrol is bureaucratically "subject to internal investigations and congressional oversight, prosecution and disciplining officers is rare" (Vitale, 2017, p. 188). Widespread bribes by private contractors for immigration service contracts go unresolved because, according to investigators, "there is currently no mechanism for investigating allegations of criminal and non-criminal misconduct conducted by contractors," despite cases with "possible national security implications" (Nixon, 2017, para. 3, 14). The absence of anti-fascist professional border patrol and immigration services exists at a time where each year from 2013 through 2017 witnessed a rise in documented far-right, anti-Latinx hate crimes (Southern Poverty Law Center, 2020).

Law professor Kevin Johnson (2019) draws a link to Trump's policies as extensions of anti-Mexican sentiment from the early and mid-20th century, arguing that

> through a series of unforgiving immigration measures, the Trump administration is engaged in nothing less than a *concerted effort to remove Latinx* people, specifically Mexicans and Central Americans, from the country in what can be characterized as *a form of ethnic cleansing*. (p. 1447, emphasis added)

In a genocidal turn, the Trump administration sought to overturn a 25-year-old court ruling against the indefinite detention of children and to instead "end judicial oversight of the detention of minor children" (p. 1491)

Genocidal Confinement of Migrant Children

In 2003 Congress authorized the Homeland Security Act that included two new agencies: Immigration and Customs Enforcement (ICE) and Customs and Border Protection (CBP). ICE is responsible for policing the interior of the United States for immigration violations. CBP, which is over the Border Patrol, can operate anywhere within 100 miles from U.S. borders, including coastal waters, an area that covers two thirds of the United States. The responsibilities between ICE and CBP are often blurred in practice (Werthan, 2018).

During Trump's presidency, CBP officials detained and separated 5,400 migrant children, *including infants*, from their parents. Trump's first attorney general, Alabama's Jeff Sessions, defended family separation by citing from the Christian Bible the "wise command in Romans 13 to obey the laws of government because God has ordained them for the purpose of order," to which Trump's press secretary simply noted, "It is very biblical to enforce the law" (as cited in Mullen, 2018, para. 1). Although Sessions sought to appease clergy who opposed family separation at the border, his reference to Romans 13 was part of the same rationale for the 1850 Fugitive Slave Law to justify capturing runaway enslaved "property" (Mullen, 2018). U.S. Supreme Court Justice Antonin Scalia appeared to draw on a similar rationale in a dissent in a case addressing immigration restrictions through state law. As if crossing state borders within the United States somehow could be interpreted as synonymous with migration from foreign nations, far-right Scalia used that logic to justify "removal of unwanted immigrants" on historical grounds because pre–Civil War slavery laws had legal standing in restricting the immigration of "freed blacks" from southern states during slavery (*Arizona et al. v. United States*, 2012, "Opinion of Scalia," p. 4). Meanwhile, Sessions skipped the verse in Romans 13 that states "Love worketh no ill to his neighbor: therefore love is the fulfilling of the law" or, as it is generally stated, "Love your neighbor as yourself," an often-referenced phrase to encourage kindness to strangers and migrants. Instead, Sessions's justification, like Scalia's, hailed back to slavery and signaled to far-right White evangelical Christians that separation of church and state existed on paper only.

Family Separation Despite Court Order

In 2018 the CBP was court ordered to end the practice of family separation at the U.S. border. In late 2020 lawyers reported to the court that they "still do not have a full accounting of the parents of the 1,500 children" (Armus & Sacchetti, 2020, para. 16). Despite the court order to end family separation, the practice continued daily through the Trump administration and into Biden's presidency (Jordan, 2021b). Investigative journalists reported an example of just one of the many horrendous conditions in detention centers: "A traumatic and dangerous situation is unfolding for some 250 infants, children and teens locked up for up to 27 days without adequate food, water and sanitation" (Attanasio et al., 2019).

Separated Children in "Concentration Camps"

A member of Congress in an on-site review of conditions at the border referred to detention centers as "concentration camps" (A. Ocasio-Cortez, as cited by Stolber, 2019, para. 1). Despite conservative backlash that contended the phrase *concentration camps* should only be referenced for the historical period of mid-20th-century fascism, modern concentration camps that originated in the late 1800s reveal a broader history. In her study of modern concentration camps globally, Pitzer (2017) writes,

> *A concentration camp exists wherever a government holds groups of civilians outside the normal legal process*—sometimes to segregate people considered

> foreigners or outsiders, sometimes to punish. . . . Detainees are typically held because of their racial, cultural religious, or political identity, not because of any prosecutable offense. (p. 5, emphasis added)

In an interview about the U.S. handling of the migrant crisis at its southern border, Pitzer reaffirmed that detention centers fit the definition of "concentration camps" because they involve "mass detention of civilians without trial" (as cited in Holmes, 2019, para. 2).

A U.S. Department of Justice (2021) report faulted its own department under the Trump administration for a "single-minded focus on increasing immigration prosecutions [that] came at the expense of careful and appropriate consideration of the impact of family unit prosecutions and child separations" ("Results in Brief," para. 2). In 2021 the lead lawyer for the court case that was to end family separation stated, "When we brought this case in 2018, we never thought there would be thousands of families separated, much less that we would still be looking for hundreds of them three years later" (L. Gelernt, as cited in Jordan, 2021b, para. 8). Yet, during Biden's 1st year as president, a lack of transparency remained as to the locations and conditions for 21,000 migrant children, many in extremely unhealthy psychological and physical conditions. Some detention facilities were unlicensed for the care of children. In one instance a detention facility was forced to close "after it was revealed that children were being given plastic bags" rather than access to toilets (Burke et al., 2021, para. 16). As might be expected under such conditions, some migrant children also lacked access to education, despite a constitutionally protected right to a public education regardless of citizenship status (see Song, 2009).

Left out of these reported numbers are the children among the more than 10 million undocumented immigrants who live in the United States after having migrated to escape poverty and violence in their countries of origin. Among these migrant families are those who come to the United States under "guest worker" visas with negligible labor protections in low-wage industries such as agriculture, a system riddled with "systemic abuse" described by a member of Congress as resembling slavery (Bauer & Stewart, 2013, p. 2). Once their visas expire, migrant workers are not allowed to stay in the United States yet find themselves "in a position of debt peonage" with unscrupulous labor brokers (p. 43). Many of these workers and their families end up staying in the United States as undocumented immigrants. Children are often who suffer the most. In linking the lingering effects of guest worker programs from the mid-20th century into the 21st, Rosas (2011) concluded, "Underestimated and hidden from view, the emotional strain of undocumented *immigrant family uncertainty continues to overburden children*" (p. 397, emphasis added).

Family uncertainty for migrant children stems from a governing willingness to permit state agencies such as ICE and CBP to use police and judicial powers with little or no oversight (see Lofgren, 2016). Where a public school civics class would normally highlight the three branches of government—executive, legislative, judicial—and how "checks and balances" ideally protect against abuses of power, far-right extremism in state agencies creates a sense of cognitive dissonance in a master narrative applauding the United States as an exceptional model of a democracy. Arbitrary detention without due process of people trying to escape untenable situations of poverty and violence contrasts a public miseducation that teaches about the welcoming of immigrants and the fairness of the nation's governing system.

As a result of the COVID-19 pandemic and global climate crisis, the influx of migrants to the U.S. southern border for the 2020s and beyond will predictably increase in ethnic diversity. People from more than 160 countries have sought to cross the border recently, including diverse speakers of not only Spanish but of various Indigenous languages, including Arabic, Haitian, Hindi, Creole, and Portuguese (Jordan, 2021a). The lack of empathy toward vulnerable migrating children and families reflects the hostility and genocidal incitement of the far right toward immigrants and refugees who fall outside fascistic White ultranationalistic criteria of "the people."

GENOCIDE OF PEOPLE OF ASIAN ORIGINS

Attacks on people of Asian origins in the 21st century represent a thread from the 19th century evident in the 1882 Chinese Exclusion Act and the 20th-century removal and internment of 120,000 innocent Japanese residents from the West Coast into concentration camps. For the Chinese, anti-Asian nativism and greed unleashed genocidal neglect and vigilantism. But it was after the Exclusion Act that Chinese were literally run out of West Coast towns such as Tacoma and Seattle and murdered in mining camps well into the early 1900s (National Park Service, 2021; Perkins, 2007).

Five years prior to the COVID-19 pandemic, the World Health Organization (WHO) noted, "Disease names really do matter. . . . We've seen certain disease names provoke a backlash against members of particular religious or ethnic communities" (as cited in Hswen et al., 2021, p. 956). In the midst of the pandemic, the WHO advised, "Don't attach locations or ethnicity to the disease, this is not a 'Wuhan Virus,' 'Chinese Virus' or 'Asian Virus'" (p. 956). Nevertheless, 1 month after the WHO plea against ethnically naming the virus, Trump publicly used his Twitter social media bullhorn to call the disease the "Chinese virus," which in turn set off anti-Asian vigilantism. After Trump racialized the virus, online data analysis of Twitter revealed that for the hashtag "#covid19" nearly 20% were anti-Chinese whereas for "#chinesevirus" 50% were (Hswen et al., 2021). For the 3-month period after Trump's tweet, observers documented over 2,100 anti-Asian hate incidents (Donaghue, 2020). A UN (2020) alert reported,

> Racially motivated violence and other incidents against Asian-Americans have reached an alarming level across the United States since the outbreak of

COVID-19. *Chinese Americans* and other Asian-Americans, including *Korean, Japanese, Vietnamese, Filipino, and Burmese* descent, among others, have been *subject to racist, xenophobic attacks.* (para. 3, emphasis added)

The UN categorized far-right anti-Asian incidents: physical attacks, vandalism, refusal of service and access, and verbal harassment. Later in 2020 when Trump and his wife contracted COVID-19, anti-Asian incidents spiked once again (Dwoskin, 2020). Reports of anti-Asian hate crimes increased an astounding 164% during the first 3 months of 2021 in comparison to the first quarter of 2020 (Levin, 2021).

One of the more horrendous attacks was by a young White man who murdered eight people, six of whom were Asian American women. He claimed his motivation was to eliminate the objects of his carnal desires because he was addicted to sex. Extremely religious adolescents apparently have higher predicted compulsive sexual behavior than secular youth (Efrati, 2019). The murderer in this case was a member of the Crabapple First Baptist Church that contends, "Lust is a huge problem in our culture today and the ease of access to materials that feed temptation is unprecedented" (as cited in Boone et al., 2021, para. 3). William Lloyd Allen, a professor of church history, placed the genocidal action in the context of evangelicalism by pointing out that the killer "was given *the theology that women are temptresses*. They teach that women tend to tempt men and *especially impure women* (as cited in Boone et al., 2021, "Your soul is at stake," para. 10, emphasis added). In addition to the evangelical gendered devaluation of women, Allen added that the shooter was socialized within a "white nationalistic subculture" that is hostile to racial and ethnic diversity, including immigrants (para. 12). As this example indicates, the White killer of Asian American women aligns ideologically with the far-right characteristic of *misogynistic postfeminism,* as introduced in Chapter 4, and the subset of "incels" who identify with *White supremacist nationalism.*

GENOCIDAL "SCIENCE" OF EUGENICS

Today eugenics is an internationally recognized genocidal crime for forcing "measures intended to prevent births" on subordinated groups (UN, 1948, Article II). By the latter part of the 19th century and into our current era, the fascistic pseudoscience of social Darwinism and cultural racisms continued as a defense by White supremacists to cull out of existence "impure" groups within the United States. Capitalistic institutions such as the Rockefeller Foundation prominently funded U.S. eugenics programs under the guise of supposedly improving the human race by reducing the number of individuals associated with alleged defective genes traits. In 1924 Hitler began his study of U.S. eugenics and eventually went on to justify Germany's ethnic cleansing of Jews and other "enemies" on the basis of U.S. eugenics blood purity "breeding" discourse. During the rise of fascism in Europe in the 1930s, individual U.S. states collectively used medical programs of eugenics as rationalization to conduct thousands of involuntary sterilizations on women who were of color, poor, and/or perceived as mentally deficient (E. Black, 2003).

The practice of unscrupulous doctors having access to vulnerable populations remains. Recently far-right Louisiana prison officials placed 10 physicians who had suspended or restricted medical licenses as the only doctors available to incarcerated people other than two fully medically licensed doctors. Using medical doctors with suspended or restricted licenses violates the codes of the National Commission on Correctional Health Care and the American College of Correctional Physicians. The Louisiana State Board of Medical Examiners, nevertheless, permits doctors who have restrictions placed on their licenses to practice and are barred from working in hospitals to provide "professional and responsive care" in prisons, despite their previously illegal medical acts (Baird, 2021, para. 7). In other words, corrupt Louisiana medical doctors "practice" in prisons in a state whose population is one third Black, but *two thirds* of the incarcerated are Black ("Louisiana profile," 2020). It is as if those responsible for the well-being of prisoners colluded to allow Trojan horses of questionable medical skills to easily pass into prisons, reminiscent of the horrendous experimental practices that White doctors performed since slavery on Black bodies and by Nazi doctors in concentration camps (Lifton, 2017; Washington, 2007, 2021).

MAINTENANCE OF FASCISTIC CULTURAL RACISMS

Accentuated by far-right extremism during this century are "new cultural racisms" that advance "cultural and religious differences as a basis for legitimating discrimination" (May, 2012, p. 474). Critical multiculturalism presumes that no one group can make a priori claims that one cultural orientation is dominant or superior over others—although that is a fundamental White supremacist ideological premise. Notably in our current politically divisive environment, hate crimes in the United States rose in 2019 against people identified as Black, Latinx, Asian, Muslim, and Jewish to the highest levels since 2008, the year Obama campaigned for president and was elected (Arango, 2020). Incorporating cultural racisms into a civic pedagogy for critical multiculturalism with an anti-fascist approach contextualizes cultural genocide historically. Such is the case with the deep roots of anti-Semitism and Islamophobia.

ANTI-SEMITIC "JUDEO-BOLSHEVISM"

To explain the dislocation much of the public experienced after World War I as an attack on an imagined and unified Christian Europe, conservatives and fascists publicized long-used anti-Semitic tropes of Jews as international conspirators. Anti-Semitism is defined as "discrimination, prejudice, hostility or violence against Jews as Jews (or Jewish institutions as Jewish)" (Jerusalem Declaration on Antisemitism, "Definition," para. 1, 2021). Key elements of "classic antisemitism" include association with "forces of evil" that possess "hidden powers" to manipulate governments, financial institutions, and media (Jerusalem Declaration on Antisemitism, "General," para. 2, 2021).

Firmly ingrained anti-Semitism in the mainstream of Europe and the United States, the slur of Judeo-Bolshevism emerged with the implication that Jews had set off the communist Russian revolution of 1917 and were, therefore, enemies of the state. Judeo-Bolshevism served to explain all that was perceived as wrong-headed with democracy, capitalism, cosmopolitanism, and multiculturalism. Receptive Christian populations—including U.S. president Woodrow Wilson's Secretary of State Robert Lansing (1914–1920)—found answers to society's ills through fascistic propaganda of an international or globalized Judeo-Bolshevism that somehow threatened the integrity and independence of the nation. Hence, stopping the spread of communism as a perceived threat to capitalism's social order eventually resulted in ostracizing, terrorizing, and murdering millions of Jews (Hanebrink, 2018; Markwick, 2018). Over a century of scapegoating Jews for society's problems remained a powerful culturally racist and nationalistic trope well into the 21st century.

During 2017, the 1st full year of the Trump presidency, anti-Semitic hate crimes in the United States increased by 37%, representing over 900 documented offenses (Cherelus, 2018). Two years later in 2019, hate crimes against Jews and Jewish institutions rose another 14% (Southern Poverty Law Center, 2020). At the Capitol siege, Katrin Meyer, the secretary general for International Holocaust Remembrance Alliance, identified displays of Holocaust denials and variations of "work sets you free" based on signs above two Nazi concentration camps. Meyer observed,

> The storming of the U.S. Capitol has shown what this kind of understanding of nationalism and patriotism is. This is where we have to be very clear and identify this as hardcore anti-Semitism. This is beyond just provocation. This is establishing anti-Semitic attitudes in the mainstream, normalizing it and therefore threatening all of us. (as cited in Brennan, 2021, para. 9–10)

The mythology created by the far right is increasingly being mainstreamed through an anti-government posture that blames society's problems on elite "globalists," an anti-Semitic term frequently used "as a code word for Jews" (Anti-Defamation League, 2018, "Quantifying Hate," para. 1). In his epilogue to his investigation into the roots of Judeo-Bolshevism, Hanebrink (2018) states that history "reveals that this myth—a potent fusion of racism and ideological defensiveness—is one of the more fertile sources for anti-Muslim and anti-Islam sentiment today" (p. 277).

ISLAMOPHOBIA

The events of 9/11 unleashed new waves of cultural racism through hate speech, physical attacks, and governmental surveillance aimed at innocent Muslims living within the United States as well as any other diverse people and groups suspected as Muslim or with Arab origins. "Despite the lack of evidence to support the claim of a new homegrown Muslim threat" (p. 4) across the United States adherents of the religion of Islam became domestic criminals through *"racialized state surveillance"* (Alimahomed-Wilson, 2019, p. 7, emphasis added; Neumeister, 2018). Beyond the government's policing and surveillance hinged to cultural racism, Islamophobia unleashed genocidal street vigilantes on innocent people.

After 9/11, far-right vengeful "patriotism" was widespread. Apple (2002) observed, "Almost immediately, there were a multitude of instances throughout the nation of people who 'looked Arabic' being threatened and harassed on the street, in schools, and in their places of business" (p. 302). Far-right extremist discourse drove vigilantism against the civil rights of Muslims who were portrayed as unwelcome aliens in an exclusionary White supremacist Christian evangelical nation. Muslims subjected to verbal abuse and violence reflect political scientist Corey Robin's (2004) observations on how liberal democracies permit nongovernmental individuals and groups to carry out "repressive fear" (p. 1062). Robin explains, "Because the Constitution makes it difficult for the state to wield weapons of fear with abandon, elites often rely upon these weapons of civil society, which are not subject to much constitutional restraint" (p. 1063). In other words, state institutions can tacitly allow selected instances of vigilantism, as did the U.S. government and New York City Police Department (American Civil Liberties Union, 2021a).

Banning Muslims

Contrary to a 1965 immigration act that lifted immigration restrictions based on countries of origins, Trump signed an executive order in 2017 to ban entry into the United States for Muslims from selected regions of the world. This decision was eventually upheld by a court because the ban was written under the guise of national security, rather than an exclusionary action against a religious group (K. Johnson, 2019). The obfuscation of cultural racism against a particular group such as Muslims by "the express absence (or explicit disavowal) of particularistic or 'racial' intent . . . *legitimates such violence"* as "group-differentiated spatial confinement" (Singh, 2017, p. 149). Most disconcerting for an anti-fascist civic education is how a blanket restriction on a specific cultural group that originated from the office of a U.S. president is indicative of far-right in-roads to political bully pulpits to oppose migration of people who would further expand the nation's racial, ethnic, and religious diversity.

To enforce exclusion of the Other is a common far-right tactic that parallels fascist violence. Fifteen years after 9/11, a wave of hate crimes against Muslims began to rise again in 2016, with a 78% increase over 2015 in what appears as a response to Trump's presidential campaign pledge to ban Muslims from legally traveling to the United States (Lichtblau, 2016). The underlying far-right rhetoric frames Muslims as "undermining and eventually replacing American democracy and Western civilization with Islamic despotism, a *conspiracy theory* known as '*civilization jihad*,'" an inspiration for over 70 Islamophobia hate groups in the United States, according to the Southern Poverty Law Center (2021, "Background," para. 2, emphasis added).

"Culturalists" and "Reformists"

Renton (2019) contrasts *culturalist* and *reformist* ideological positions toward anti-Muslim cultural racism. In this construct, the far-right "culturalist" political supporters of President George W. Bush's Islamophobia "portrayed the West and Islam as in a permanent conflict" (p. 43). By characterizing the conflict and justification for war shortly after 9/11 as a "crusade" to "rid the world of evil-doers," President Bush (2001–2009) drew on the medieval Christian military campaigns against Muslims (Waldman & Pope, 2001, para. 1). Populations in the contemporary Muslim world interpreted Bush's reference to a "crusade" as equivalent to a declaration of war on Islam. In line with a politicized evangelical Christianity, Bush fondly evoked references to God to validate his military invasions. As the commander in chief, Bush's words echoed the crusading charge of Pope Urban II in 1095 for preemptive attacks on Muslims:

> Let this then be your war-cry in combats, because this word is given to you by God. When an armed attack is made upon the enemy, let this one cry be raised by all the soldiers of God: It is the will of God! It is the will of God! (as cited in Halsall, 1996, "Robert the Monk," para. 6)

Culturalists, like Pope Urban II and President Bush more than 900 years later, adhere to a politicized religious absolutism to warrant attacks on Muslims.

Liberal and conservative "reformists," on the other hand, accept that there is a conflict, but instead "argue that it can be managed if the state isolates the extremist minority within Islam from those who wish to live in peace" and can be assimilated (Renton, 2019, p. 43). For the reformist, young Muslims in particular are "potentially the enemies of Britain, the US and France" (p. 43). The imaged holy war against Muslims and the desire to suppress Islam created "a far wider audience since 2001 than at any stage before" (p. 43). Whether culturalist or reformist, the eventual outcome is the same: the genocidal cultural racialization and fascistic discrimination of innocent Muslims.

INCORPORATION OF GENOCIDAL CHARACTERISTICS
INTO AN ANTI-FASCIST CIVIC EDUCATION

Due to lax local law enforcement reporting hate crimes, figures underestimate the actual number of hate crimes (Southern Poverty Law Center, 2020). As described in this chapter, far-right extremism directed at Indigenous populations and migrants of color is a racist and nativist thread woven into U.S. history with genocidal consequences, especially for children. Mainstream curriculum and instruction ignore these genocidal conditions. By incorporating a genocidal framing of fascistic discourse of the contemporary far right and their conservative enablers, critical multiculturalism can provide basic curricular knowledge such as found in this chapter as part of a civic education that emphasizes the lived experiences of millions who suffer. Why anti-fascists choose to take direct action both online and in the streets becomes clearer with these examples of undemocratic policies and practices of the state and the negligent and hostile behaviors of those with governmental responsibilities. In the context of critical multicultural education's identification of such undemocratic practices, anti-fascist responses are a valid source for inclusion in a critical pedagogy devoted to advancing civic reasoning and discourse in and out of the classroom.

CHAPTER 7

Political Economy of Fascistic Land and Property Confiscation

The sacred status of property in the forms of land taken from Indigenous farmers and of Africans as chattel was seeded into the drive for Anglo-American independence from Britain and the founding of the United States.

—Roxanne Dunbar-Ortiz, *An Indigenous People's History of the United States*

Contested within studies of fascism is the extent to which capitalism encourages and accepts fascist politics. A strict Marxist position contends that monopoly capitalism—a 20th- and 21st-century deepening concentration of capital and wealth in the hands of a very small minority—is central to the making of fascism. In the midst of the Great Depression, Mauritz Hallgren defined fascism as "a political philosophy based upon the need of capitalism to employ the power of the state to protect the institution of production for private profit" (as cited in Roberto, 2018, p. 295). A recognized major strength of Marxist analyses during the interwar years "was to place fascism within the context of the wider social struggles of the 20th century" (Passmore, 2002, p. 16). But one did not have to identify as a Marxist to grasp the deleterious effects on social relations of capitalism. Even an alarmed President Franklin Roosevelt, as we found in Chapter 3, equated fascism with monopoly capitalism.

Griffin (2018), along with most scholars of fascism, tempers the claim that capitalism per se can be equated with fascism by noting that no fascist economic model was historically adopted as long as the political economy was in step with an ultranationalistic promotion of a mythic rebirth of the nation. Whether or not business leaders and workers supported fascism was dependent on specific contexts of fascist regimes and what it claimed to offer (Passmore, 2002). Despite the general vagueness of fascism toward economic policies, fascist movements *"invariably act in the interests of the corporate-financial oligarchy when in power,* no matter what anti-capitalist rhetoric they may have used before coming to power" (Patnaik, 2020, p. 38, emphasis in original).

CIVIC EDUCATION WITH AN ANTI-FASCIST POLITICAL ECONOMY KNOWLEDGE BASE

A critical citizenship education necessitates a foundation in how economic inequality began with the creation of land as a speculative property for profit through proto-fascist appropriation and accumulation. An anti-fascist multicultural education is vested in mutual aid of a participatory, equitable, and democratic political economy. In contrast, a political economy of capitalism creates social relations where a wealthy class can live primarily off the the labor and debts of other people and organizations through interest accrued from borrowers and production of products and services intended to ultimately benefit private stock investors. *Teaching Anti-Fascism* incorporates a knowledge base on how historical roots of land as private property originated and how such a political economy arrangement affects contemporary discriminatory conditions of devastating wealth and income inequality that affects the well-being of millions of young people and their families.

Next is a brief overview of the contemporary effects of monopoly capitalism on property. This background information leads to subsequent sections on the effects of economic dispossession and forced segregation.

MONOPOLY CAPITALISM AND PROPERTY

Monopoly capitalism, with its ever-increasing concentration of wealth, reduces competition and contrasts with the classical economic assumption that unregulated capitalism produces a fairness of perfect competition. For instance, the nation never fully recovered after 2007–2009 Great Recession from

> A toxic mix of irresponsible financial deregulation, bankers' exploitive practices and reckless gambling and borrowing, and too little transparency [that] resulted in an estimated *$7 trillion in home equity stripped from American families*. . . . Black people had nearly half . . . of wealth removed from their grasp. . . . This was *a white-collar heist of epic proportions*. (Price, 2020, p. 17, emphasis added)

Monopolistic banks, not families losing their homes, were bailed out by the federal government. During the COVID-19 pandemic the Federal Reserve, the central banking system of the United States, did help some people struggling financially. However, Federal Reserve policies also created a stock market boom that further *increased wealth inequality* that benefited the wealthiest 10% of the population who own 89% of all shares of stocks and mutual funds. Despite middle-class homeowners witnessing a speculative explosion in the equity of their home values, the rise in the value of the stock market—trumpeted as evidence of a robust economy—"makes the increase in homeowners' equity look negligible" (Sloan & Podkul, 2021, para. 14).

Astronomical concentrations of wealth exist in equity companies that operate as private banks by managing investments from institutions, both public and private, to acquire equity ownership of other companies. Take the example of the world's biggest private equity company Blackstone and its off-shot BlackRock, which is largely unregulated and manages $10 *trillion* in public assets, adding to its status as "the world's largest bank" (Brown, 2018, para. 7; Brush & Wittenberg, 2022). After buying up homes and rental properties at below market rates during the Great Recession, Blackstone profited by charging high rents.

Who controls access to and ownership of land as both tangible and financial properties is a key determinant of wealth and inequality in a capitalistic political economy. The explosive costs to buy or rent housing that Blackstone helped fuel resulted in increases in homelessness and food-insecure hungry children. Such exploitative practices originate from a state-supported capitalism that is extremely dysfunctional and punishing for people in need. The viable alternative of states socially owning their own public banks is so rare, in comparison, that North Dakota is the only U.S. state to use this model, which has been more financially efficient than the most prominent Wall Street banks. In the best interest of their citizens, the Bank of North Dakota is able to funnel profits back into the state's general fund and, for example, reduce loan burdens for holders of rural mortgages and student loans (Brown, 2019).

For now, we turn to analyses of the relation between genocide and land appropriation that results in forced segregation, a feature of a critically informed anti-fascist civic education.

GENOCIDAL APPROPRIATION AND ACCUMULATION OF LAND THROUGH SEGREGATION

A primary way European Americans gained and maintained control of economic opportunities was through proto-fascist dispossession of people from ancestral lands and economically segregating non-Whites from living within desirable properties. By definition *segregation* is "the separation of distinct groups into separate conditions" (Jargowsky, 2018, p. 209). *Racist segregation* evolves from land appropriation and inequitable accumulation of wealth and represents the forced separation of a community or person from spaces that beneficially serve the rest of society. Enforced segregation results in the breakup of the collective unity of racialized people to secure White spaces. Most harmful, segregation—whether de jure or de facto—holds negative economic consequences for marginalized people to access suitable land, housing, food, and employment and to accumulate wealth.

Restrictive policies and practices designed to dispossess and segregate the racialized Other conflict with the UN (1948) Convention on the Prevention and Punishment of the Crime of Genocide. Legal expert John Powell (2021) notes that the practice of segregation was not just about separating people by race, but was and continues to be "primarily about preserving White supremacy and opportunity" (p. 21). The institutional and extralegal White supremacist practices of racialized segregation are contrary to the convention. Land dispossession and forced segregation clearly violate key elements of Article II:

- "Deliberately inflicting on the group conditions of life calculated to bring about its physical destruction in whole or in part"
- "Causing serious bodily or mental harm to members of the group"
- "Killing members of the group"

To grasp the genocide of land confiscation and dispossession of property, consider one example of many elicited in the recent centennial remembrances of the proto-fascist massacre and utter destruction of a prosperous Black community in Tulsa, Oklahoma, along with other bloody "Red Summer" racist expulsions during an era with multiple lynchings of African Americans in nearly every state (Brown, 2021; Nowatzki, 2020).

Fascist politics as "an exclusionary will to power," Nikhil Pal Singh (2017) explains, manifests "itself in *zones of internal exclusion* within liberal-democratic societies" with such examples as "plantations, reservations, ghettos, and prisons" (p. 109, emphasis added). Forced segregation represents internal zones of exclusion from White economic opportunities. Our exploration of a discriminatory political economy begins with the effects of exclusionary access to *land* as speculative private property for financial gain. In addition to presenting brief historical trajectories to explain genocidal practices to securing property rights by the Other, the negative effects on low- and middle-income Whites are discussed later in this chapter. Also addressed in this chapter is how land and property rights affect the well-being of marginalized people in pursuit of the basic necessities of housing and food under an inequitable political economy maintained through fascist politics.

LAND

People generally are unaware that the geographical location of land and whatever is on it exists with a history predating the commodification of land. For descendants of colonial settlers, the history of land usually begins with their ancestors' first homestead. In common practice when a house and the land on it are sold, the property deed lists the previous owner and age of structures. Lost in this financial transaction is how the process of property rights to land actually originated. Whereas the Declaration of Independence lauded the pursuit of "life, liberty, and . . . *happiness*," the Fifth Amendment to the U.S. Constitution states that no one should be deprived of "life, liberty, or *property*." Equating happiness with property stems from the founders' reliance on the patriarchal political philosophy of John Locke

(1690/2003) for whom liberty was synonymous with property rights as a biblical natural right based in heritable private property. Hence, in the rise of the modern nation-state in the late 1700s, "capitalists and states arose hand in hand, each facilitating the ascendancy of [each] other" (Beckert, 2014, p. 440).

How then did land become a commodity that is economically exchangeable? What kind of political economy determined land was an exchangeable commodity with property rights that could increase wealth through financial valuation? To begin to address these questions takes us back historically to the genocidal invasion by Europeans into the Americas more than 500 years ago to clarify what exactly "discovery" meant both then and now.

EUROPEAN INTERNATIONAL LAW OF "DISCOVERY"

The previous chapter described Indigenous land confiscation and the relationship between fascist politics and genocide, with particular attention to the effects on non-European children in the Americas. Here we examine more closely the moral and legal justifications used by Europeans for their genocidal practices. Spain, Portugal, England, and other imperialists used Europe's international law *Doctrine of Discovery* to rationalize the occupancy and near extermination of Indigenous peoples from the Americas. Based on the 15th- and 16th-century Christian application of the Doctrine of Discovery, conquered Indigenous people immediately lost significant property and governing rights upon their "discovery" (Miller et al., 2010). In effect, the dispossession of Indigenous people from their ancestral lands created landless populations. The enclosed lands—"reservations"—that the Europeans allowed Indigenous people to eventually live on were always of marginal value and in many locations today are inhospitable environments (Flavelle & Goodluck, 2021).

Origins of the Doctrine of Discovery

The roots of the Doctrine of Discovery originated when the Roman Catholic Church sought to create a Christian worshipping world. The Crusades (1096–1271) "led to the idea of justified holy war by Christians against infidels to *enforce the Church's vision of truth* on all people" (Miller et al., 2010, p. 9, emphasis added). In providing financial backing to Portuguese navies in search of riches and ports to establish trading posts along the coast of Africa, Pope Nicholas in 1455 directed Portuguese King Alfonso

> to invade, search out, *capture, vanquish, and subdue* all Saracens [i.e., Muslims] and pagans . . . and other *enemies of Christ,* . . . [and] whatsoever held and possessed by them and to *reduce their persons to perpetual slavery*, and to apply and appropriate . . . dominions, possessions, and goods, and to convert them to his and their use and profit. (as cited in Shenk, 2015, p. 16, emphasis added)

For centuries, popes advocated preemptive war—as "just" and godly—for the "defense" of the Church's land theft (Miller et al., 2010, p. 9).

Terra Nullis. Related to the political economy of land confiscation, the doctrine's element *terra nullis*, or *vacuum domicilium*, meant that lands discovered were deemed empty or vacant. Legal scholars Miller et al. (2010) explain that the application of *terra nullis* assumed that lands were not possessed by anyone or only by non-Europeans in conflict with the doctrine and, therefore, could be claimed. Even when Indigenous groups farmed, hunted, and lived on their lands, the logic of the papal doctrine still considered such lands *terra nullis* "if they were not being properly used according to European laws and customs" (p. 8). Properly used land for Europeans was synonymous with *improved* land for agriculture. In other words, Europeans viewed Indigenous lands as *wastelands* and as an affront to European civilization and technological progress and, therefore, necessitated the removal of native populations.

First Discovery and Occupancy. The Doctrine of Discovery served as the rationale for the formation of settler colonies throughout the Americas, Australia, and New Zealand. Peruvian sociologist Aníbal Quijano (2000) labeled this process of occupancy the *coloniality of power* and explained that "[w]hat is termed globalization" began with the invasion and occupancy of the Americas to create a "colonial/modern Eurocentered capitalism as a new global power" (p. 533). In other words, "capitalism and territorialism were indistinguishable from one another" (Arrighi, 1994, p. 59).

Land mixed with Euro-American settler labor was what created economic value under what to Indigenous people was a very foreign and abusive political economy and a spiritually profane interaction with the natural world. The doctrine element of *first discovery* initially provided Europeans property rights to Indigenous lands. Competition for lands among European powers required an additional legal element: occupation of the discovered land with military forts and settlers. *Occupancy* provided preemptive title to the land by a discovering European nation over any other government trying to possess Indigenous land.

During the discovery process, Indigenous nations in effect had their sovereignty severely limited. Their conquering discoverers restricted Indigenous economic ability to trade only with their uninvited landlords and not with any other European nations (Miller et al., 2010). The Doctrine applied proto-fascist violence to remove and segregate the surviving Native Americans from their lands and common trading partners. Proto-fascist ideology constructed *Indigenous people as foreigners* on their own customary territorial lands, a process much like what fascist regimes did centuries later to Jews. With an ideology of land as a commodity that can be "improved" for a "profit," the process of a European-imported political economy form of social relations was culturally incongruous for Indigenous populations. Land confiscation initially was for extraction of natural resources from Indigenous lands and eventually became key to the development of the exchange of transnational capital under imperialistic control of European financial centers.

English and U.S. Discovery Legacies

In 1607 the English secularized the religious doctrine element of first discovery to make claims on Indigenous ancestral lands in North America over those of other European nations. Isenberg (2016) explains, "In British law, ownership was measured by *standing one's ground*—that is, *holding and occupying the land*" (p. 12, emphasis added). The colonies that broke away from England and formed the United States retained the elements of the doctrine's ideological perception of Indigenous territories as empty.

The discovery legacy includes President Jefferson's 1803 authorization to gather military intelligence on Native Americans in order to eventually acquire control of their lands west of the Mississippi River. Under the command of Army Captain Meriwether Lewis, the military expedition was purposely named *The Corps of Discovery*. The Doctrine of Discovery was affirmed in U.S. law by the Supreme Court in 1823; in the 2000s two court cases continued to apply the doctrine to settle land disputes (Miller et al., 2010).

Indigenous battles with powerful commercial interests and the U.S. Army Corps of Engineers continue over such concerns as pipelines that transport fossil fuel, with the very real possibility of leaks harming reservation water supplies and other infringements on sacred lands (Keeler, 2021; Sisk, 2021). Overall, uncertainty remains for Indigenous cultural patrimonial land claims and treaty rights, especially when the U.S. Supreme Court in 2020 ominously stated, "History shows that Congress knows how to withdraw a reservation when it can muster the will" (*McGirt v. Oklahoma*, 2020, p. 8).

Contemporary Case of Far-Right Land "Occupancy"

Following in the footsteps of violent land confiscation under the Doctrine of Discovery's right of occupancy, far-right anti-government White nationalists associated with paramilitaries, and a self-styled sovereign citizen movement occupied the Malheur National Wildlife Refuge in the U.S. northwest state of Oregon in 2016. The fascist politics of this group were in line with far-right groups who embrace acceleration of violent confrontations to realize an "ultimate goal which is an independent nation state in the Pacific north-west, *an ethnostate*" for Whites nationalists (R. Nazzaro, as cited in Wilson, 2020, "Speculation that Nazzaro," para. 3, emphasis added).

The wildlife refuge "occupiers," who were self-proclaimed "patriots," were ideologically and materially closely aligned with the wealthiest 1% of the population in their self-interested *private* goal to open protected *public* lands for ranchers to graze their livestock wherever desired. The anti-government rhetoric of the militias at Malheur drew from the far-right corporate-funded American Legislative Exchange Council (ALEC) that writes bills, which Republican state legislators have introduced verbatim and passed (Casey, 2016b; Riley, 2013). Half of all public lands leased for grazing "are controlled by billionaires like the Koch brothers, the Hilton family, and even a Hewlett-Packard heiress" (Keeler, 2021, p. 50).

ALEC's agenda coincided with the Malheur occupation "to have states take control of federal property, easing the way for development, resource extraction and privatization" (Casey, 2016b, "ALEC and the Koch Brother," para. 2). The heavily armed far-right participants in the 41-day occupation were arrested on conspiracy charges for impeding Malheur federal employees through intimidation and threats. Together the defendants had previous arrest records for domestic violence, illegal firearm possession, and terrorist threats, including some who had violated court orders not to possess weapons and one who in 2014 "threatened to kill everyone" in a Georgia municipal court (Levin, 2016, para. 9). However, they all were acquitted and *"may have normalized armed protest,* leading to more acts of violence in the future" (Casey, 2016a, "What Comes Next," para. 1, emphasis added; see also Wilson, 2021a).

Diné/Ihanktonwan Dakota writer Jacqueline Keeler emphasizes that "the central issue" of both the far-right Malheur occupation and Indigenous contemporary fight to maintain sovereignty over their lands is Indigenous "domination by a colonial government" (as cited in Wilson, 2021d, para. 2). For Keeler (2021) the thread of a coloniality of power that continues with the U.S. government necessitates resistance both for survival and the regaining of sovereignty. Resistance points to an urgency for rebellions against contemporary fascistic genocidal aggression of "uninterrupted practices of colonialism":

> Continuous mobilization—such as defensive wars, uprisings, subversions, riots, insurgencies, popular demonstrations, and revolutions intended to repel, undermine or over-throw the dominating power since the "discovery," in addition to the more institutionalized resistance channeled through the work of political parties, unions, student organizations, and the like—constitute persistent testimony of an ongoing liberating struggle that traverses the limits of historical and geocultural demarcations. (Moraña et al., 2008, p. 10)

The struggle against a continuing legacy of a coloniality of power is directly related to emancipatory movements such as Black Lives Matter and the legacy from which it draws. As Harvard historian Sven Beckert (2014) makes clear, "Slavery, colonialism, and forced labor, among other forms of violence, were not aberrations in the history of capitalism, but were at its very core" (p. 441).

BLACK STRUGGLE FOR PROPERTY RIGHTS

The previous chapter provided an overview of genocidal practices focused on people of African descent and the lasting effects on many families. What follows here is a political economy orientation to examine fascistic genocide with the case of enslaved and segregated Black Americans that follows law professor Cheryl Harris's (1993) research in "Whiteness as Property": "*The origins of property rights in the United States are rooted in racial domination*" (p. 1707, emphasis added). For the colonial elites who became founders of the United States, Foner (1995) explains, "Representative government could only rest on a citizenry enjoying the personal autonomy that arose from the ownership of productive property" (p. xii). In addition to the romanticized pioneer White settler farmer, the task of large-scale farmlands owned by wealthy White colonists depended on exploited enslaved African labor. Hacker's (2020) data analysis, for example, found that slaves in the United States from 1619 to the end of the Civil War in 1865 "contributed *410 billion hours of labor*" (p. 842, emphasis added).

In the brief period after the Union victory over the Confederacy of the States, Blacks freed from slavery were assured of access to land confiscated from plantations only to have that promise broken by southern sympathizer Andrew Johnson who assumed the presidency after a dissident White supremacist murdered President Abraham Lincoln. Kendi (2016) contextualizes how racist ideas defended skewed land distribution policies: "White settlers on government provided land were deemed receivers of American freedom; Black people, receivers of American handouts" (p. 231). Johnson eventually pardoned the Confederate secessionists and returned the agricultural lands of the plantations back to the former slave owners and northern White purchasers (Foner, 1990; Kendi, 2016). As Nathan Rosenberg, a lawyer and researcher working with Black farmers who are seeking reparations, puts it, "If you want to understand wealth and inequality in this country, you have to understand *black land loss*" (as cited in Presser, 2019, p. 29, emphasis added).

Inventing and Enforcing Segregated "Race"

The colonial elites feared continuing labor revolts by groups of indentured English servants and Africans working and living together. The solution of the property-owning ruling class was to invent two races—"White" and "Negro"—to segregate the English from the Africans through legal means and sanctioned terrorism (Baum, 2006). Legalized corporal punishment resulted from any evidence of cooperation or relationship between the White English and the Black African populations.

The historical, legal, and political economy story of *Whiteness* is one in which skin color, cultural practices, and geographic origins became a way to determine status rankings and the eventual right to own property. However, this "legacy of the political project of white supremacy expresses itself by obscuring the class antagonism among whites" (Taylor, 2016, p. 210). Evident of class differences are the 15 million Whites living in poverty, according to a recent report published by the U.S. Census Bureau (Semega et al., 2020), a topic returned to later in this chapter. The particular political economy imposed during the colonial era and advanced by governing and business classes normalized the United States as an exclusively White nation, a position embraced by the contemporary far right and their Republican allies.

Contemporary Manifestations of Forced Segregation

Efforts to maintain institutionalized segregation of millions of African Americans from mainstream society by White power structures is a fact of American life from the colonial era to the present. Through legal and extralegal measures White society created practices of forced segregation and confinement to specific land spaces, a legacy that helps account for the existence of a paucity of racially integrated neighborhoods and schools. The 20th-century civil rights movement, for example, was fought against a background of segregated schools, restaurants, hotels, public transportation, and residential housings. Blacks also faced segregation through limitations on employment opportunities, including White-controlled labor unions. Some regions publicly confined African Americans to designated inferior spaces in institutions such as hospitals, libraries, and theaters. As Loewen (2005) documents extensively in *Sundown Towns*, the historical and sociological record shows that the quest of White economic advantages through enforced segregation stemmed from an anti-Black ideology.

After World War II, racialized real estate policies provided White citizens a massive boost in wealth accumulation over people of color who were denied access to low-interest home ownership loans through the Federal Housing Administration and Veterans Administration (Loewen, 2005). A manipulative capitalistic form of real estate devalued Black neighborhoods and communities by artificially lowering property values through the practice of "redlining." The term *redlining* is literally derived from the red lines drawn on maps used by bankers and real estate agents to indicate a self-fulfilling prophecy for a neighborhood as a poor financial risk and, therefore, provided White capitalists a reason to refuse loans and insurance. Despite congressional legislation with a stated goal for "the development of well-planned, *integrated*, residential neighborhoods" (Library of Congress, 1949, emphasis added), practices justified by racist ideas held long-term consequences that in effect isolated residents of color "from decent jobs, quality education, and basic health and safety" (Silverstein, 2018, para. 3).

During the late 1960s the federal government pursued the development of housing to advance racial integration in urban areas. Although the Fair Housing Act at that time was intended to eliminate discriminatory practices of exclusion, enforcement "has never been seriously monitored" (Frankenberg, 2013, p. 563). As Keeanga-Yamahtta Taylor (2019) explains, anti-Black racist assumptions became a "defense of private property, including the cultural cues that came along with it, [and] inspired the maniacal reaction to the possibility of Black neighbors" (p. 259).

Toxicity of Enforced Segregation

If a participatory, equitable, and democratic political economy prioritized healthy alternatives for housing, no Black or Brown family would willingly choose to live next to environmentally hazardous land or polluting factories as many do today. Nor would any parent willingly send their child to a school if it were known that the school was built on top of a landfill that "leaches dangerous chemicals into the school's water supply" (R. Bullard, as cited in Washington, 2019, p. 10; e.g., New Orleans), or schools and playgrounds next to industries associated with asthma (e.g., South Camden, NJ), or a water treatment plant that "covers eight blocks near a school" (p. 11; e.g., New York's West Harlem, Chicago's South Side). No White affluent suburb would tolerate state officials disconnecting their healthy water treatment system to their neighborhoods and creating a polluting alternative as a far-right governor of Michigan allowed in Flint, a genocidal travesty that has continued for nearly a decade with little indication of a satisfactory resolution for lead-poisoned Black children and their families (Tuser, 2021).

Fascist politics of forced segregation on or near unhealthy land fits within the UN (1948) genocide element of "causing serious bodily or mental harm to members of a group" (Article II). The healthy development of young people suffers when exposed to a brew of unregulated and legalized toxic chemicals. Washington's (2019) research finds, "African American and other marginalized Americans of color are preferentially affected by chemicals known or strongly suspected to lower intelligence because they are far more likely to live in 'sacrifice zones'—communities assaulted by environmental poisons and hazards" (p. 12). Furthermore, in comparison with Whites, recent research also reveals Black, Asian American, and Latinx populations are exposed disproportionally to "*every source*" of air pollution (Tabuchi & Peopovich, 2021, p. A12, emphasis added).

Racial Segregation of Children Today

Despite that de jure segregation of public school children ended with the 1954 *Brown v. Board of Education* case, low-income Black and Latinx children remain in disproportionally segregated schools nearly 70 years later. Black children attend schools that are (a) segregated ethnically and racially at a rate 5 times that of Whites and (b) located in high poverty areas 2.5 times that of Whites. Just 3% of Black students attend schools with a majority of students of color where their classmates are not poor (García, 2020). With lax oversite by the U.S. Department of Justice, some White politically controlled communities redrew school district lines to limit Black access to resource-rich schools as part of *a secessionist movement* as well as creating segregated opportunities within integrated school buildings (Felton, 2017; Orfield & Jarvie, 2020). Black and Latinx parents overall recognize that the failure by governmental officials to desegregate public schools "bolsters segregation by economic status" (García, 2020, p. 1).

Effects of Economic Segregation

Economic segregation refers to the separation of "social classes to different types of communities . . . [and] most often refers to racial residential segregation" (Jargowsky, 2018, p. 209). Along with reducing social cohesiveness in marginalized communities, the structural violence of economic segregation excludes poor people and their neighborhoods "from the opportunities and protections offered to their wealthier and more powerful counterparts" (Pilisuk & Rountree, 2015, p. 172). In addition to inadequately funded schools, economic segregation limits access to basic resources such as suitable housing and health care. Since the 1980s economic segregation as measured by household income has steadily increased between neighborhoods in nearly all metropolitan regions. Because segregation is so extensive, economic segregation of African Americans "produces much poorer neighborhoods than if Blacks were interspersed with the much less poor White population" (Jargowsky, 2018, p. 225).

Lack of access to living-wage jobs due to economic segregation negatively affects parental mobility and material assets in ways that can shape a child's access to equitable educational resources, especially in schools located in low-income communities (cf. U.S. Department of Education, 2013). Representative of the persistence of economic segregation, Stainback and Tomaskovic-Devey (2012) found that by 1980 "progress for black Americans in the workplace came to an abrupt stop" (para. 5; also Ajilore, 2020). The same discrimination that a parent of color finds in employment is often what awaits their children.

Black Farmers' Continual Fight Against Economic Segregation

Black farmers remain a resilient group that has faced continual economic and land confiscation since the end of the Civil War. Black farmers formed the Colored Farmers Association in the late 1800s as a cooperative means for mutual aid to one another and their segregated communities. During its brief history the association had an estimated 250,000 to 1 million members. The association collaborated with poor White farmers and "proposed radical political and economic reforms, organized alternative enterprises, and launched boycotts and workers strikes" (Taylor, 2012, p. 223).

Property ownership provided political power for Whites, which enabled the enactment of barriers to Black farmers. Many of the Black farmers worked on White farms under debt peonage and threats of violence that often resulted in murderous outcomes. Lynchings of Black males, for instance, were often a function of Whites wanting Black farmlands for themselves (Presser, 2019). The association did not survive boycotts by banks, agricultural distributors, and the railroads coupled with the rise of White populism within the agrarian poor. The Black Farmers Association "dared to pursue bolder programs and died violently for its efforts" (Holmes, 1975, p. 200).

Black farmers' "struggle to end legal apartheid" continued despite having lost an estimated 90% of their land between 1910 and 1997 (Taylor, 2012, p. 224; see also Presser, 2019). Governmental programs such as the 1930s New Deal agricultural legislation and loans by the U.S. Department of Agriculture (USDA) that were delegated to White supremacists to administer resulted in Black displacement from farmlands, as documented by civil rights reports from 1964 to 1982 (Environmental Working Group, 2021; Perea, 2011). The Reagan administration undid the USDA's civil rights division in the mid-1980s to eliminate *"reverse racism"* (House of Representatives Subcommittee on Civil and Constitutional Rights, 1984, p. 199, emphasis added), a *"white-coined conservative term . . .* suggesting, *erroneously . . .* that there was a societal reality of blacks discriminating against whites on a large scale" (Feagin, 2012, p. 149, emphasis added). From the 1990s into the 2020s governmental reports continued to find within the USDA a continuation of racial discrimination against Black farmers (Environmental Working Group, 2021; Holloway, 2021).

In an attempt to rectify a history of economic segregation and land dispossession, Biden signed into law a bill that included $4 billion in debt relief to farmers who faced racial discrimination (Holloway, 2021). A backlash came immediately from banks whose representatives claimed that immediate payoff of loans would harm the profitability of their financial interest rate gains accrued through long-term loans on Black farmers. Banks also threatened to withhold future loans to farms owned by Blacks if the debt relief funds were distributed as planned. Using the racist idea of reverse discrimination, far-right White farmers in the Midwest sued the USDA over the plan. Funding the lawsuit was "America First Legal," led by Trump's far-right nativist former senior policy advisor and speechwriter Stephen Miller. Due to the backlash from the banks and "at least 13 lawsuits filled" by White farmers, none of the $4 billion in debt relief to Black farmers had been distributed during the writing of this book (Holloway, 2021, para. 12; Rappeport, 2021, 2022).

CLASS, ECONOMIC STRATIFICATION, AND LAND

The creation stories of the original colonies in North America and the eventual founding of the United States tells of a people in search of freedom of religion and a classless democracy. However, the religious "Puritans were obsessed with class rank," and after the 1630s "less than half came to Massachusetts for religious reasons" (Isenberg, 2016, pp. 7, 33). In practice, the colonies were about maintaining British elite class privileges and the continuing subordination of those viewed as inferior. What is left out of standard historical accounts is how the colonies served as a dumping ground for a designated class of English citizens viewed as surplus populations. Such White people were generally poor and from the lower socioeconomic classes and looked down on as "dregs of society" (p. 21).

Like slave labor under Jim Crow and fascist regimes, castoff English subjects did not own land in the colonies and were objectified as "expendable 'rubbish'" (Isenberg, 2016, p. 13) and portrayed as strange "breeds" (p. 2), "thriftless" (p. 22), "scum of the land" (p. 29), and "waste people" (p. 20). From afar English royalists considered North America a wasteland and the indentured, lower class settlers as waste—or *White Trash*, as the title of Nancy Isenberg's (2016) meticulous study of class relations makes clear. The colonial poor, she explains, "were thought to be fertilizing wasteland with their labor . . . as a disembodied commercial force" (p. 24). In other words, English ruling class discourse constructed White indentured servants who lived under debt slavery, enslaved Africans and Indigenous people, and the land in the Americas as undeveloped waste. Only through supervision and dictatorial control, wealthy colonial elites rationalized, could this collective waste of land and people ever become developed and productive.

Isenberg (2016) also brings to our attention the 1648 English *Laws and Liberties* in which people who could be deprived of their freedom were cast as "strangers . . . [who] willingly sell themselves, or are sold to us" (p. 30). In addition to enslaved Africans, the "strangers" were poor Whites who were often homeless children, seamen, and convicts. They worked lands of the propertied class, especially for export of raw materials back to England. In assessing the colonial era's influence on the prosperity of capitalists in the 19th century, Marx (1887/2001) vividly observed how both White and Black expendable child labor was central to the development of capitalism: "A great deal of capital, which appears to-day in the United States without any certificate of birth, was yesterday, in England, *the capitalized blood of children*" (p. 1081, emphasis added).

As "servant" and "slave" were nearly synonymous in the early years of the British colonies, children of indentured poor women were simply objectified as commodities to till the land of the prosperous and then discarded like trash. Ultimately, "[w]hat separated rich from poor was that the landless had nothing to pass on" as an inheritance, especially in the fabled Jamestown where "the *orphans of dead servants were sold off*" (Isenberg, 2016, p. 34, emphasis added). The exploited labor of White indentured servants and especially enslaved Africans enabled the eventual blossoming of state-supported capitalism throughout the 1800s, accompanied with outcomes that have financially benefited the majority of Whites to this day (Beckert, 2014; Reece, 2020).

CONTEMPORARY CLASS RELATIONS AND LAND FOR HOUSING

In what is touted as the wealthiest nation in the world, the U.S. political economy continues to permit a widening rich–poor wealth and opportunity gap. Family wealth is measured by all household assets. In 2019 just prior to the COVID-19 pandemic, which further fueled inequality, the median net wealth of Black families was just 13% of White families ($24,100 compared to $188,200) (Bhutta et al., 2020). White families accumulate more wealth than any other racial or ethnic group because Whites are more likely to receive inheritances and other gifts that contribute to intergenerational transmission of wealth. White families also have a higher rate of home ownership, employer-sponsored retirement plans, and emergency savings (Bhutta et al., 2020).

Wealth accumulation declined during the pandemic from 2020–2021 for most of the nation, but "the combined fortune of the nation's 660 billionaires . . . was $4.1 trillion," nearly a 40% increase in less than 1 year (Collins, 2021, "January 25, 2020 update," para. 3). Cozy governmental rules for capitalists guarantees that equity firms avoid audits and have nearly all their assets or wealth sheltered from taxation that leave the ultra rich often paying less than 3% of their income in taxes (Drucker & Hakim, 2021; Eisinger et al., 2021). For example, Amazon's Jeff Bezos wealth grew over a 4-year period to $99 billion, but his taxable income over that time was equivalent to just 4% of his wealth (Eisinger, et al., 2021). Meanwhile, during the pandemic over half of the families with children lost their jobs, with the highest levels among low-income families. As the pandemic began to slightly subside, White workers were able to return to jobs at a higher rate than other racial groups (Children's Defense Fund, 2021).

Racial disparities in wealth are not based on individual merit. Instead, wealth inequities began with the long history of land and property ownership that originated with land confiscation and the racist invention of segregated housing and employment. Quick and Kahlenberg (2019) summarize the durability of capitalism's governing policies and practices of racist exclusion: "Black–white residential segregation is a major source of unequal opportunity for African Americans: among other things, it perpetuates an enormous wealth gap and excludes black students from many high-performing schools" (p. 1). Moving out of segregated housing is fraught with physical dangers for Blacks at the hands of far-right violence and puts the burden of integration on African Americans rather than through systemic policies and enforcement changes at all levels of government. To this day "the dictates of the market have been impossible to surmount when housing is a commodity and thus malleable to the social desires and expectations of a public molded by racial consciousness" (Taylor, 2019, p. 260).

In the meantime, the ultra rich voluntarily segregate themselves on land set aside for private gated communities within exclusive housing associations with their own parks and amenities—and in some cases with their own "survivalist" facilities—located in spaces increasingly undetected by online maps (Allen, 2016; Osnos, 2017). The segregated enclaves "of well-off whites often carries a religious-like faith in the superiority of the free market and a denigration of important concerns of central city residents who are not affluent or white" (Feagin, 2012, p. 134). In contrast, according to the U.S. Census Bureau (2021) data, Black and Latinx people have a home ownership rate of

45% and 49%, respectively, compared to 74% for Whites. When segregated from affordable housing, people turn to rental properties with the highest rates charged for Blacks and Latinx populations. Nearly half of renters are low income. Households headed by females represent 75% of federally subsidized housing, with one third of them single mothers (USA Facts, 2021). Compared to nondisabled adults, twice as many disabled adult renters are poor. Living in poverty with limited income-earning opportunities and accessible housing options, disabled adults fall behind on rent payments more so than the general population (Lake et al., 2021).

Through late fees and fines on poor renters, landlords seek to maximize their profits (Garboden & Rosen, 2019). According to the National Alliance to End Homelessness (2020), for those living below the poverty threshold, more than 50% of their income goes to housing, an unsustainable financial condition. For low-income and an increasing number of middle-income groups with monthly home mortgage or rental payments, the threat of eviction and the possibility of homelessness looms large. When renters become debtors, poor women with children are the most likely group to face eviction. Desmond (2016) notes that evicted families "lose not only their home, school, and neighborhoods, but also their possessions: furniture, clothes, books" (p. 296) along with any savings; likelihood of job loss; and exclusion from "access to government aid" for those in extreme debt (p. 297). The general practice of landlords is to pass over any future renters who may have been evicted elsewhere (Goldstein, 2021). For student learning, children having to regularly relocate among housing locations "results in disruptions to academic progress and peer networks and is highly correlated with poor academic achievement and behavioral problems" (Garboden & Rosen, 2019, p. 641).

Homelessness

Without permanent and stable housing, people who are unhoused seek nearly any available land for shelter. Overall, the actual number of people who are homeless are undercounted (National Academies of Sciences, Engineering, & Medicine, 2018). Counting people who are homeless through annual surveys misses those who are in shelters or some kind of temporary housing doubling up with acquaintances and relatives. With homelessness rising steadily across the United States since the mid-2010s, more than half a million people were officially counted as homeless on a 1-day annual survey, and within that total approximately 30% were families with children (Security.org., 2021).

A record number of school-age children and youth at some point experience homelessness—an estimated 1.5 million—a spike of 11% in recent years, all a foreboding indicator of not graduating from high school and limiting future living wage employment (School House Connection, 2020). For example, Seattle Public Schools, in a 4-year period, had a 7% growth in its student population but an 80% increase in homeless students (Morton & Greenstone, 2018). Lacking reliable locations for their housing and their schools, homeless children and their families also have to cope with food insecurity.

Hunger and Food Insecurity

"Hunger," according to USDA (2020), is the likely consequence of "food insecurity," defined as "a household-level economic and social condition of limited or uncertain access to adequate food" (para. 11–12). An estimated 11 million children—one of six of all children—are food insecure. For U.S. military active service members and their families, 16% report experiencing food insecurity (Shull, 2021). A higher percentage of Black, Latinx, and Indigenous individuals than Whites suffer food insecurity. For instance, 21% of Blacks face food insecurity compared to 11% of Whites (Feeding America, 2021). A significant explanatory variable for food insecurity is enduring "structural racism and discrimination" that is perpetuated by an intersecting web of a lack of affordable housing, high health care costs, and a scarcity of reliable transportation to access employment opportunities (Feeding America, 2021, p. 2). Programs originally set up for those in poverty now also support the more than 7 million people designated as the *working poor* (LeBlanc, 2020; U.S. Bureau of Labor Statistics, 2020). Food insecurity is not simply a short-term emergency like a house fire that can normally be eliminated by a temporary solution in a reasonable amount of time. Instead, hunger experienced through food insecurity is a function of longstanding practices of forced segregation allowed by "an increasingly *punishing nature of the American economy*, especially for people of color" (LeBlanc, 2020, pp. 10–11, emphasis added).

CLAIMING PUBLIC SCHOOL LAND AS ANTI-FASCIST CIVIC EDUCATION SITES

Public schools as landed property are needed sites for anti-fascist civic education that can build on previous battles of multicultural educators in collaboration with local communities to stop school closures that disproportionately affect students of color (see Bryant, 2016; Fabricant & Fine, 2013; Younge, 2013). With the rise in the privatization of public schools for the benefit of hedge fund managers and the religious right, most recently evidenced in Trump's billionaire Secretary of Education Betsy DeVos's advocacy, public funds for such projects as overdue maintenance of buildings on school lands are transferred to private interests. Concurrently, capitalistic austerity governance contends that social welfare programs must be reduced. This fascistic political economy contributes to not only underfunded school buildings but to a weakening of a social safety net that poor White students and those of color along with their families depend on.

Added to this capitalistic skewed political economy is a school curriculum that miseducates about the actual workings of the economy and the realities that await young people. From his vantage point in a Detroit automobile factory, Black industrial worker James Boggs (1970) was prescient in anticipating the predominance of "cyberculture" (p. 42) and a political economy that trains Blacks "for industrial tasks that are fast becoming . . . obsolete" (p. 43). More than 50 years after Boggs's prediction, graduating high school students face dwindling sustainable career opportunities along with the replacement of human labor with automation (Coles, 2018; Davis, 2020).

State-supported capitalism and its associated hierarchies of inequality and racialized discrimination are the total opposite of the ideal characteristics of anti-fascism as presented in Chapter 5. Schools are valid sites to incorporate both the effects of capitalism on the life opportunities of young people and potential political economy alternatives. In recent years acknowledgement of socialism as a political economy based on social needs, rather than capitalism's bottom line of profit margins, has increasingly found acceptance. Half of young adults over the past decade expressed a positive attitude toward socialism and a declining acceptance of the value of capitalism (Saad, 2019). "Given the wide-spread advocacy of socialism . . . at the end of Black insurgency" in the late 1960s, Keeanga-Yamahtta Taylor (2016) finds that "it is almost odd when socialism is dismissed as incapable of explaining racism or Black oppression" (p. 200). Like their fascist predecessors of an earlier generation, the contemporary far right, along with conservatives and liberals, constructs socialism as a demon that must not be allowed to grow. The anti-fascist traits of democratic socialism that are nonhierarchal with the equity aim for an emancipation of oppressed populations is an orientation that a capitalistic political economy will not tolerate gracefully. Nevertheless, the 2020s continue to witness a growing trend in an increase of socialist city councilors and candidates for city councils (Burns, 2021).

Public support by educational policymakers and civic educators can provide young people a critical multicultural education for civic engagement that reveals and challenges the anti-democracy of rampant monopoly capitalism. Multicultural educators and their students can work in tandem with community members who grasp the urgency of an anti-fascist, nonhierarchical democratic socialism. Critical pedagogical courage in and out of schools is prerequisite to challenge and resist genocidal appropriation and accumulation of land through segregation and dispossession—including public schools—and the resultant devastating effects on life opportunities for marginalized youth and their families who are closely policed. Accordingly, we next take up cases of fascistic social control through policing and militarism.

CHAPTER 8

Fascist Warriors

Police and Military as Fictitious Guardians

> The police have always been political.... Today, states portray their police
> forces as value-neutral protectors of public safety, but in reality, states
> continue to monitor and disrupt all kinds of political activity through
> surveillance, infiltration, criminal entrapment, and repressing protests.
>
> —Alex S. Vitale, *The End of Policing*

Whether by police, street militias, or the military, fascist aesthetics glorify and find purifying redemption in the use of political violence. During the lead up to WWII, fascists spoke of the "sacred violence of action" as part of a sanctifying self-renewal process (Finchelstein, 2020, p. 38). Fascists replaced reasoned civic debate with the immediate sensual experience of sacrificing one's individuality to a collective engagement in violence with the "ultimate fascist aesthetic experience . . . war" (Paxton, 2004, p. 17). In doing so, fascist violence blurred the differences between peace and war. In *The Anatomy of Fascism* Paxton (2004) explains that *fascist violence* was considered not only useful, but *beautiful.* He points out how fascist regimes successfully bet that the middle class "would take some vicarious satisfaction in a carefully selective violence, directed only against 'terrorists' and 'enemies of the people'" (p. 85). The fascist violence of ethnic cleansing and eugenics was aimed toward an ultranationalistic vision of "an aesthetic of the perfect body" (p. 13). The flip side of this fascist reasoning was the Other as the embodiment of imperfection who needed to be eliminated from the nation—all of which, as outlined in the previous two chapters, leads to genocide.

At the height of his presidency, Donald Trump enthused about the curative powers of police attacks against journalists and protesters, calling such violence *"a beautiful sight"* (as cited in Solender, 2020, para. 6, emphasis added). Echoing fascist leaders of the past, Trump encouraged violence throughout his electoral campaign. His response to a protester during a campaign rally was, "I'd like to *punch him in the face"* (as cited in Diamond, 2016a, para. 2, emphasis added). Trump then complained, "We're not allowed to push back anymore" (para. 6). After Whites who spewed racial slurs and beat a Black Lives Matter protester, Trump responded supportively, "Maybe he should have been *roughed up"* (as cited in Diamond, 2015, para. 2). In an attack on mainstream journalists whom he described as "scum" and "horrible," Trump watched approvingly as his Michigan crowd of supporters angrily faced off with news reporters (as cited in Schleifer, 2015, para. 1). At an Iowa rally Trump bragged that on a busy New York street "*I could . . . shoot somebody and I wouldn't lose voters*" (Diamond, 2016b, para. 2, emphasis added). Apparently his assessment was correct: Such fascistic expressions in support of far-right violence did not deter 63 million people from voting for Trump in 2016, nor 72 million voters in 2020, nor the near uniformity among the ranks of Republican legislators who continued to stand up for him and his fascist politics after his presidential defeat, his rousing of his supporters minutes before the Capitol siege, and his second impeachment trial.

Such violent attitudes prompted far-right recommendations and legislation to arm teachers. Students were reconceived from developmental learners to potential enemies to be controlled by any means necessary, including teachers who receive "mindset development" and imagine killing their favorite students if necessary (Gunter, 2018, para. 5). In fact, despite the spotlight on school shootings, they are relatively rare, with only 1% of all homicides of 5–18-year-olds occurring on public school grounds. Instead, no research exists that any current gun policies prevent school shootings, because "most students killed with firearms are shot in their own homes, typically because of a domestic dispute, accidental or negligent discharge of a gun, or suicide" (Gun Policy in America, 2020, para. 6).

Trump and other leaders with authoritarian impulses are attracted to unrestrained policing, like fascist rulers of the past who "relied on a society of self-surveillance and denunciation" with violence a complementary aspect of improving the nation (Reichardt, 2012, p. 59). The fascist reliance on culling certain populations to advance mythic ultranationalism depended on wide acceptance of violence among the middle classes as essential to policing for the creation of a good society (Lipset, 1959/2003), a concept contrary to the original notions of policing.

ORIGINS OF CONCEPT OF POLICE AND POLICING

The roots of the term *police* stem from the Greek city-state concept of *polis*, broadly understood as the *body politic* of a state or society that creates a sense of community, and from the Latin *polity* and *policy/policies* as the organization and management of civil society through a specified authority. Historically, *policing* in principle was concerned with maintaining the general welfare of a territory's people. Prior to the 18th- and 19th-century rise of nation-states and 20th-century fascist regimes, the phrase *police state* and *policing* were ideally regarded as a responsibility in governing a territory to ensure the survival of all of its inhabitants. The German *Polizeistaat*, which translates into English as "police state," captured this older concept of policing but acquired a much more menacing connotation when Nazis deployed widespread modern technology tools for repression as a central policy for controlling the population (Chapman, 1970).

Today the concept of police state in its less benign intention is more in line with legalized impunity to use force and widespread governmental surveillance/spying on its own citizens, including children who are required by law to attend school. Police are more likely described as warriors rather than guardians of society. Fascist policing in the United States asks us to return to the following questions: Who are the domestic enemies who must be controlled? and What segment of the population needs police state protection?

"FIRST CIVIL RIGHT"

Murakawa (2014) helps us zero-in on U.S. racialized policing priorities. She documents how U.S. presidents considered the "first civil right" to keep a White public free from violence. This particular perception of group-oriented civil rights remains a pitch to Whites who fear people of color demanding equity and equal rights in all aspects of public life. In the 2020s the "first civil right" is foundational to far-right distractive attacks on any curricular element or teacher professional development that hints at a multicultural civic education informed by critical race theory, as a front-page headline captured: "Venom of Political and Culture Battles Seeps Into School Halls" (Mervosh & Heyward, 2021, p. A1).

White-privileged civil rights align with historical threads that weave through slave patrols, militias, the Second Amendment, policing, soldiering in foreign lands, government-sponsored torturers, and FBI domestic extralegal surveillance and violence. This braided account is bathed in violence, a fascistic bloodletting from the colonial era to our current historical moment. Today this history manifests in far-right religious justifications for unrestrained brutality against the Other, as previous chapters observed. A historical background of the origins of anti-Black policing contributes to an anti-fascist framework for critical multicultural education. Incorporating modern policing through a lens of anti-fascism provides pedagogical opportunities to account for a context of historical tendrils that twine around embedded contemporary structures of discrimination and violence.

With a history of Indigenous dispossession and the human bondage of people of African descent, U.S. proto-fascism holds a different lineage to fascist policing than in Europe. During the British colonial era in North America no formal police departments existed. Instead, communities had volunteer watchmen and home guards. A primary concern among the White colonial elites were Indigenous acts of self-defense and enslaved African insurrections. Blacks in bondage as well as those who were free could be stopped, interrogated, and subjected to physical abuse. Slave patrols served plantation owners and urban civic leaders to stop any Black-skinned persons to determine if they had permission from their "masters" to be unattended. Cases existed where freed Blacks were regularly rounded up by slave patrols and put in bondage or, worse yet, tortured and murdered (Singh, 2017; Vitale, 2017).

Terms for controlling Black bodies by slave patrols are now commonly associated with modern policing. For instance, the "beat" was the geographic area where designated Whites would "patrol" their rounds (Hadden, 2001, p. 219). As historian Jill Lepore (2020b) puts it, "The government of slavery was not a rule of law. It was rule of the police," a condition that remains in contemporary America (p. 65). Consequently, we find disproportionate *patrols* of poor and Black neighborhoods and schools as an officer's *beat*.

During the formative years of the U.S. founding as a nation-state, communities and individual states created more formal systems of patrolling in the defense of White fears of people of African descent. The former colonies depended on limited hunting gear of White males for watchmen and guards because communities did not actually possess enough armament to respond against any major insurrections. As slave revolts periodically presented themselves, communities and states formed paramilitaries or militias because the federal government did not maintain a standing army or navy of sufficient size to fend off every action perceived as hostile.

During the 1830s we also find Horace Mann riding by horseback through Massachusetts to advocate for publicly funded common schools to help eliminate what he interpreted as unpoliced social disorder among young people and to instill his vision of a moral order (Spring, 2011). In a like manner, by the mid- and late 1800s urban areas such as New York, Boston, and Chicago witnessed the formation of police departments, not because of a rise in crime, but to enforce codes of morality on culturally different immigrants and to regulate the movement of free Blacks. Police in this formative era "were both corrupt and incompetent" and at the beck and call of business owners intent on suppressing voting and worker organizations (Vitale, 2017, p. 38). By the early 1900s cities turned to more professional training of police by using strategies gained from the colonial management of subjugated populations.

Modern policing in the United States draws from military techniques that controlled Indigenous populations domestically and abroad, especially from the late 1890s in the Philippines and the 1960s and early 1970s in Vietnam to the 21st century in Afghanistan and Iraq (Singh, 2017; Vitale, 2017). The tactics of the military abroad involved little oversight. As one Vietnam war veteran who was involved in torturing civilians put it, "We could do pretty much whatever we wanted [to local villagers], as long as we didn't leave scars" (as cited in Singh, 2017, p. 68). During the Vietnam War when genocidal actions became more evident, French philosopher and activist Jean-Paul Sartre (1968), who witnessed mid-20th-century fascism, observed

Now we can recognize . . . the truth of the Vietnam war: it meets all of Hitler's specifications. Hitler killed Jews because they were Jews. The armed forces of the United States torture and kill men, women, and children in Vietnam merely *because they are Vietnamese.* Whatever lies or euphemisms the government may think up, the spirit of genocide is in the minds of the soldiers. (p. 82, emphasis in original)

A quarter of a century after the end of the Vietnam War, Bush administration lawyers in 2002 justified torture under U.S. law and concluded "that *certain acts may be cruel, inhuman, or degrading*, but still not produce pain and suffering of the requisite intensity to fall within [a U.S. statute's] proscription against torture" (National Security Archive, 2002, p. 1). Furthermore, "to prove 'severe mental pain or suffering,' the statute requires proof of 'prolonged mental harm'" that was caused by interrogation techniques (p. 7). Despite criticism of the memorandum, U.S. law clearly can be construed to shield U.S. personnel and contractors from what many would likely describe as torture, not euphemistically as "enhanced interrogation," as partially revealed from a 6,700-page report on the deep state CIA torture program that still remains classified and for which no one has been held accountable (Prasow, 2021). What we do know, for example, is that one interrogator told a detainee, "We can never let the world know what I have done to you" (U.S. Senate Select Committee on Intelligence, 2014, p. xiii). Among numerous gruesome acts of torture, CIA officers issued "threats to harm the children of a detainee, threats to sexually abuse the mother of a detainee, and a threat to 'cut [a detainee's] mother's throat'" (p. xiii). More recently we learned about torture described by military jurors who condemned the treatment of a 9/11 detainee by the CIA in Pakistan, Afghanistan, and an unnamed third nation. The jurors stated that the detainee "was subjected to physical and psychological abuse well beyond approved enhanced interrogation techniques" and compared the mistreatment as "being *closer to torture performed by the most abusive regimes in modern history*" (as cited in Rosenberg, 2021, p. A1, emphasis added).

Individuals trained under vague fascistic interpretations of torture and the violence of military technologies disproportionally fill the ranks of contemporary police forces, not as defensive guardians of society but as aggressive warriors supported by a financially lucrative domestic police training industry (A. Stephens, 2020). Furthermore, statistically the veterans who are employed by police departments suggest that some of those recruits are far-right extremists. For example, the *Military Times* reports that more than one-third of active-duty soldiers observed among their ranks those who engage in neo-Nazi, White nationalistic, and other racist discourse (Shane, 2020).

Policies justified by racist ideas are foundational in explaining police actions in undeclared foreign wars and the disproportionate domestic policing of Brown and Black populations. Emblematic of state-sanctioned use of excessive force administered with near impunity, policing stems from a historical investment in "police with a formless authority . . . elaborated through colonial and racial violence" for the despised Other (Singh, 2017, p. 144). A fascistic desire extends to embolden and arm private citizens and public school teachers to protect the "homeland" and classroom, all of which leaves us with another question: How is it that individuals have nearly unrestricted access to and display of weapons? For this, we turn to the Constitution and the twisted contemporary history of the Second Amendment.

THE CONSTITUTION AND THE SECOND AMENDMENT

"Congress shall have the power to . . . provide for calling forth the militia to execute the laws of the union, suppress insurrections and repel invasions," so declares Article 1, Section 8, of the Constitution. The only "insurrections" that worried the new nation's ruling class were those that might arise among Indigenous and enslaved people. Mixed into this transitional founding period was the Second Amendment to the Constitution, which states: "A well-regulated Militia, being necessary to the security of a free State, the right of the people to keep and bear Arms shall not be infringed." Based on records of the debates and communications among the founders, a primary purpose of the amendment was to assure colonial elites that the federal government would not disband existing paramilitaries designed to control the enslaved (Bogus, 2002; Horwitz & Anderson, 2009). Each state eventually gained access to more formidable weapons, which were usually kept locked away except in the case of a foreign invasion or insurrection. The state militias eventually became what we know today as the National Guard. Modeling techniques acquired from the military occupation of the Philippines, Pennsylvania formed the first National Guard unit in 1905 to suppress labor organizing at the behest of business owners (Vitale, 2017).

Today the normative assumption is that the Second Amendment allows individual access to any kind of militarized weaponry for "defense" against domestic enemies rather than for simple possession of a personal hunting rifle. For 217 years the courts consistently ruled the Second Amendment represented a *collective right*, not an individual one. In 1939, a few months prior to when German fascists invaded Poland and prompted the start of WWII, the U.S. Supreme Court *ruled against individual gun rights* by citing English and colonial laws along with the intent of the U.S. Constitution authors to reaffirm the collective right of the Second Amendment. In *U.S. v. Miller et al.* (1939) the court explained that possession of weapons per se in this case did not have "some reasonable relationship to the preservation or efficiency of a well regulated militia" (para. 5). In other words, possessing and transporting weapons—beyond traditional hunting gear—was understood by both Congress and the Supreme Court as the providence of a governmentally controlled and "well regulated militia" or National Guard.

During the 1960s a small number of prolific writers began to creatively reinterpret the Second Amendment as an individual right in what Spitzer (2002) describes as a "law journal breeding ground" (p. 32). As the National Rifle Association (NRA) moved away from an organization of hunters, it took on a far-right ideology toward individual possession of lethal weapons.

This was the era when Harlon Carter—the murderous former head of the Border Patrol (see Chapter 6)—was active on the executive board of the NRA, eventually ascending to its presidency. The NRA aggressively funded legislative lobbying and even offered prize money to anyone who wrote the most persuasive law journal article that contributed to the reinvention of the Second Amendment's collective rights purpose to an individual right approach (Spitzer, 2002). Late in the 2000s the Supreme Court sided with the individual rights approach in *District of Columbia v. Heller* (2008). That decision was within the documented 5-year period from 2005–2010 when the Supreme Court decisions moved politically to the right and "became the most conservative [court] in living memory," a position further cemented for the 2020s and beyond with additional Republican-friendly appointments (Liptak, 2010, para. 2; see also Liptak, 2021; *The New York Times*, 2010). Carol Anderson (2021) concludes that the Second Amendment "is lethal; steeped in anti-Blackness, it is the loaded weapon laying around just waiting for the hand of some authority to put to work" (p. 165).

Today far-right gun rights advocates are also among anti-government "patriots" in their justification for lethal weapons. Far-right ideology twists the Second Amendment for those who want to overthrow the U.S. government if necessary. Private militias, however, remain unconstitutional despite some far-right local governing bodies and militias seeking a legal shield for paramilitaries in their communities (McCord, 2020; Robertson, 2020). Legitimized by Trump's successful 2016 presidential candidacy, hard-core far-right insurrectionists' discourse moved into mainstream politics. As a result, the far right today feels more confident to use violence with impunity as if it had never happened, a legacy of how African Americans have lived under the threat and application of excessive force upon their very existence.

AS IF IT HAD NEVER HAPPENED: USE OF EXCESSIVE FORCE

Colonial laws provided impunity for White people disciplining Blacks with excessive force. A 1669 Virginia law specified that if a slave "should chance to die" in the process of "correction" by a White person, the African American's "death shall not be accounted a felony, but the master (or that other person appointed by the master to punish him) be acquitted from molestation" (Digital History, "October 1669," 2021). The 1705 Virginia Slave code added that such a murder at the hands of a White person would be "*as if such incident had never happened*" (General Assembly of Virginia, 1705, "XXXIV", emphasis added).

Three hundred years later in a secret detention center in a warehouse district, members of the Chicago Police Department—some of whom were associated with the KKK—subjected people to torture and "disappearances" by illegally taking them into custody without arrest warrants (Johnson, 2019). Black and Latinx civilians, along with at least one White female protester of U.S. foreign policy, were among the victims of this CIA-like extralegal interrogation center (Ackerman, 2015b). After an investigative report revealed the operation of the detention center and the Chicago Police Department admitted to its previously secret location, the "fact sheet" the department distributed was "*as if that* [i.e., unlawful detention, torture, and disappearances] *has never happened* in Chicago, that *there's no history* there, there's no legacy there" (Ackerman, 2015a, para 41, emphasis added). A year earlier, in 2014, during news reporting on protests in Ferguson, Missouri, against police violence, *The Washington Post* reporter Wesley Lowery tweeted how he and another journalist were detained, roughed up by the local police SWAT team, and then were "released without any charges, no paperwork whatsoever. *It's as if the arrest and the assaults never took place*" (as cited in Hannon, 2014, para. 10, emphasis added). During the 2020 urban uprisings in response to the police killing of George Floyd, police literally removed from the streets individual Black Lives Matter and anti-fascist protesters like a fascist squad disappearing innocent people. In her essay "Road to Fascism," former public defender Tiffany Cabán (2020) depicted the process of authorities releasing illegally detained protesters without any charges as "the state acting *as if nothing had happened*—until the next raid" (p. 4, emphasis added). At the school district level, frustrated parents report that racial bias and slurs that their Black and Brown children experience are too often treated by school officials as if they never happened. Such parents are left uncertain as to who to call on to ameliorate hostile schooling environments.

FASCIST HISTORY OF 9-1-1 AS RESPONSE TO CIVIL RIGHTS PROTESTS

Police overreaction to protests was the main cause that fueled urban riots in the 1960s (Hahn & Jeffries, 2003). In response to 159 protests for civil rights in 1967, the executive branch authorized the 9-1-1 emergency phone system to suppress future protests, a technology that aided U.S. efforts in 1963 to stamp out public protests and any pro-democracy counterinsurgency in Venezuela. The creation of 9-1-1 went hand in hand with a new Department of Justice training program that "advise[s] state and federal law enforcement to intervene in civil disorders, *recommends local police departments adopt militaristic riot control* training and equipment . . . and encourages police departments to *infiltrate black communities*" (Feldkamp & Neusteter, 2021, "Emergence of 911," para. 6, emphasis added). Since the implementation of the 9-1-1 system, White citizens' racially biased calls have "resulted in police violence and murder of civilians, and funneled millions of Black, poor and oppressed individuals into the criminal justice system" (Feldkamp & Neusteter, 2021, "Emergence of 911," para. 13). Schools experience police overreach when SWAT squads are called in to quell normal youthful misbehavior. And the racist abuse of 9-1-1 continues: In 2021, for instance, after a White couple in Michigan called 9-1-1 when they saw two Black men in a nearby house, police officers arrived and promptly handcuffed the two men. One of the Black men was a real estate agent showing a home on the market to a Black military veteran and potential buyer who ended up fearing for his Black adolescent son's life during the encounter (Edwards, 2021). An anti-fascist critique understands White consensus and violence are two faces of the same coin for fascist regimes, which relies on a society of self-surveillance and denunciation (Reichardt, 2012).

GANGS AND KKK IN POLICE UNIFORMS

The aftermath of the 2020 police killing of Floyd and the 2021 far-right Capitol siege revealed what was already known: White supremacists, neo-Nazis, and advocates of violent anti-government insurrection represented a threat to public safety and any sense of democratic governance. Far-right police advocates of extralegal violence were allowed within their departments even when their superiors were aware of them. Without fear of accountability, far-right police ideologically set a tone of acceptability for other officers while engaging in blatantly illegal acts. The FBI offers no reassurance given its record of "civil rights abuses" and its "long history of acknowledging the abuses, promising to change, and rarely coming through on meaningful reform" (Sekkarie, 2020, "A Long History," para. 1).

The Los Angeles County Sheriff's Department, the world's largest sheriff's department with 18,000 employees, is an example of policing out of public control. Since 1991, evidence presented in legal cases has identified a significant number of deputies with ties to neo-Nazis who targeted Black and Latinx residents (Johnson, 2019). Recently revealed were the existence of *multiple gangs* in the department and the defiance of the White male Los Angeles County sheriff to cooperate in the investigations of his department (Gumbel, 2018; Solis, 2021). Nationally, over 90% of county sheriffs are White men but represent just 30% of the overall populations. Holding sheriffs accountable is legally difficult because "county leaders can find themselves powerless to discipline or remove sheriffs implicated in malfeasance. Governed mainly by state constitutions, sheriffs can act with unique impunity" (Reflective Democracy, 2020, "The Rap Sheet," para. 4). This lack of accountability includes the nearly untouchable power of county sheriffs who wield disproportionate clout, including leading the "Second Amendment sanctuary" charge for communities who embrace far-right ideologies (e.g., Wenzelburger, 2021).

Like the LA deputies, police departments across the United States hold widespread racist and fascistic beliefs among officers as verified by (a) associating with neo-Nazis and the KKK, (b) modifying of their bodies with White supremacist tattoos, (c) calling Blacks derogatory names during encounters and among other officers, (d) mocking interracial relations, (e) fabricating evidence, and (f) wearing Confederate apparel under uniforms (Johnson, 2019).

Law professor Vida Johnson (2019) further observed that the "dozens of instances of overt racism by law enforcement officers captured on video or on social media, texts or emails, [were] stunning" (p. 227). She added that police violence and a "lax response to white supremacist attacks in communities of color . . . [create] legitimate fears . . . as members of the community stop turning to law enforcement for help" (p. 227). Noteworthy is the fact that school districts with school resource officers lack a reliable means to screen out such far-right police from patrolling school hallways and grounds.

FAR-RIGHT POLICE UNIONS

A far-right, anti-labor union governor of Wisconsin successfully led a campaign to eliminate unions for public employees while exempting police (Finnegan, 2020). The governor understood the advantages of supporting police unions that abhor accountability and any substantive reforms. Police union members are the antithesis of any other type of labor union, including those for teachers. Police unions represent a history of brutality toward people of color, laborers seeking to improve their working conditions and wages, anti-fascist and Black Lives Matter activists, journalists, and other citizens protesting fascistic policies and policing. Like county sheriffs, police unions are notorious for shielding their members from any type of external accountability and cannot be depended on to assist their own departments to investigate any officer misdeeds with any sense of timeliness or validity (Hardaway, 2019). Rather than an independent body concerned with public safety, police unions operate "like a protection racket and sounding more like the Mafia" (Bunch, 2020, para. 5). Police unions use their members' dues and other resources to block reforms and any disciplining of any of their members. Police unions tacitly or publicly endorsed Trump for a second presidential term because he would give them free rein and impunity to use excessive force. The New York City *public employee* police union went so far as to issue a threatening communique: "Mayor DeBlasio, *the members of the NYPD are declaring war on you!* . . . This isn't over, Game on!" (as cited in Cheney-Rice, 2020, para. 2, emphasis added). Yet, these same police organizations remain relatively quiet in condemning far-right attacks on police officers guarding against the Capitol siege after Trump's presidential defeat.

WHITE NATIONALISTS' NIGHTMARE: BLACK LIVES MATTER MOVEMENT

Black Lives Matter (BLM) originated after the 2012 killing of Black, unarmed 17-year-old Travon Martin. BLM leaders made clear after the killer's exoneration under Florida law that the movement "is an ideological and political intervention in a world where Black lives are systematically and intentionally targeted for demise" (Garza, 2014, para. 2). This historical recognition, according to one of the three Black women who founded the movement, "is an affirmation of Black folks' contributions to this society, our humanity, and our resilience in the face of deadly oppression" (Garza, 2014, para. 2). After the 2014 police killing of recent high school graduate Michael Brown by a White police officer in Ferguson, Missouri, BLM became a more nationally recognized tag for racial justice protests. Following the 2020 police murder of George Floyd and subsequent protests, Trump characterized BLM as a "symbol of hate" (as cited in Cohen, 2020, para. 1); his personal lawyer and former New York City mayor Rudy Giuliani, drawing from the fascist politics playbook of distraction, called BLM "a Marxist organization" (para. 20), an extension of far-right anti-Semitic claim of "cultural Marxism" (see Berkowitz, 2003; Wilson, 2015). The tactics by both Trump and Giuliani represented efforts to sidestep debates over police use of violent tactics disproportionally on Black populations, especially because BLM "is an acknowledgement [that] *Black poverty and genocide [are] state violence*" (Garza, 2014, para. 10, emphasis added).

Millions exist in economically neglected neighborhoods with job opportunities outsourced abroad and vital social services cut for children and their families living under a "production of fear" by state institutions: "the threat, the fear, the sense that people are walking [arrest] warrants, that they're targets in American cities right now because the threat of their removal, their bodily violations, their beatings, their killing, hang over people so profoundly" (Heatherton, 2020, 27:12–28:04). A fear of police actions is merited given that between 2013–2019 no charges resulted from 99% of killings by police in communities where no geographic correlation existed with high crime rates (Mapping Police Violence, 2020). Under liberalism and its associated color-blind vision of the rule of law, police impunity in the use of excessive force remains nearly unabated.

LEGALIZED STATE KILLING OF THE OTHER

Since the Ferguson police killing of Brown, an average of 1,000 people, or nearly three per day, are shot and killed by police annually (*The Washington Post*, 2020). This figure, however, is likely underestimated because the federal government remains amiss in collecting data on those who die while in police custody, despite Congressional legislation to do so. According to criminal justice researchers, "The highest levels of inequality in mortality risk are experienced by black men . . . [who] are about 2.5 times more likely to be killed by police over the life course than are white men," an indicator of a public health crisis (Edwards et al., 2019, p. 16794).

An anti-fascism pedagogy critiques problematic federal statutes that shield police from criminal changes in light of (a) the widespread policing of public schools, especially in marginalized Black neighborhoods where the odds are high that a young Black person may be harassed, arrested, or harmed by police; and (b) the existence of 1,772 juvenile jails (Cremin, 2020; Sawyer & Wagner, 2020). By examining the intersections of three branches of government with policing, multicultural educators can contribute to increasing the impact of the BLM movement through a civic education in both their schools and over-policed communities. Using an anti-fascist context, educators can engage with young people and local communities about legal barriers that must be eliminated as a necessary step to reimagining public safety without police impunity to kill in nearly any encounter with civilians. Yet, as is evident in these pages, fascist politics embedded in a liberal democracy go to extreme lengths to legally justify policing compatible with a modern police state.

CRITICAL EFFECTS FROM FERGUSON LEGAL RULINGS

The uprisings after Floyd's 2020 death evoked memories of Ferguson, such as the headline "Ferguson Prepared America For This Moment" (Reilly, 2020). Overlooked within this discourse, however, are federal statutes and White supremacist discourse that provide police immunity from criminal charges in nearly all cases—statutes and practices that continue on the books whether or not police departments are "reformed" beyond liberal procedural tinkering. Even a progressive St. Louis County prosecutor in 2020 was unable to find a legal means to prosecute the policeman who killed Brown 6 years earlier. The prosecutor concluded that "our investigation does not exonerate [Officer] Darren Wilson," noting that if the officer had handled the confrontation differently, "Michael Brown might still be alive" (W. Bell, as cited in Salter, 2020, para. 7). In other words, given the way the law is interpreted and applied limited this prosecutor, especially lacking any video evidence such as was available to convict the police officer who murdered George Floyd (Pfosi & Allen, 2021). To better understand why the Ferguson officer and other police officers continue to use excessive force with impunity, including killing a suspect without a warrant, we next consider two 2015 Department of Justice (DOJ) reports related to White Officer Wilson's actions and the practices of Ferguson governance that parallel behaviors in numerous communities (e.g., McIntire & Keller, 2021). An analysis of these two reports reveals underlying reasons young people of color in and out of schools remain disproportionately in the cross-hairs of unrestrained police violence, particularly with "school resource officers" patrolling school hallways as their beat. For teachers who affirm in their classrooms that Black Lives Matter, an understanding of DOJ reports on Ferguson helps place the challenges of systemic changes in a broader anti-fascist context.

Basis of DOJ Decision That Officer Wilson Did Not Violate Federal Law

The investigation into the killing of unarmed Brown concluded, "Darren Wilson's actions do not constitute prosecutable violations under the applicable federal criminal civil rights statute, 18 U.S.C. § 242, which prohibits uses of deadly force that are 'objectively unreasonable,' as defined by the United States Supreme Court" (DOJ, 2015b, p. 5). To go forward with a prosecution of Wilson or of any officer under 18 U.S.C. § 242, the DOJ explained that the federal government would have to prove "Wilson fired the shots with the requisite 'willful' criminal intent" (p. 10). Citing Supreme Court cases, the DOJ stated, "The use of deadly force is justified when the officer has 'probable cause to believe that the suspect pose[s] a threat of serious physical harm, either to the officer or to others'" (p. 10). Furthermore, "the government must also prove that the officer acted willfully, that is, 'for the specific purpose of violating the law'" (p. 10).

Carelessness, blunders, and prejudicial perceptions of the Other are protected under statute 18 U.S.C. § 242, according to the DOJ (2015b): "Mistake, fear, misperception, or even poor judgment does not constitute willful conduct prosecutable under the statute" (p. 11). To go forward with prosecution, the DOJ contended, "The only possible basis for prosecuting Wilson under Section 242 would therefore be if the government could *prove that his account is not true*" (p. 78, emphasis added). The DOJ prefaced that remark with "Wilson's account of Brown's actions, *if true*"—an acknowledgment that Wilson's version of events served as the benchmark to be proved as false "beyond a reasonable doubt" (p. 78, emphasis added).

The DOJ (2015b) drew attention to the fact that "the Constitutional right at issue is the Fourth Amendment's prohibition against unreasonable seizures, which encompasses the right of an arrestee to be free from 'objectively unreasonable' force" (p. 10). Both police and prosecutors determine, however, what is "objectively unreasonable" use of excessive force. In nearly all cases of police use of excessive violence, *objectivity* rests primarily on the *subjectivity* of the police and, therefore, rarely results in arrest and prosecution of police officers (see Human Rights Watch, 2014). The broad leeway provided police includes the 1989 interpretation of *Graham v. Connor* that a "split-second" judgment by an officer "must be judged from the perspective of a reasonable officer on the scene, rather than with the 20/20 vision of hindsight" (as cited in DOJ, 2015b, pp. 10, 79). *Graham v. Conner* is so engrained in police training that officers come away with the impression they can act with impunity (Kirkpatrick, 2021).

If the police believe they are threatened in nearly any manner, they can kill by shooting or choking if deemed "reasonable," including when the final shot to a wounded and unarmed Brown was executed to the top or "apex of his head" (DOJ, 2015b, p. 7). The DOJ report noted, "Brown could not have been standing straight when Wilson fired this bullet because Wilson is slightly shorter than Brown. The Black youth was likely bent at the waist or falling forward when he received this wound" (p. 17). Apparently, police have the legal right to shoot civilians who even raise their arms in surrender yet continue walking toward the officer, according to a 2012 federal court decision (DOJ, 2015b). The DOJ further concluded, "Even if, with hindsight, Wilson could have done something other than shoot Brown, *the Fourth Amendment does not second-guess a law enforcement officer's decision* on how to respond to an advancing threat" (p. 85, emphasis added). Despite the conviction of the officer in George Floyd's case, protective statues and color-blind reasoning remain the norm in the 2020s.

Wilson's Perception of Brown as a Menacing Other

The contact between officer Wilson and victim Brown lasted no more than 90–120 seconds. During that very short duration, Wilson viewed Brown as something other than human. After Wilson's patrol car door slammed against Brown and a scuffle of an underdetermined nature between Wilson and Brown at the vehicle window resulted in Brown being shot in the hand, Wilson said that Brown "looked like a *demon*" (DOJ, 2015b, p. 14, emphasis added). At the point that Brown had stopped running away from Wilson and turned around, Wilson testified that Brown appeared "'*psychotic*,' '*hostile*,' and '*crazy*,' as though he was '*looking through*' Wilson" (p. 14, emphasis added). According to Wilson, the now severely wounded Brown had the "'*most intense aggressive face*' that he had ever seen on a person" (p. 15, emphasis added). Wilson did admit that he used the derogatory "N-word" after shooting Brown (V. Johnson, 2019). Wilson's racialized perception fits with law professor Jeffrey Fagan's point that statistical analyses strongly suggest "police are more likely to form this sense of imminent danger when confronting a Black person than a white person" (as cited in Kirkpatrick, 2021, p. A13). In other words, Wilson saw a dark-skinned Other who he perceived as a threat rather than a fellow human in great pain. School personnel and parents are justifiably wary of any claims of color-blind neutrality in how police view a racialized student population, as the DOJ narrative and other research indicates.

Institutionalization of Policing as Fascist Governance

The second DOJ (2015a) report that considered the governance practices of Ferguson is instructive to help bring to the forefront elements of fascistic policing that generally go unnoticed unless a high-profile police killing surfaces in protests. A qualitative content analysis of patterns found in the DOJ report revealed six categories of concern, each of which are addressed next.

Racialized Political Economy of Revenue Generation. City officials encouraged police to issue tickets and make arrests, not to protect public safety, but for financial reasons: "Ferguson police officers from all ranks told us that revenue generation is stressed heavily within the police department, and that the message comes from City leadership" (DOJ, 2015a, p. 2). This practice resulted in police acting as revenue-generating warriors rather than protective guardians for local residents; the city officials saw Black citizens as commodified "sources of revenue" (p. 2). The DOJ bluntly stated, *The municipal court does not act as a neutral arbiter of the law or a check on unlawful police conduct.* Instead, the court primarily uses its judicial authority as the means to compel the payment of fines and fees that advance the City's financial interests" (p. 3, emphasis added). Officials at all levels colluded so that "the code enforcement system had been honed to produce more revenue" (p. 10).

Neo-Peonage System of Fines. Ferguson basically created a neo-peonage system of assessing and collecting fines. Technically, a peonage system involves debtors held in some form of servitude by a creditor until their debt is repaid. Although Black residents in Ferguson burdened with unjust fines and bail were not technically held in strict captivity, their freedom of movement and ability to find employment sufficient to pay off their growing fines were hindered by racial segregation and job discrimination (DOJ, 2015a). Such judicial financial practices are unconstitutional, according to the Eighth Amendment, which states that "excessive bail shall not be required, nor excessive fines imposed." Ferguson police increased their "productivity" for generating revenues by nearly any means they chose, legal or extralegal, because the police "department has little concern with how officers do this" (DOJ, 2015a, p. 11).

Despite the unconstitutionality of excessive fines and bail costs, profitable systems of cash bail disproportionately target poor people nationally. Cash bail systems encourage an increase in arrests that "assign higher bail amounts, which drive up incarceration rates, underline racial inequities, and perpetuate poverty" (Fernandez, 2020, p. 27). Nationally, because 70% of those arrested cannot make bail to secure their release, over half a million people find themselves in lengthy pretrial detention despite no conviction or sentencing (Covert, 2017). The deviousness of Ferguson's debt collection represents an extension of proto-fascist brutality of Black bodies, both enslaved and freed.

Jim Crow Practices of White Supremacy. Under Jim Crow practices White police historically arrested Blacks for nearly any reason. A prominent practice was not following the orders of White police officers by failing to immediately demonstrate subservient respect to them. Indicative of Jim Crow's legacy, Ferguson

> officers frequently make enforcement decisions *based on what subjects say, or how they say it.* Just as officers reflexively resort to arrest immediately upon *noncompliance with their orders, whether lawful or not,* they are quick to overreact to challenges and verbal slights. These incidents—sometimes called "contempt of cop" cases—are propelled by officers' belief that arrest is an appropriate response to disrespect. (DOJ, 2015a, p. 25, emphasis added)

For example, Ferguson police, under a quota system, routinely detained and arrested residents for such code violations as "Manner of Walking in Roadway," "High Grass and Weeds," "Barking Dog and Dog Running at

Large" (p. 7) and "Failure to Comply" (p. 19). Like the Jim Crow practices in the late 1800s and into the 1960s, Ferguson police took great liberty in citing residents for such violations.

Mirroring the formal era of Jim Crow, Ferguson police regularly used attack dogs to force compliance, a common practice in some departments to this day (Meacham, 2020; C. Stephens, 2020). Pointedly, the DOJ (2015a) stated that Ferguson's police department "engages in a pattern of deploying canines to bite individuals when the articulated facts do not justify this significant use of force . . . [that leaves] serious puncture wounds to nonviolent offenders, *some of them children*" (p. 31, emphasis added). Only Black residents were singled out for this treatment: "*in every canine bite incident . . . the subject was African American*" (p. 31, emphasis added). Furthermore, this Jim Crow practice was unrelated to police encountering physical resistance but instead was used "to inflict punishment" and fear (p. 33).

Lack of Community Trust in Police. Police and city officials habitually denied Black resident concerns over patterns of mistreatment. When protests did erupt after the shooting of Michael Brown, police and city officials contended with a common far-right reframing that the public protests were the work of "outside agitators" who do not reflect the opinions of "real Ferguson residents" (as cited in DOJ, 2015a, p. 5). The DOJ countered this assertion by noting that the city's official "view is at odds with the facts we have gathered during our investigation. Our investigation has shown that *distrust of the Ferguson Police Department is longstanding and largely attributable to Ferguson's approach to law enforcement*" (p. 5, emphasis added). Ferguson police tactics toward Black residents "undermine community trust," and, therefore, "law enforcement is seen as illegitimate, and the partnerships necessary for public safety are, in some areas, entirely absent" (p. 5). Similar to the disposition of anti-fascist activists described in Chapter 5, African Americans have valid reasons to distrust police for their safety. Six years later and shortly after the murder of George Floyd at police hands, far-right U.S. Attorney General William Barr nevertheless wanted the public to imagine police as "trusted and effective guardians of our communities" (as cited in Goff, 2020, p. A23).

Blurred Governing Structures. Government claims of fairness theoretically rest on the separation of judicial, legislative, and executive branches to balance power among these three governmental divisions. Ferguson, however, was an example of no discernable separation of powers in accordance with this American ideal taught in public schools. The DOJ (2015a) provides ample evidence of Ferguson's autocratic and blurred governing structures in ways similar to the merging of state powers by fascist regimes.

Ferguson's judicial system—specifically the municipal court—"operates as part of the police department," which given the separation of powers should be under the executive branch (DOJ, 2015a, p. 8). "The court," in this instance, "is supervised by the Ferguson Chief of Police, is considered part of the police department for City organizational purposes, and is physically located within the police station. *Court staff report directly to the Chief of Police*" (p. 8, emphasis added). The court clerk, who was under the supervision of the executive branch through the police department, regularly strayed into judicial proceedings and had "disposed of charges *without the Municipal Judge's involvement*" (p. 8, emphasis added). A municipal judge confirmed to the DOJ (2015a) that "it is not uncommon for him to add charges and assess additional fines when a defendant challenges the citation that brought the defendant into court" (p. 49).

Fascistic Criminalizing of School-Age Youth. In its 102-page report the DOJ (2015a) addressed the unreasonable force used by police against Ferguson's public school children, 80% of whom were Black. For example, school-age youth could forcibly be arrested for "play fighting" (p. 25), wounded by an attack dog where officers were "laughing about the incident" (p. 32), slammed against a locker for a hallway fight and then told "she was under arrest for Failure to Comply" (p. 37), or arrested and shot with a stun-gun for refusing "to leave the classroom after getting into a trivial argument with another student" (p. 37). The DOJ recommended reforms but failed to acknowledge a body of research on the inherent problem of having any police presence in schools, research that continues to find racially biased disciplining of students (Green, 2018).

RACIST IMPETUS FOR POLICE IN SCHOOLS

From its racist origins, policing in schools was never colorblind. The impetus for placing police in schools began in the 1950s at the behest of White communities wishing to assert their protective "First Civil Right" as schools slowly desegregated and included Black, Latinx, and Indigenous students in formerly White spaces (Cremin, 2020). In 1974, a congressional act labeled poor young people as "potentially criminals"—understood by legislators as coded language for Black children (as cited in Hinton, 2015, p. 810). Law enforcement agencies gradually absorbed social services in targeting and surveilling urban youth. The congressional act required schools to partner with police in order to receive federal grants, a process that led to the proliferation of "widespread use of police-school liaisons to patrol urban junior high and high school campuses, the cameras installed to monitor children on school buses, the metal detectors at the entrances, and the use of ultrasonic alerters by teachers" (Hinton, 2015, p. 815).

In 1979 just 1% of all schools had armed police, but by 2008 the figure was up to 40%. The dramatic increase in the presence of police in schools was the result of the DOJ's "COPS in Schools" grant program from 1999–2005, which provided generous funding to 3,000 police departments (Na & Gottfredson, 2013). Koon's (2013) research revealed how schools with a high population of students of color continually have transitioned "from rehabilitation and services to criminalization" with an increase of police in schools (p. 3). Furthermore, data indicate that police in schools is associated with "a surge in arrests or misdemeanor charges for essentially non-violent behavior . . . that sends children into criminal courts" (Eckholm, 2013, p. A1). Na and Gottfredson (2013) note,

> To the extent that minor behavioral problems are redefined as criminal problems and teachers are expected to rely on police in dealing with disciplinary problems, discipline responsibilities tend to be shifted away from teachers, administrators, and other school staffs to the SROs [school resource officers]. (p. 623)

This program, created by the DOJ, not only needs reexamination in light of the negative consequences it has created, but abolishment. This is especially the case in light of Na and Gottfredson's conclusion of their research that "found *no evidence suggesting that SRO or other sworn law-enforcement officers contribute to school safety*. That is, for no crime type was an increase in the presence of police significantly related to decreased crime rates" (p. 642, emphasis added; see also Cremin, 2020).

The infamous school-to-prison pipeline leads to euphemistically named "correctional facilities" that disproportionately imprison students of color (Sawyer & Wagner, 2020). During the first 2 decades of this century, many states began to acknowledge some of the major injustices and abuses that result from youth incarceration and significantly reduced the number sent to detention centers. Nevertheless, approximately 75% of adolescents who are jailed continue to be detained for relatively minor transgressions such as "property offenses, drug offenses, public order offenses" and "simple assaults" such as fighting (Rovner, 2015, p. 4).

MILITARIZATION OF POLICE

The Department of Defense inundated over 8,000 local law enforcement agencies with a $7 *billion* transfer of "surplus" weapons designed for foreign wars to use domestically on civilians, including Black Lives Matter protesters (Brancaccio et al., 2020). During the late 2010s school-based police officers in at least 22 school districts in eight states had access to "M-14 and M-16 rifles, extended magazines, automatic pistols, armored plating, tactical vests, SWAT gear, Mine-Resistant Ambush Protected, or MRAP, vehicles, and grenade launchers, which are used by police agencies to deploy tear gas and smoke in crowd-control situations" (Blad, 2020, para. 7). The warrior orientation of police is enhanced with nearly 20% of officers being military veterans compared to 6% in the population overall. In 2009 the DOJ published a guide that warned, "Sustained operations under combat circumstances may cause returning officers to mistakenly blur the lines between military combat situations and civilian crime situations, resulting in inappropriate decisions and actions—particularly in the use of less lethal or lethal force" (as cited in Weichselbaum & Schwartzapfel, 2017, "The Vet-to-Cop Pipeline," para. 8). In other words, former members of the military, especially those with untreated posttraumatic stress disorder, too often bring war zones to domestic streets and schools they patrol as police officers.

TWENTY-FIRST-CENTURY EMPIRE BUILDING AND MILITARIZATION OF STUDENTS

The violent and militaristic impulse of fascist regimes during the mid-20th century described in Chapter 3 resulted in an imperialistic drive. Among the concessions to fascism by liberal democracies was the acceptance of Mussolini's military invasion and occupation of Ethiopia and his warnings of White extinction by the Other. Mainstream media supported the invasion in line with many Italian Americans and New York City's mayor who publicly presented $100,000 to Italy. A coalition of "Black and White anti-racists and antifascists came together around the world to organize" against the invasion (Ben-Ghiat, 2020b, para.2), but the outbreak of the Spanish Civil War and growing German fascism "soon made Ethiopia's plight of marginal concern for most Whites" (para. 12), a fascist military adventure that took an estimated 250,000 Ethiopian lives between 1936–1941. White mainstream concern shifted to the European theater when fascist empire builders began to apply colonial violence to Europe itself.

After WWII, the United States reorganized its empire of territories by shedding most of its colonies and replacing them with military bases (800), which are spread across the planet. During the past 70 years new technologies provided the United States a way "to enjoy the benefits of empire without claiming populated territories" as colonies (Immerwahr, 2019, p. 264). The imperialistic unilateral extension of military power over the governance of a foreign nation or territory is also part of the long history of the United States. As presented in public school textbooks, imperialism is constructed as a reasonable extension of American exceptionalism. For example, despite the nonexistence of weapons of mass destruction, the United States directed this false narrative in the lead-up to a unilateral invasion of Iraq for the real purpose, as described on the front page of the capitalist-friendly *Investor's Business Daily*, of providing an opportunity for "releasing fresh oil supplies onto the world markets" (Graham, 2002, p. A1). At the same time a lead economist for a major international investment firm quipped, "The start of a war may be good" for stock market trading (R. Berner, as cited in Graham, 2002, p. A16). Presented as a common aspect of a liberal democracy rather than as a trait of far-right extremism or fascism, U.S. unprovoked invasions of foreign lands are in practice *"the harshest versions of white supremacy* . . . recast in the language of racial uplift and 'benevolent assimilation'" (Singh, 2006, p. 72, emphasis added).

Twenty-First-Century Colonial Imagery

The spillover of imperialistic cultural racisms into 21st-century foreign policy is most evident in the U.S. invasion and occupation of both Afghanistan and Iraq, two nation-states that did not pose military threats. Instead of treating 9/11 as a criminal act and taking advantage of the UN's International Criminal Police Organization, the United States illegally framed 9/11 as an act of war even though terrorism of the 9/11 attackers—three fourths of whom were from Saudi Arabia—were "outside the context of war to which the laws of war apply" (Paust, 2003, p. 327). Since 9/11 when President Bush first declared a global war on terrorism, the United States expanded the number of military installations internationally, which now includes 40% of the world's nations, or 80 nations on six different continents, at a cost of over $2 trillion (Savell & 5W Infographics, 2019).

Much of the work of the military remains obfuscated, even from members of Congress who vote for military appropriations, including a bipartisan vote adding $25 billion on top of President Biden's astronomical $715 billion request (Johnson, 2021). For example, after four U.S. soldiers died in military combat in the landlocked African nation of Niger, Republican Senator Lindsey Graham was among other legislators who did not know U.S. troops were in Niger. Graham stated on national television, "I didn't know there was 1,000 troops in Niger. . . . We don't know exactly where we're at in the world, militarily, and what we're doing" (para. 3, 8, as cited in Diaz, 2017). Graham added that "this is an endless war with no boundaries" after assuring the families of the deceased soldiers that "they were there to defend America" (19:31, as cited in Diaz, 2017). How the U.S. nation was defended, however, is never made clear beyond assertions of patriotism.

From the dispossession of Indigenous lands to an endless war on terrorism, fascistic cultural racism remains. In the pages of the *Wall Street Journal* prominent journalist Robert Kaplan (2004) defended imperialism as a necessity and belittled journalists who questioned military preemptive attacks on foreign populations. Kaplan, whose writing Bush admired, compared the manufactured war on terrorism to what the Calvary did against Indigenous warriors in the 19th century, telling readers that *"the American military is back to the days of fighting the Indians"* (para. 1, emphasis added). While defending his cultural racism by contending this was not a "slight" on Native Americans, he proclaimed, "The red Indian metaphor is one with which a liberal policy nomenklatura may be uncomfortable, but Army and Marine field officers have embraced it because it captures perfectly the combat challenge of the early 21st century" (para. 2).

Most troubling are findings that neo-Nazis, White supremacists, and anti-government personnel are known and allowed to remain in the military (Shane, 2020). A segment of retired military officers is also an anti-fascist concern. "Open Letter from Senior Military Leaders" noted how 317 generals and admirals had warned prior to the 2020 election that "our historic way of life is stake" if Biden won (Flag Officers 4 America, 2021, para. 2). After the election, the 124 signatories to the letter implied that the reason Trump lost had to do "with election irregularities" that were overlooked (para. 3). Using fascistic tropes, these divisive retired military "leaders" contended that survival of the nation stemmed from a "conflict between supporters of Socialism and Marxism vs. supporters of Constitutional freedom and liberty" (para. 1; see also Golby & Feaver, 2021). If fascistic politics are left unchecked within the active and retired ranks of the military, the United States could find itself advancing toward the current situation in Germany where neo-Nazis have widely infiltrated the ranks of the police and military (Bennhold, 2021).

Recruitment of Young People Into Fascist Violence

The U.S. military has to recruit large numbers of potential soldiers annually to maintain its global police presence. Each year the military needs approximately 184,000 individuals recruited into the military to replace departing personnel (Youth.gov., 2020). When unemployment is low, military recruitment is more challenging. With automation increasingly replacing human labor in factories and many service industries and the outsourcing abroad of manufacturing jobs, young people will continue to struggle to find living-wage employment. In this context, the Pentagon seeks to entice young people into the military with promises of economic gains.

Army Junior Reserve Officers' Training Corps (JROTC) programs for adolescents are disproportionately populated with students of color who are poor (Goldman et al., 2017). In the absence of a military draft since 1973, military recruitment today "essentially amounts to a *poverty draft*" for young people from low-income communities seeking a means to overcome economic indebtedness (Barber, 2020, para. 2, emphasis added). The military also offers a financial incentive to young people who are among those with soaring college student debts.

The Army has turned to producing competitive video gaming that "will help connect with young people" and to make "soldiers more visible and relatable," as reported in the Department of Defense publication *Stars and Stripes* (Garland, 2018, para. 10). This recruitment effort is on top of the JROTC presence in over 1,700 public and private schools and juvenile jails. JROTC minimizes the deadly experiences of soldiering and military conditions, for example, behind the $17 billion spent on a million veterans with PTSD in just a single year, 2018 (Nuwer, 2021). JROTC literature instead ironically claims that it is "one of the largest *character development* and *citizenship* programs for youth in the world" (U.S. Army Junior ROTC, 2021, para. 1).

Money also is the driver for young people living in towns along both the northern and southern U.S. borders who are recruited into one of the 45 Border Patrol Explorers posts, a collaboration between the Boy Scouts and the Border Patrol. Adolescents role-play xenophobic games, tracking, shooting, and arresting people. Most jobs in the low-income regions where most of these boys and girls live are with law enforcement, including the Border

Patrol. The actual training of Border Patrol Explorers is far from transparent, as an investigative reporter who uncovered this program discovered after 2 years of promised but then denied access numerous times to these publicly funded programs (Musick, 2020).

DEFUND OR ABOLISH PRISONS AND POLICE?

Efforts to defund or simply abolish prisons and police departments in their current form is not a new issue, although the topic was amplified after George Floyd's death (Kaba, 2020; Samuels, 2010). Any belief in the rehabilitative effects of prisons is misplaced (e.g., Alexander, 2010; Brown, 2022). Historically, the economic development of the colonies was dependent on prison labor, such as White indentured servants, orphaned children, "vagrants," and enslaved Africans. As prisons developed in the new nation, they were places of hard labor for the incarcerated. After Reconstruction the South opposed using taxes to build prisons to house an increasingly large criminalized Black population. White elites instead turned to privatized, inhumane forced labor prison camps that benefited both Southern economic interests and those of corporations in the North (Blackmon, 2008). In the 21st century over 4,100 corporations "'lease' the labor of prisoners and pay them pennies per day/hr. . . . and still get to put 'Made in America' on the label" (Brinson, 2016, para. 3; McDowell & Mason, 2020).

Space does not allow vetting debates around defunding or abolishing prisons and police. Suffice to say that calls for defunding are generally pleas for funding for more robust social services:

> Homelessness, poverty, substance abuse—we've criminalized a range of human behaviors and we've relied on the police to be the social service agency not just of first resort, but sometimes our only social service agency that deals with these issues. (S. Stoughton, as cited Merrefield, 2021, "Different Interpretations," para. 9)

Anti-fascism favors the abolishment of both prisons and police in their current forms, replacing them with more humane institutions and practices. The abolishment alternative requires a rethinking of the normalization of the cruel and unjust punishment inflicted through fascistic policing and incarceration.

A necessary starting point for abolition is advocacy to overturn federal statute 18 U.S.C. § 242, which provides nearly unlimited police impunity on use of excessive force, and to stop the federal and state bleeding of funding from social and health services that have been significantly reduced and transferred to militarized policing since the late 1960s (see Lepore, 2020b). Anti-fascist abolition envisions as a beginning (a) schools' grounds free of police, (b) juvenile recipients of nonpunitive and community-based treatment for minor infractions, and (c) the increased use of health providers as first responders instead of police for concerned citizen calls for mental health concerns. The advocacy group Dignity in Schools (2018) offers anti-fascist educators detailed measures in their "Counselors Not Cops" policy recommendations as alternatives to militarized police in schools.

FASCISTIC CREEP INTO YOUTH SOCIALIZATION

Young people as a captive audience in schools are vulnerable to far-right propaganda. Anti-fascist multicultural educators have an opportunity to place policing and the military into its historical context through a critical citizenship pedagogy. Any resemblance of the "Officer Friendly" program should be abandoned by schools. Created in 1966 by the notoriously brutal Chicago Police Department in collaboration with the Sears-Roebuck Foundation, the program targeted elementary school students and spread through the 350 communities (Onion, 2020). The National School Resource Network (1979) urged support of the Officer Friendly program to overcome a "public image of law enforcement officers—especially as perceived by children—[that] suffers from negative attitudes expressed by parents, siblings, and friends" (para. 1).

The United States is apparently the only liberal democracy that allows military recruiters to operate within public schools. Some schools provide unlimited access to students, including coaching athletics and eating in cafeterias with students. Districts can legally restrict military recruiters to one location rather than be allowed to make presentations in classrooms. Nearly 90% of students contacted by the military in a follow-up study reported that they never received information about the risks of military service, including losing many of their constitutional rights (Kershner & Harding, 2015; cf. Hedges, 2003).

The accessible ease of both the police and military recruiters to students is reminiscent of the aims of fascist educational socialization, as described in Chapter 3, for building an entirely militarized culture. The Pentagon budget alone reflects a fascistic funding priority that would have resonated with the regimes of Mussolini and Hitler. This is especially the case when the U.S. military budget today is *more than the combined defense spending* of China, India, Russia, the United Kingdom, Saudi Arabia, Germany, France, Japan, South Korea, Italy, and Australia. The military budget allocation accounts for nearly half of all U.S. government discretionary spending that skimps on social services and housing assistance and enriches the arms industry (Peter G. Peterson Foundation, 2021; Stockholm International Peace Research Institute, 2020).

Clearly, critical civic educators alone cannot change a militarized society that preys on vulnerable young people. Nevertheless, an anti-fascist civic education can increase awareness of these conditions among local community residents and school district personnel and students. Teacher educators can incorporate the very real nature of fascist politics in policing and the military to strengthen civic reasoning and discourse for public school teachers and their students. An anti-fascist civic education is an important step toward a demilitarized and more humane society for the future of young people.

Part IV

AN ANTI-FASCIST "READING THE WORLD"

Part IV is organized around Paulo Freire's (1970) concept of the development of a critical consciousness and applied to teacher education. "Reading the world" (Freire, 1985) is fundamental for anti-fascist civic education. In this Freirean civic context of critical knowledge, skills, and dispositions, Chapter 9 provides five anti-fascist multicultural assessment rubrics for teacher education programs. Because Freire (1985) reminds us that educators are learners, too, concluding Chapter 10 includes recommended introductory readings correlated with each of the previous chapters for further exploration.

"Reading the World"

Civic Anti-Fascism for Teacher Education

In a society that often fosters alienation, passivity, and disengagement, we need to foster among our students a sense of community, vibrant connections through shared learning and optimism about the world…[and] to help them understand how people have joined together in social movements to work to make things better.

—Michael Charney, Jesse Hagopian, and Bob Peterson,
Teacher Unions and Social Change, 2021

In a literacy experiment in 1962 Paulo Freire taught 300 peasants how to read and write within 45 days, which led to his Brazilian government's support to create thousands of classes, or "cultural circles" (Bentley, 1999, para. 5). Laborers learned not only "to read the word" but were also "reading the world" in the process of developing a critical consciousness of the world around them (Freire, 1970, 1985). Freire (1970) refers to this process as *conscietização* for learners. Conscietização develops when critical reflection leads to a more complete grasp of barriers dispossessed and marginalized populations can face. *Conscietização* is not a passive exercise but *involves taking action* against social, economic, and political oppression. Two years after the spread of his literary experience that resulted in farm workers questioning their working conditions and wages, a military coup and subsequent dictatorship in cahoots with feudalistic landlords had Freire imprisoned for 70 days for his effort. For 15 years Freire remained exiled from Brazil (Bentley, 1999).

Because Freire's pedagogy of the oppressed was effective, a far-right government silenced him. During the U.S. era of legalized slavery, those who were caught teaching enslaved Africans to read and write could be punished and silenced. The slave-owning founders of the United States never imagined a fully educated populace but instead saw formal education as an exclusive right of the elite. For the masses, the colonial vestiges of the Puritan-style reading of the Christian Bible was sufficient to be an educated person. For a century after the end of the Civil War, the South, under the control of White supremacist governments, adequately funded schools for Whites while leaving substandard resources for Black children who were able and allowed to attend school. Leadership at the federal level lauded industrial education for freed Blacks and was dismissive of the idea that a liberal arts education, especially as it might lead to questioning the norms of Jim Crow. Beyond hegemonic lip service, the notion of a literate and critically knowledgeable population through public education *for all* regardless of class, race, ethnicity, gender, and sexuality remains unrealized in the United States.

Today, as noted in previous chapters, the far right stirs a beehive of White anxiety and the necessity of policing educational boundaries. The far right seeks to limit civic learning so that school-age children are insulated from historical facts and hegemonic practices that propel American exceptionalism and White supremacy in exclusionary and genocidal ways (e.g., Pollock & Rogers, 2022). For Freire (1985), however, the educational challenge "is how not to separate reading the word and reading the world, reading the text and reading the context" (p. 20). Furthermore, the world and context of civic engagement is not static for Freire. Instead, citizenship is "never finished" (Freire, 1998, p. 90). Citizenship "demands commitment [and] political clarity," which in turn leads to an acknowledgment that "a democratic education cannot be realized apart from an education of and for citizenship" (p. 90).

YOUTH ACTIONS INDEPENDENT OF A STATUS QUO EDUCATION

Beyond the school house and in their communities, many young people have taken it upon themselves to figure out solutions to the multiple problems that face their generation now and in the coming decades. Their problem-solving efforts are disconnected from their status quo schooling experiences that have inadequately prepared them to confront some of the biggest political and social issues facing the planet. Students have walked out of their classes when they find discrimination ignored by school personnel (e.g., Kingkade, 2021). As an adolescent Greta Thunberg surfaced internationally as one of clearest examples of drawing attention to the climate crisis that is affecting all of humanity and the natural world. She began protesting outside the Swedish Parliament when she was 15, addressed the United Nations 2 years later, and as an 18-year-old gave a blistering evidence-based attack on the political inaction of those in power and in her audience for the Austrian World Summit who, as usual, politely applauded and thanked Thunberg for her comments (Schwartzenegger 2021). After months of background research, a group of anti-fascist teenagers lured a far-right school board candidate to share his anti-Semitic, anti-Black racist ideology and goal for a White ethnostate where he wrote: "We are advocates of white nationalism and or a pro-western Christian theocracy with a protected white majority status. Whichever one is more obtainable" (J. Wells, as cited in Smith, 2021, para. 5). These adolescent described themselves as "a leaderless collective of young anarchists and anti-fascists" (as cited in Smith, 2021, para. 14). In an effort to raise the critical consciousness of local citizens, three New York City women in their early 30s researched on their own and designed stickers that looked similar to street signs but featured the names and details of prominent New Yorkers who owned slaves. A Black woman who encountered one of the stickers was astonished as to what she learned about one of the slavers: "I didn't know anything about that. He could've owned me" (V. Thompson, as cited in McShane, 2021, para. 3).

In the majority of public schools, however, an engaged civic education appears as an afterthought at best. Conklin (2021) explains that teachers' reluctance to teach topics that might be controversial results in a "sanitized" version of the "ideals of our democratic values" (p. 357; also, Pollock & Rogers, 2022). Despite the impossibility of a neutral appearance in politicized schooling, too many school administrators try to foster an atmosphere that in effect restricts teaching histories and contemporary evidence of "racism, sexism, genocide, and oppression" (p. 357). In this mainstream environment Rhode Island high school students and parents filed a suit after students did not receive any civics education beyond history courses that focused on American exceptionalism in waging wars (Goldstein, 2018). Apparently less than half of U.S. states require coursework in civics despite the modest citizenship education purpose set in the 19th century for the common school (Goldstein, 2018; Spring, 2011). Two years after the suit made it to a federal court, the judge ruled that the U.S. Constitution does not include the right to civic education (Sawchuk, 2020). Hence, education as the responsibility of each individual state is where such battles over civics and multicultural education ensue.

POSSIBILITIES AND CHALLENGES OF A CRITICALLY INFORMED CIVIC EDUCATION

John Dewey's (1938/1974) *Experience and Education*, which is often assigned in teacher education programs, broadly framed his book in the preface's first sentences: "All social movements involve conflicts which are reflected in intellectual controversies. It would not be a sign of health if such an important social interest as education were not also an arena of struggles, practical and theoretical" (p. 5). Intellectual controversies are contested ideologies that shape the political and educational terrains. Writing during the interwar years of historical fascism, Dewey acknowledged that "it is so difficult to develop a philosophy of education" when there is a departure from the status quo of "custom and tradition" (p. 5). Hence, "the conduct of schools, based upon a new order of conceptions, is so much more difficult than is the management of schools which walk in beaten paths" (p. 5).

Dewey's observation helps put in perspective challenges to advance antifascism into mainstream educational discourse. Political leaders do understand that schools are sites for building support for a particular nation-state vision, one that is congruent with dominant interests. Nevertheless, when public educators assume an anti-fascist stance like the New York City Teachers Union and Black teachers during the racially segregated interwar years and WWII, schools become sites to resist and challenge the fascist politics of oppression. Teacher education programs with a critical approach can enable teachers to engage in civic reasoning and discourse to confront repressive practices in schools and society.

Helping students to develop *conscietização*, or a critical consciousness for reflection and action, holds challenges. Most prominent for the 2020s and beyond is the resurrection by the far right of the so-called "cultural wars." The Republican Study Committee called on members to "lean into the culture war" as one way to make electoral gains in future election cycles (as cited in Benen, 2021, para. 5). The shrill of the cultural war narrative finds far-right legislators passing laws that attempt to control the public school curriculum teachers provide if it is deemed "divisive" (Schwartz, 2021). The far-right model of governance with its false alarms of stolen elections and cultural wars, however, is simply a distraction from legislating in ways that benefit the planet and those most marginalized by an unjust political system. The drumbeat of far-right constructed cultural wars reaches back decades to any curriculum that attends to White supremacist practices and domestic fascist politics. The divisive pedagogy that Republican legislators and their far-right media mouthpieces whine about was created by a fascistic legacy of centuries of genocidal practices. Teachers are only considered divisive when, in the Freirean sense, they join with their colleagues and students in the spirit of *conscietização* to learn about viewpoints and material realities necessary for critical civic engagement.

The far right goes so far in some states to ban a pedagogy of civic engagement or "action civics" (Schwartz, 2021, "Banning," para. 1). Because conservatives and the far right recognize the politically contested nature of citizenship, reasoned dialogue and debate is out of the question. In contrast, the American Historical Association notes, "Learning how to identify and evaluate *conflicting interpretations* is an essential citizenship skill" (Stearns, 1998, para. 14, emphasis added). Yet, citizenship is not one-dimensional and equal for every citizen. For example, Banks's (2020) citizenship typology ranges from "failed citizenship" to that which is "recognized" and "participatory" in the political process. Banks's ideal trait of a transformative multicultural citizenship culminates in individuals being able to use personal agency "to implement and promote policies, actions, and changes that are consistent with human rights, social justice, and equality," even when civil disobedience may be necessary (p. 155). In regard to what constitutes civic engagement, Peterson (2019) contends that in our era of far-right politics, educators "need to equip students with the tools to fight effectively against deeply entrenched systems of power. *Notions of activism do not need to be separated from civil disobedience*" (pp. 6–7, emphasis added).

By the beginning of 2022 nearly 8,000 teachers had already signed a pledge to teach history truthfully (Zinn Education Project, 2022). In signing the pledge, a high school English teacher explained, "Lying to students means hiding the past and rewriting the history of this country" (M. Graziose, as cited in Zinn Education Project, 2022, para.30). A history teacher explained why she was resisting the potential repercussions of her state's censoring:

"The truth is worth more than the $5,000 fine the State of Arizona wants to slap on me if I allow my students to become critical thinkers" (E. Chisholm, as cited in Zinn Education Project, 2022, para. 32). An elementary teacher in North Carolina knew which side he wanted to be on:

> I want it to be known that I was one of countless educators nationwide who taught kids to identify, understand, and work to end racism, sexism, white supremacy culture, and the silencing of marginalized voices from our curricula. *Teaching the truth does not mean teaching kids to hate America. It is teaching them that we all play a role in helping our country become a more perfect union.* (K. Sathy, as cited in Zinn Education Project, 2022, para. 33, emphasis added)

Another elementary school teacher noted how students are not simply empty vessels without a sense of the injustices that affect the daily lives of many: "To think children are not aware of the inequalities that exist in their everyday lives is ignorant and insulting" (S. Green, as cited in Zinn Education Project, 2022, para. 40). Collectively, critically aware and courageous teachers, such as the thousands of teacher signatories pledging to teach truth to power along with the support of their unions, are a vital force to resisting the fascist politics of educational absolutism increasingly visible across the United States (e.g., Charney et al., 2021).

THE ANTI-FASCIST CIVIC ROLE OF TEACHER EDUCATION

The majority of both pre-service and in-service teachers likely hold a background insufficient for teaching anti-fascism. Therefore, a reconfiguration of professional education is a requisite to develop the knowledge, skills, and dispositions for a critical multicultural pedagogy for civic engagement. Lee et al. (2021a) explain:

> To truly understand the challenge of division and alienation in society, civic learning and discourse needs to be informed by a broader research literature that helps us to understand issues of implicit bias, identity orientations, and the intersection between identity, perceptions, and thinking. (p. 12)

The teacher education fetish of "methods" courses and an ongoing curricular erosion of even a single required course in the social and philosophical foundations of education hampers fostering a critically informed teaching force. Having multicultural concepts incorporated into a teacher education curriculum has been a struggle against an instrumental cookbook approach that unwittingly can align with the far right's relentless attacks on ethnic studies and other multicultural topics (M. Vavrus, 2002; Vavrus, 2015). Public school institutional constraints, often perpetuated by veteran teachers themselves, place limits on teacher interns to practice implementation of multicultural concepts.

Conservative and far-right ideological orientations by experienced teachers in some cases accounts for a reluctance or even outright hostility toward multiculturalism, especially in recent scapegoating of critical race theory (Will et al., 2021). Alternatively, Journell (2011) found that many "teachers also chose not to include multicultural elements within their instruction because they did not feel competent with non-traditional versions of history" (p. 13). Like the teachers noted earlier who defy far-right legislative censorship, teacher educators can incorporate civic reasoning and discourse across curriculum and instruction courses in a manner that opens a dialogue on anti-fascism as a valid pedagogical orientation. Workplace alienation for teachers, however, exists in an era where teachers fear silencing over topics framed as un-American by the far right (e.g., Ferlazzo, 2021; Soza, 2015). More than ever pre-service and classroom teachers can benefit from mentoring and support from teacher educators and teacher unions in an era of rising far-right constraints on the school curriculum. Fascist politics are clearly anti-democratic and, therefore, provide an opening for anti-fascism as a valid corrective to corrosive far-right discourse.

The following sections offer examples of rubrics for a teacher education faculty to evaluate their programs. One purpose of the five rubrics is to stimulate dialogue among teacher educators, teacher candidates, classroom teachers, and policymakers. The rubrics are adaptable for the contingencies of in-service professional development. Importantly, as Freire (1970) reminds us, we are "*co-investigators*" or co-learners with our students, teachers, and community members in developing practices that advance an anti-fascist civic engagement (p. 97, emphasis in original). Each of the rubric assessments that follow have three levels: *unacceptable*, *acceptable*, and *target*.

TEACHER EDUCATION ANTI-FASCIST RUBRICS

Teacher candidates with critical mentoring can learn how to access state teaching standards that would allow featuring anti-fascism in their lesson plans. Table 9.1 attends to a teacher education program's responsibility to mentor teacher candidates.

Table 9.1. Awareness of State Teaching Standards That Validate Anti-Fascism in Lesson Plans

Unacceptable	Acceptable	Target
The teacher education program provides perfunctory references to teaching standards without helping teacher candidates make valid anti-fascist civic linkages for lesson plans.	The teacher education program provides access to teaching standards and directs teacher candidates to independently make valid anti-fascist civic linkages for lesson plans.	The teacher education program provides access to teaching standards and mentors collaboratively with teacher candidates on how to make valid anti-fascist civic linkages for lesson plans.

To create anti-fascist lesson plans, however, certain preconditions are needed in teacher education programs before preservice teachers have the confidence and realization of the civic importance to read the world. Teacher education programs need faculty who not only infuse their own pedagogy with an anti-fascist knowledge base, but who can critically evaluate anti-fascist expectations and course content in relation to various forms of documented inequities among population groups attempting to exercise their citizenship rights. Table 9.2 offers a way teacher educators can assess their program designs and pedagogy.

Table 9.2. Modeling Best Anti-Fascist Multicultural Professional Practices in Teaching

Unacceptable	Acceptable	Target
Faculty do not model in their own teaching an anti-fascist knowledge base in relation to civic reasoning and discourse that includes inequities among population groups in exercising their citizenship rights.	Faculty incorporate in their own teaching an anti-fascist knowledge base in relation to civic reasoning and discourse that includes inequities among population groups in exercising their citizenship rights.	Faculty not only incorporate in their own teaching an anti-fascist knowledge base, but can critically evaluate program expectations and anti-fascist course content that includes inequities among population groups in exercising their citizenship rights.

The curriculum that program faculty offer should incorporate sufficient historical and contemporary background information for their students to recognize and appreciate the significance of anti-fascism as a critical element within a civic education. The aim for candidates is to demonstrate in *developmentally appropriate* lesson plans content to redress negative impacts of U.S. historical foundations and manifestations of proto-fascism, historical fascism, and far-right extremism in contemporary political, economic, and educational systems through various forms of documented inequities. This can result in teacher interns who are able to articulate a knowledge base as to how an anti-fascist multicultural education can serve to benefit *all* students in a pluralistic democracy. In this process, faculty can help future teachers become critically aware of multicultural challenges inherent in a U.S. history of opposition and suppression of anti-fascism as an aspect of civic engagement. Table 9.3 addresses program anti-fascist curricular adequacy in the preparation of teachers.

Programs moving toward an anti-fascist multicultural orientation curriculum and instruction will need adequate "resources that allow for exploration of non-traditional historical narratives" (Journell, 2011, p. 13). Teacher education programs should aim to provide a broad array of historical and contemporary anti-fascist multicultural resources (e.g., see Chapter 10) so that candidates know how to access such materials in relation to various forms of documented

Table 9.3. Anti-Fascist Multicultural Historical and Contemporary Foundations for Teacher Candidates

Unacceptable	Acceptable	Target
(a) Candidates are unfamiliar with U.S. historical foundations of proto-fascism, historical fascism, and far-right extremism that manifest in contemporary political, economic, and educational systems through various documented inequities.	(a) Candidates articulate a familiarity as to how U.S. historical foundations of proto-fascism, historical fascism, and far-right extremism manifest in contemporary political, economic, and educational systems through various documented inequities.	(a) Candidates demonstrate in *developmentally appropriate* lesson plans ways to redress negative impacts of U.S. historical foundations of proto-fascism, historical fascism, and far-right extremism that manifest in contemporary political, economic, and educational systems through various documented inequities.
(b) Candidates lack a critical civic awareness of politicized opposition to incorporation of anti-fascism in education and are unable to use civic reasoning to counter such anti-democracy challenges.	(b) Candidates articulate a critical civic awareness of politicized opposition to incorporation of anti-fascism in education but are unable to use civic reasoning to counter such anti-democracy challenges.	(b) Candidates articulate a critical civic awareness of politicized opposition to incorporation of anti-fascism in education and are able to use civic reasoning to counter such anti-democracy challenges.
(c) Candidates lack an anti-fascist multicultural knowledge base to incorporate into lessons plans to aid the development of civic reasoning and discourse for their students.	(c) Candidates hold an anti-fascist multicultural knowledge base but lack the pedagogical skill to incorporate this knowledge into lessons plans to aid the development of civic reasoning and discourse for their students.	(c) Candidates incorporate an anti-fascist multicultural knowledge base into lessons plans to aid the development of civic reasoning and discourse for their students.

inequities that affect students, their families, and communities. Table 9.4 provides a means to evaluate the resource capacity of a program.

With a civic education background steeped in an anti-fascist multicultural foundation, future teachers are in a process of developing a critical consciousness that supports a disposition congruent with anti-fascism. Such a disposition can inform developmentally appropriate contributions to student

Table 9.4. Anti-Fascist Multicultural Teacher Educational Resources

Unacceptable	Acceptable	Target
The teacher education program lacks accessibility to anti-fascist multicultural education resources for a critical civic education such that candidates do not know where and how to locate such resources.	The teacher education program has accessibility to limited historical and contemporary anti-fascist multicultural education resources such that candidates know where and how to locate such resources.	The teacher education program has accessibility to a broad and robust array of historical and contemporary anti-fascist multicultural education resources to the extent that candidates know where and how to locate such resources.

learning and school improvement activities. In modeling best practices, faculty can assist future teachers in gaining the confidence and skills to make a well-developed commitment to teaching anti-fascism. Table 9.5 provides assessments to help pre-service teachers move from critical reflection to a habit of mind that is visible, for example, in candidates' educational philosophy statements that inform their pedagogical goals (cf. Dewey, 1938/1974).

Table 9.5. Anti-Fascist Multicultural Dispositions for Teacher Candidates

Unacceptable	Acceptable	Target
A civic commitment to an anti-fascist multicultural orientation is unobservable in candidates' written and oral educational philosophy statements that inform their pedagogical goals.	An emerging civic commitment to an anti-fascist multicultural orientation is observable in candidates' written and oral educational philosophy statements that inform their pedagogical goals.	A well-developed civic commitment to an anti-fascist multicultural orientation is observable in candidates' written and oral educational philosophy statements that inform their pedagogical goals.

MOVEMENT TOWARD AN ANTI-FASCIST CIVIC EDUCATION

Recalling the 1930s and 1940s anti-fascist intercultural education and pedagogical activism of the New York Teachers Union against their racist peers and the resolution of Black educators living and teaching surrounded by the ever-real threat of White supremacist violence (see Chapter 2), inspired educators and policymakers today can collectively move toward an anti-fascist civic education. Also important to remember is that within 2 years after the end of WWII, the mainstream turned its back on teaching anti-fascism. Throughout the 1950s the focus was on the bogeyman of a manufactured threat in our midst of communists and socialists who were among those who supported racial justice and equality (Conklin, 2021). Like the German and Italian fascist regimes of the mid-20th century, today we witness a movement toward educational absolutism as far-right state legislators attempt to censor discussions of the effects of a patriarchal and racialized history of the United States, often cloaked under the guise of "parents' rights" (see Chapters 3–4; Schwartz & Pendharkar, 2022, para. 14). The struggle for social justice among marginalized racial and ethnic groups is a primary taboo for the far-right's White supremacist claims of divisiveness and un-Americanism. To imagine that "it can't happen here" or that Trump and his far-right politicized mafia learned their lesson is a pipe dream that policymakers and educators should avoid (Bowden, 2021), especially when the Republican National Committee chairwoman recasts the Capitol siege as "legitimate political discourse" (as cited in Dawsey & Sonmez, 2022, para. 3). An anti-fascist framework serves as a starting point for educators' and policymakers' deliberations and practices (see Chapter 5). Without an anti-fascist orientation, a looming nightmare of rising fascist politics awaits the United States unless policymakers and civic-minded educators join with their peers and local communities in resisting by means still available to forcibly and knowledgeably confront far-right fascist politics in and outside our schools (see Chapters 6–8).

Teaching Anti-Fascism is not intended as a closure to a reading of the world. The next and final chapter highlights introductory and accessible texts to further explore to enhance the knowledge, skills, and dispositions for an anti-fascist citizenry who can move toward a more humane and equitable just world.

CHAPTER 10

Continuing to Read the World Through a Critical Civic Lens

[W]e are not just teachers but teacher learners. It is really impossible to teach without learning as well as learning without teaching.

—Paulo Freire (1985)

Policymakers and educators ideally will take, build on, and modify what the previous chapters have presented and create policies and practices suitable for their respective settings. No book, including this one, can capture the totality and depth of a knowledge base available to advance an anti-fascist civic education. This closing chapter lists articles and books with brief descriptions associated with each of the preceding chapters for further reading. The purpose is to offer *introductory readings*. With adequate instructional scaffolding, all readings described are also suitable for advanced college students with faculty facilitation. Complete bibliographic information for each recommendation is located in the reference list.

"U.S. GOV'T IS SOFT ON FASCISM" (CHAPTER 1)

- Giroux's *American Nightmare: Facing the Challenge of Fascism* (2018)

Giroux's book is a call to stop denying the possibility of fascist politics through vivid examples and critiques and to face the very real threat of fascism.

- McLaren's "Are Those Whiffs of Fascism That I Smell? Living Behind the Orange Curtain" (2020a)

This accessible narrative journal article brings readers to ground level through McLaren's own lived experience of a recent event that provides an example as to how micro fascisms can seep into everyday life.

- Lee et al.'s executive summary of "Educating for Civic Reasoning and Discourse" (2021b)

The executive summary to this timely and comprehensive monograph provides an overview with a broad range of recommendations for various targeted audiences to advance a critical civic education.

- Au's "A Pedagogy of Insurgency: Teaching and Organizing for Radical Racial Justice in Our Schools" (2021)

Wayne Au's invited keynote lecture for the 2019 annual meeting of the American Educational Studies Association incorporates the concept of an educational "insurgency" as a necessary response to many of the ills of fascist politics described in this book.

"IT CAN'T HAPPEN HERE": FASCIST POLITICS IN AMERICA (CHAPTER 2)

- Taylor's "To be a Good American: The New York City Teachers Union and Race During the Second World War" (2011)

Clarence Taylor's chapter in his edited book focuses on a progressive teachers union that understood the fight against fascism included responding to racism and anti-Semitism. This union in the largest city in the United States coexisted with another teachers union that sympathized with fascism.

- Beadie and Burkholder's "From the Diffusion of Knowledge to the Cultivation of Agency: A Short History of Civic Education Policy and Practice in the United States" (2021)

This chapter's "short history" is packed with detailed background on the rich and uneven history of civic education. Seven historical phases of civics education are accessibly provided. Of particular relevance is the advancement and challenges prior to, during, and after WWII in advancing an anti-racist civic education, including the efforts of Black teachers in the Jim Crow South.

HISTORICAL FOUNDATIONS OF FASCIST POLITICS (CHAPTER 3)

- Passmore's *Fascism: A Very Short Introduction* (2002)

Given the overwhelming literature devoted to the study of fascism, Passmore's book provides a broad and balanced perspective on historical fascism. The text is a helpful introduction to historical fascism.

- Stanley's *How Fascism Works: The Politics of Us and Them* (2018)

This book by a Yale philosophy professor links to contemporary conditions and is quite accessible about elements of historical fascism and how fascist politics manifest today.

- Finchelstein's *A Brief History of Fascist Lies* (2020)

Finchelstein's short text zeroes in on truth claims that are accessible and enlightening in an era of far-right "fake news" assertions.

- Fallace's "American Educators' Confrontation With Fascism" (2017)

This analytical *Educational Researcher* journal article examines how U.S. educators in interwar years initially misinterpreted the implications of the rise of fascism as a positive development.

CONTEMPORARY FAR-RIGHT EXTREMISM (CHAPTER 4)

- Renton's *The New Authoritarians: Convergence on the Right* (2019)

Renton's text covers the international terrain of the political theory and practice of the far right. The book helps differentiates historical fascism from the contemporary right.

- Miller-Idriss's *Hate in the Homeland: The New Global Far Right* (2020)

This text is very accessible and attends to the lure for young people to far-right extremism. Miller-Idriss's chapters on the far-right's "Grooming and Recruiting: Cultivating Intellectual Leadership" and "Whose Homeland? Inoculating against Hate" are particularly relevant.

- Ross's *Against the Fascist Creep* (2017)

Ross provides extensive documentation about neo-fascist and far-right individuals and organizations historically and into the era of the Trump presidency.

- Lyons's *Insurgent Supremacists: The U.S. Far Right's Challenge to State and Empire* (2018)

With its focus on the United States, the book offers a timely background on the contemporary rise of far-right extremism. For accessibility Lyons has divided the text into thematic sections.

EVERYDAY ANTI-FASCISM AND THE STRUGGLE FOR A MULTICULTURAL DEMOCRACY (CHAPTER 5)

- Bray's *Antifa: The Anti-Fascist Handbook* (2017)

Bray's "handbook" covers the international history and actions of anti-fascists. In light of the sparse literature on anti-fascism, this ground-breaking book serves as a much-needed compilation of anti-fascism in theory and practice.

- Vysotsky's *American Antifa: The Tactics, Culture, and Practice of Militant Antifascism* (2021)

Vysotsky, a sociologist of social movements, provides educators a timely and scholarly book on anti-fascism in the context of the United States. Vysotsky brings both his experience as an anti-fascist activist and sociologist to create a valid research-based exploration of anti-fascism and its relationship to anarchism.

- Moore and Tracy's *No Fascist USA! The John Brown Anti-Klan Committee and Lessons for Today's Movements* (2020)

Moore and Tracy retrace the rise of contemporary anti-fascism through interviews with activists and examples of artifacts from the late 20th century. This well-researched book provides concrete examples of linkages between movements for anti-racism and anti-fascism.

- Burley's *Why We Fight: Essays on Fascism, Resistance, and Surviving the Apocalypse* (2021b)

An anti-fascist journalist takes readers into both anti-fascist and far-right subcultures that mainstream media generally overlooks. Burley helps us conceptualize and consider various forms of anti-fascist praxis.

OTHERING: GENOCIDAL RACIST AND NATIVIST FASCIST POLITICS (CHAPTER 6)

- United Nations' *Convention on the Prevention and Punishment of the Crime of Genocide* (1948)

The itemized listing of the elements that comprise the internationally recognized definition of genocide is an invaluable background to make valid tie-ins between what constitutes genocide and far-right discourse, including practices of racialized land dispossession and segregation.

- Adams's *Education for Extinction: American Indians and the Boarding School Experience, 1875–1928* (1995)

Adams thematically links ideologies with actual practices of policymakers and boarding school administrators and teachers. Adams's use of diaries and letters makes this book relevant for our current era to grasp the lingering trauma of settler colonialism on Indigenous populations.

- Blackmon's *Slavery by Another Name: The Re-Enslavement of Black Americans From the Civil War to World War II* (2008)

Blackmon's meticulously researched county records in the South unearths a revealing history of the misuse of the 13th Amendment to perpetuate slavery well into the 20th century. As a compliment to this book, the Public Broadcasting Service (2012) offers a film by this name that features Blackmon's research approach and findings.

- K. R. Johnson's "Trump's Latinx Repatriation" (2019)

Johnson's law journal article provides historical background and legal perspectives on far-right policies that are nativist and anti-Latinx. The article contextualizes the legal and extralegal actions that Latinx populations experience.

POLITICAL ECONOMY OF FASCISTIC LAND AND PROPERTY CONFISCATION (CHAPTER 7)

- Miller et al.'s *Discovering Indigenous Lands: The Doctrine of Discovery in the English Colonies* (2010)

Written in accessible language by law professors, this volume is an exceptional source for understanding the roots, effects, and continuation of the Doctrine of Discovery. The first two chapters offer an excellent introduction.

- C. Harris's "Whiteness as Property" (1993)

Cheryl Harris's seminal and in-depth *Harvard Law Review* article provides an early example of how a critical race theory that includes personal storytelling can reveal the proto-fascist and racist underbelly of U.S. law and governmental practice.

- K. Taylor's *Race for Profit: How Banks and the Real Estate Industry Undermined Black Homeownership*, 2019

Keeanga-Yamahtta Taylor brings a critical political economy perspective to disentangling the long history of racist governmental and real estate policies that helped to create segregated neighborhoods and communities.

- Isenberg's *White Trash: The 400-Year Untold History of Class in America* (2016)

In contrast to liberalism's ideology of a mythic classless society of equal individuals, Isenberg goes to the roots of inequality of class stratification. The book negates any notions that White populations have ever been a homogenous socioeconomic class.

- Roberto's *The Coming of the America Behemoth: The Origins of Fascism in the United States, 1920–1940* (2018)

A unique presentation that examines the role of capitalism in the rise of fascism in the United States during the interwar years. Well-researched, Roberto's text includes extensive primary sources from that era.

FASCIST WARRIORS: POLICE AND MILITARY AS FICTITIOUS GUARDIANS (CHAPTER 8)

- Vitale's *The End of Policing* (2017)

An outstanding text that examines the roots of modern policing and provides researched perspectives conducive for arguing to dismantle rather than reform police departments in light of their continuing history of use of excessive force and repressing movements for social justice.

- Singh's *Race and America's Long War* (2017)

Singh's text relates well with Chapters 6–7 but is particularly germane to Chapter 8's focus on racialized policing and the U.S. military.

- Bogus's "The History and Politics of Second Amendment Scholarship: A Primer" (2002)

A succinct overview on how the Second Amendment morphed from a collective right for state militias such as National Guard units to a relatively recent interpretation as an individual right to own and display arms, including ones normally associated with military personnel.

- Anderson's *The Second: Race and Guns in a Fatally Unequal America* (2021)

Anderson shatters any illusions that the Second Amendment was a benign individual gun rights addition to the Constitution by skillfully establishing the deep connection of the Second Amendment to the oppression of enslaved and freed African Americans.

- Onion's "Playing Good Cop" (2020)

Rebecca Onion's short researched article addresses the era of "Officer Friendly" that was prior to the expansion of police into problematic school resource officers. The article helps contextualize the early propaganda efforts to move policing into schools.

"READING THE WORLD": CIVIC ANTI-FASCISM FOR TEACHER EDUCATION (CHAPTER 9)

- Lee et al.'s "Recommendations for Practice, Policy, and Research" (2021c)

Carol Lee and her colleagues provide an itemized listing with explanations for an education that emphasizes civic reasoning and discourse. Importantly, the extensive outline goes beyond normative civics classroom approaches by including recommendations for classes in social studies, government, geography, history, literacy/language arts, mathematics, and science, as well as what state and district policies and funding are necessary for civic learning.

- Conklin's "Pedagogical Practices and How Teachers Learn" (2021)

This chapter contains constructive steps to scaffold civic education in relation to student identities and lived experiences. Conklin's approach is useful for designing a developmentally appropriate anti-fascist curriculum. She offers a compelling and succinct history of the ebb and flow of progressive civic education.

- Hill's *The Antifa Comic Book: 100 Years of Fascism and Antifa Movements* (2018)

Although labeled a "comic book," this text is a graphic nonfiction with a detailed history of anti-fascist responses internationally to fascist and far-right politics. In addition to being appropriate for policymakers and educators, the text—when scaffolded and chunked by chapters—provides an accessible introduction to fascism and anti-fascism for students "reading the world."

- Journell's *Unpacking Fake News: An Educator's Guide to Navigating Media With Students* (2019)

In this edited text, chapters attend to critical media literacy that combines theory and practice, which is helpful in an age of far-right disinformation.

- Riccó's "Teaching *It Can't Happen Here* in the Trump Era" (2020)

Based on her experiences teaching an upper-level undergraduate seminar "Global Fascism: Legitimizing State Violence across the Atlantic," Guilia Riccó provides insights in teaching Lewis's 1935 satire that ties into current far-right politics. In addition to sharing student assignments she found effective, Riccó makes clear that background information should first be provided to students before reading the novel. She notes that the novel "requires pedagogical caution, as students find it overwhelming, especially in the post-2016 election era" (p. 172). In the Freirean sense, Riccó's students were learning to read their world.

In recommending these resources for further reading in addition to the content of *Teaching Anti-Fascism*, policymakers, educators, and students will ideally take away critical perspectives about how to break through the political and educational resistance to the incorporation of anti-fascism in a multicultural civic education. Collectively, we can move toward transformative pedagogical models and strategies to connect with community anti-fascists and other concerned citizens to assist young people develop into active citizens who are critically informed with the knowledge, skills, and dispositions reflective of a vision and ideals of a democratic society. Paulo Freire would expect nothing less from us.

References

Ackerman, S. (2015a, May 15). As Chicago pays victims of past torture, police face new allegations of abuse at Homan Square (interview). *Democracy Now!* http://www.democracy now.org/2015/5/15/as_chicago_pays_victims_of_past

Ackerman, S. (2015b, February 26). Held for hours at secret Chicago "black site": You're a hostage. It's kidnapping. *The Guardian.* https://www.theguardian.com/us-news/2015/feb/26 /ortlan-police-homan-square-vic-suter

Adams, D., & Snow, D. A. (2010). *Readings on social movements: Origins, dynamics and outcomes* (2nd ed.). Oxford University Press.

Adams, D. W. (1995). *Education for extinction: American Indians and the boarding school experience, 1875–1928.* University Press of Kansas.

Adelman, W. J. (1986). *Haymarket revisited: A tour guide of labor history sites and ethnic neighborhoods connected with the Haymarket affair* (2nd ed.). Illinois Labor History Society.

Aez, P. A., Casado, A., & Wade, J. C. (2009). Factors influencing masculinity ideology among Latino men. *Journal of Men's Studies, 17*(2), 116–128. https://doi.org/10.3149/jms.1702.116

Ajilore, O. (2020, September 28). *The persistent Black-White unemployment gap is built into the labor market.* Center for American Progress. https://www.americanprogress.org/article /persistent-black-white-unemployment-gap-built-labor-market/

Albright, M. (2004, July 30). *Democracy now! confronts Madeleine Albright on the Iraq sanctions: Was it worth the price?* Democracy Now! https://www.democracynow.org/2004/7/30 /democracy_now_confronts_madeline_albright_on

Albright, M. (2018). *Fascism: A warning.* HarperCollins.

Alexander, D., Peterson-Withorn, C., & Tindera, M. (2019, July 25). White House wallets: The definitive net worth of Donald Trump's cabinet. *Forbes.* https://www.forbes .com/sites/michelatindera/2019/07/25/the-definitive-net-worth-of-donald-trumps -cabinet/?sh=2b17b436a157

Alexander, M. (2010). *The new Jim Crow: Mass incarceration in the age of colorblindness.* The New Press.

Alimahomed-Wilson, S. (2019). When the FBI knocks: Racialized state surveillance of Muslims. *Critical Sociology, 45*(6), 871–886.

Allen, K. (2016, August 27). How the super-rich are making their homes "invisible." *Financial Times.* https://www.ft.com/content/7a707048-648d-11e6-8310-ecf0bddad227

Alltucker, K. (2019, August 4). Who is the El Paso shooter? Investigators search for links, motive in anti-immigrant screed. *USA Today.* https://www.usatoday. com/story/news/nation/2019/08 /04/el-paso-wal-mart-shooting-patrick-crusius-probed-hate-crime/1914874001/

Almendrala, A. (2016, December 19). Native American youth suicide rates are at crisis levels. *Huffington Post.* https://www.huffpost. com/entry/native-american-youth-suicide-rates-are -at-crisis-levels_n_560c3084e4b0 z768127005591

Alterman, E. (2021, October 8). *Altercation: What takes the place of local news ain't news.* The American Prospect. https://prospect.org/politics/altercation-what-takes-the-place-of-local -news-aint-news/

Amend, A. (2020, July 9). *Blood and vanishing topsoil: American ecofascism past, present, and in the coming climate crisis.* Political Research Associates. https://www.politicalresearch .org/2020/07/09/blood-and-vanishing-topsoil

American Civil Liberties Union. (2021a). *Factsheet: The NYPD Muslim surveillance program.* https://www.aclu.org/other/factsheet-nypd-muslim-surveillance-program

American Civil Liberties Union. (2021b). *Surveillance under the USA/PATRIOT Act.* https://www.aclu.org/other/surveillance-under-usapatriot-act

American Library Association. (2021). *Hate speech and hate crimes.* http://www.ala.org/advocacy/intfreedom/hate

Anderson, C. (2021). *The second: Race and guns in a fatally unequal America.* Bloomsbury.

Anti-Defamation League. (2018). *Quantifying hate: A year of anti-Semitism on Twitter.* https://www.adl.org/resources/reports/quantifying-hate-a-year-of-anti-semitism-on-twitter#globalist-as-code-word-for-jew

Anti-Defamation League. (2021). *When women are the enemy: The intersection of misogyny and White supremacy.* https://www.adl.org/resources/reports/when-women-are-the-enemy-the-intersection-of-misogyny-and-white-supremacy

Apple, M. (2002). Pedagogy, patriotism, and democracy: On the educational meaning of 11 September 2001. *Discourse: Studies in the Cultural Politics of Education, 23*(3), 299–308. https://doi.org/10.1080/0159630022000029795

Arango, T. (2020, November 16). Hate crimes in U.S. rose to highest level in more than a decade in 2019. *The New York Times.* https://www.nytimes.com/2020/11/16/us/hate-crime-rate.html

Arizona et al. v. United States, 567 U.S. 387 (2012). http://www.supremecourt.gov/opinions/11pdf/11-182b5e1.pdf

Armus, T. (2021, January 7). Rep. Matt Gaetz and other GOP politicians baselessly suggest Antifa is to blame for pro-Trump mob rioting into Capitol. *The Washington Post.* https://www.washingtonpost.com/nation/2021/01/07/antifa-capitol-gaetz-trump-riot/

Armus, T., & Sacchetti, M. (2020, October 21). The parents of 545 children separated at the border still haven't been found. The pandemic isn't helping. *The Washington Post.* https://www.washingtonpost.com/nation/2020/10/21/family-separation-parents-border-covid/

Arnold. A. (2020, September 30). So you want to get involved in mutual aid. *The Cut.* https://www.thecut.com/2020/09/what-exactly-is-mutual-aid-how-to-get-involved.html

Arrighi, G. (1994). *The long twentieth century: Money, power, and the origins of our times.* Verso.

Association of Qualitative Research. (2013). *Typology.* https://www.aqr.org.uk/glossary/?term=typology

Attanasio, C., Burke, G., & Mendoza, M. (2019, June 20). *Lawyers: 250 children held in bad conditions at Texas border.* Associated Press. https://apnews.com/article/a074f375e643408cb9b8d1a5fc5acf6a

Au, W. (2021). A pedagogy of insurgency: Teaching and organizing for radical racial justice in our schools. *Educational Studies, 57*(2), 109–132. https://doi.org/10.1080/00131946.2021.1878181

Baird, A. (2021, May 10). *Louisiana bars problem doctors from practicing medicine in most hospitals. So they treat incarcerated people instead.* BuzzFeed News. https://www.buzzfeednews.com/article/addybaird/ortland-prison-doctors-licenses-suspended

Banjerjee, A., & Sawo, M. (2021, August 9). *The racist campaign against "critical race theory" threatens democracy and economic transformation.* Economic Policy Institute. https://www.epi.org/blog/the-racist-campaign-against-critical-race-theory-threatens-democracy-and-economic-transformation/

Banks, C. A. M. (2012). United States, intercultural/intergroup education in. In J. A. Banks (Ed.), *Encyclopedia of diversity in education* (Vol. 4, pp. 2239–2244). SAGE.

Banks, J. A. (Ed.). (2012). *Encyclopedia of diversity in education* (Vols. 1–4). SAGE.

Banks, J. A. (2020). *Diversity, transformative knowledge, and civic education: Selected essays.* Routledge.

Barbaro, M. (2016, September 16). Donald Trump clung to "birther" lie for years, and still isn't apologetic. *The New York Times.* https://www.nytimes.com/2016/09/17/us/politics/ortla-trump-obama-birther.html

Barber, B. (2020, January 15). *The student debt crisis is fueling the poverty draft.* Facing South. https://www.facingsouth.org/2020/01/student-debt-crisis-fueling-poverty-draft

Barker, K., & Jurasz, O. (2019). Online misogyny: A challenge for digital feminism? *Journal of International Affairs, 72*(2), 95–114. https://www.jstor.org/stable/26760834

Barton, M. S. (2015, April). The global war on anarchism. *Diplomatic History, 39*(2), 303–330. https://www.jstor.org/stable/2637665

Bauer, M., & Stewart, M. (2013). *Close to slavery: Guestworker programs in the United States.* Southern Poverty Law Center. https://www.splcenter.org/20130218/close-slavery -guestworker-programs-united-states

Baum, B. (2006). *The rise and the fall of the Caucasian race: A political history of racial identity.* New York University Press.

BBC. (2015, July 6). *Bill Clinton regrets "three strikes" bill.* https://www.bbc.com/news /world-us-canada-33545971

Beachy, R. (2010, December). The German invention of homosexuality. *Journal of Modern History, 82*(4), 801–838. https://doi.org/10.1086/656077

Beadie, N., & Burkholder, Z. (2021). From the diffusion of knowledge to the cultivation of agency: A short history of civic education policy and practice in the United States. In C. D. Lee, G. White, & D. Dong (Eds.), *Educating for civic reasoning and discourse* (pp. 109– 155). National Academy of Education. https://doi.org/10.31094/2021/2

Beckert, S. (2014). *Empire of cotton: A global history.* Vintage Books.

Beckett, L. (2020a, July 27). Anti-fascists linked to zero murders in the US in 25 years. *The Guardian.* https://www.theguardian.com/world/2020/jul/27/us-rightwing-extremists-attacks -deaths-database-leftwing-antifa

Beckett, L. (2020b, October 20). White supremacist behind majority of US domestic terror attacks in 2020. *The Guardian.* https://www.theguardian.com/world/2020/oct/22/white -supremacists-rightwing-domestic-terror-2020

Ben-Ghiat, R. (2020a). *Strongmen: Mussolini to the present.* Norton.

Ben-Ghiat, R. (2020b). When fascist aggression in Ethiopia sparked a movement of Black solidarity. *The Washington Post.* https://www.washingtonpost.com/outlook/2020/08/03 /when-fascist-aggression-ethiopia-sparked-movement-black-solidarity/

Benadusi, L. (2004). Private life and public morals: Fascism and the "problem" of homosexuality. *Totalitarian Movements and Political Religions, 5*(2), 171–204. https://doi .org/10.1080/1469076042000269211

Benen, S. (2021, June 25). *Republican leaders advise members to "lean into the culture war."* MSNBC. https://www.msnbc.com/ortla-maddow-show/republican-leaders-advise-members -lean-culture-war-n1272372

Benner, K. (2021, October 27). Republicans assail Garland over Justice Department school memo. *The New York Times.* https://www.nytimes.com/2021/10/27/us/politics/merrick-garland -justice-department-schools-memo.html

Bennhold, K. (2021, June 24). Is there a shadow army in Germany? *The New York Times.* https://www.nytimes.com/interactive/2021/06/28/podcasts/dayx.html

Bennhold, K., & Schwirtz, M. (2021, January 25). Global far right finds potential in Capitol riot. *The New York Times,* A1, A10.

Bentley, L. (1999, December). *A brief biography of Paulo Freire.* Pedagogy and Theater of the Oppressed. https://ptoweb.org/aboutpto/a-brief-biography-of-paulo-freire/

Berkowitz, B. (2003, August 15). *"Cultural Marxism" catching on.* Southern Poverty Law Center. https://www.splcenter.org/fighting-hate/intelligence-report/2003/cultural-marxism-catching

Berlin, I. (1969). Two concepts of liberty. In I. Berlin, *Four essays on liberty* (pp. 118–172). Oxford University Press. (Original work published in 1958)

Bernard, D. (2018, December 9). The night thousands of Nazis packed Madison Square Garden for a rally—and violence erupted. *The Washington Post.* https://www .washingtonpost.com/history/2018/12/09/night-thousands-nazis-packed-madison-square -garden-rally-violence-erupted/

Bhutta, N., Chang, A. C., Dettling, L. J., & Hsu, J. W. (2020, September 28). *Disparities in wealth by race and ethnicity in the 2019 survey of consumer finance.* Board of Governors of the Federal Reserve System. https://www.federalreserve.gov/econres/notes/feds -notes/disparities-in-wealth-by-race-and-ethnicity-in-the-2019-survey-of-consumer -finances-20200928.htm

Black, E. (2003). *War against the weak: Eugenics and America's campaign to create a master race*. Four Walls Eight Windows.

Black, J. (2003). *Oxford dictionary of economics* (2nd ed.). Oxford University Press.

Blackmon, D. (2008). *Slavery by another name: The re-enslavement of Black Americans from the Civil War to World War II*. Doubleday.

Blac, E. (2020, June 1). Senator aims to end military equipment program used by school police. *Education Week*. https://www.edweek.org/policy-politics/senator-aims-to-end-military-equipment-program-used-by-school-police/2020/06

Blais, M., & Dupuis-Déri, F. (2012). Masculinism and the antifeminist countermovement. *Social Movement Studies, 11*(1), 21–29.

Blake, A. (2017, February 13). Stephen Miller's authoritarian declaration: Trump's national security actions "will not be questioned." *The Washington Post*. https://www.washingtonpost.com/news/the-fix/wp/2017/02/13/ortlan-millers-audacious-controversial-declaration-trumps-national-security-actions-will-not-be-questioned/

Boggs, J. (1970). *Racism and the class struggle: Further pages from a Black worker's notebook*. Monthly Review Press.

Bogus, C. T. (2002). The history and politics of Second Amendment scholarship: A primer. In C. T. Bogus (Ed.), *The Second Amendment in law and history: Historians and constitutional scholars on the right to bear arms* (pp. 1–15). The New Press.

Boone, C., Joyner, C., Redmon, J. (2021, March 26). Is sex addiction really a thing? Science is skeptical. *The Atlanta Journal-Constitution*. https://www.ajc.com/news/crime/is-sex-addition-really-a-thing-science-is-skeptical/C4Y5L3PHANASZC2PXLLJL47XRA/

Boorstein, M. (2021, January 4). D.C. houses of worship beef up security as Trump defenders descend on the nation's capital. *The Washington Post*. https://www.washingtonpost.com/religion/2021/01/04/black-lives-matter-banner-proud-boys-dc-black-church-asbury/

Boschma, J. (2021, June 30). *Seventeen states have enacted 28 new laws making it harder to vote*. CNN. https://www.cnn.com/2021/06/30/politics/voter-suppression-restrictive-voting-laws/index.html

Bouie, J. (2021, September 14). George W. Bush 2021, meet George W. Bush 2001. *The New York Times*. https://www.nytimes.com/2021/09/14/opinion/ortla-w-bush-911-speech.html

Bowden, J. (2021, February 4). Collins: Trump has learned "a pretty big lesson" from the impeachment. *The Hill*. https://thehill.com/homenews/senate/481486-collins-trump-has-learned-a-pretty-big-lesson-from-impeachment?rl=1

Brancaccio, D., Conlon, R., & Wrenn, C. (2020, June 12). *How police departments got billions of dollars of tactical military equipment*. Marketplace. https://www.marketplace.org/2020/06/12/police-departments-1033-military-equipment-weapons/

Bray, M. (2017). *Antifa: The anti-fascist handbook*. Melville House.

Bray, M. (2018). Foreword. In G. Hill (Ed.), *The Antifa comic book: 100 years of fascism and Antifa movements* (pp. 7–12). Arsenal Pulp Press.

Bray, M. (2020). Five myths about Antifa. *The Washington Post*. https://www.washingtonpost.com/outlook/five-myths/five-myths-about-antifa/2020/09/11/527071ac-f37b-11ea-bc45-e5d48ab44b9f_story.html

Bray, M., Namakkal, J., Riccó, G., & Roubinek, E. (2020, October). Fascism and anti-fascism since 1945: Editors' introduction. *Radical History Review, 138*, 1–9. https://doi.org/10.1215/01636545-8359223

Brennan, D. (2021, March 29). U.S. Capitol attack shows far-right is "mainstreaming" anti-Semitism, Holocaust group says. *Newsweek*. https://www.newsweek.com/us-capitol-attack-far-right-mainstreaming-anti-semitism-holocaust-group-ihra-1579372

Brinson, C. (2016, October 10). *Prison & capitalism*. Civil Liberties Defense Center. https://cldc.org/prison-capitalism/

Brodkin, K. (1998). *How Jews became White folks and what that says about race in America*. Rutgers University Press.

Bronfenbrenner, K. (2000). *Uneasy terrain: The impact of capital mobility on workers, wages, and union organizing*. Cornell University, New York School of Industrial and Labor Relations.

Brown, A. (2022, Feb. 12). Boiling behind bars. *The Intercept*. https://theintercept.com/2022/02/12/prisons-texas-heat-air-conditioning-climate-crisis/

Brown, D. L. (2021, June 1). In Tulsa, solemn remembrances of a century-old race massacre by survivors and descendants. *The Washington Post.* https://www.washingtonpost.com /history/2021/05/31/tulsa-massacre-anniversary-survivors-descendants/

Brown, E. (2018, May 30). *Blackstone, BlackRock, or a public bank? Putting California's funds to work.* Truthout. https://truthout.org/articles/blackstone-blackrock-or-a-public -bank-putting-california-s-funds-to-work/

Brown, E. (2019). *Banking on the people: Democratizing money in the digital age.* The Democracy Collaborative.

Brush, S., & Wittenberg, A. (2022, January 14). BlackRock assets hit record $10 Trillion, powered by ETFs. *Bloomberg.* https://www.bloomberg.com/news/articles/2022-01-14 /blackrock-s-assets-pass-10-trillion-for-the-first-time

Bryant, J. (2016, September 6). The racism of school closures. *The Progressive Magazine.* https:// progressive.org/public-schools-advocate/racism-school-closures/

Bryant, J. (2021, October 19). The Proud Boys are coming for the public schools. *The Progressive Magazine.* https://progressive.org/public-schools-advocate/proud-boys-coming-public -schools-bryant-211019/

Buchanan, T. (2016). "Beyond Cable Street": New approaches to the historiography of antifascism in Britain in the 1930s. In H. Garcia, M. Yusta, X. Tabet, & C. Clímaco (Eds.), *Rethinking antifascism: History, memory and politics, 1922–present* (pp. 61–75). Berghahn Books.

Buchwald, T. F., & Keith, A. (2019). *By any other name: How, when, and why the US government has made genocide determinations.* U.S. Holocaust Memorial Museum. https://www .ushmm.org/m/pdfs/Todd_Buchwald_Report_031819.pdf

Bump, P. (2021, January 7). Most congressional Republicans supported the effort to block Biden's win. *The Washington Post.* https://www.washingtonpost.com/politics/2021/01/07 /most-congressional-republicans-supported-effort-block-bidens-win/

Bunch, W. (2020, June 7). Why do police unions talk and act like the Mafia? How can we stop them? *The Philadelphia Inquirer.* https://www.inquirer.com/opinion/commentary/police -unions-defend-brutality-george-floyd-protests-20200607.html

Burke, G., Linderman, J., & Mendoza. (2021, May 11). *Migrant children held in mass shelters with little oversight.* Associated Press. https://apnews.com/article/ortla-trump-immigration -health-coronavirus-pandemic-government-and-politics-3b4e480c9021e6a8e02313 f4c73a497e

Burley, S. (2021a, July 13). The great 2020 Antifa scare. *Political Research Associates.* https:// politicalresearch.org/2021/07/13/great-2020-antifa-scare

Burley, S. (2021b). *Why we fight: Essays on fascism, resistance, and surviving the apocalypse.* AK Press.

Burley, S. (2022, January 4). *Community bonds and mutual aid sustain anti-fascists targeted by the state.* Truthout. https://truthout.org/articles/community-bonds-and-mutual-aid-sustain -anti-fascists-targeted-by-the-state/

Burns, R. (2021, October). Meet the "sidewalk socialists." *In These Times,* 14–23.

Cabán, T. (2020, August 24/31). Road to fascism. *The Nation,* 4.

Calloway, C. R. (1977). Group cohesiveness in the Black Panther Party. *Journal of Black Studies, 8*(1), 55–74. http://www.jstor.org/stable/2783689

Campion, K. (2020, August 24). Women in the extreme and radical right: Forms of participation and their implications. *Social Science, 9*(9), 1–20. https://www.mdpi.com/2076-0760/9/9/149

Canadian Civil Liberties Union. (2020). *Understanding bill C-51: The Anti-Terrorism Act, 2015.* https://ccla.org/understanding-bill-c-51-the-anti-terrorism-act-2015/

Capps, K. (2021, January 7). *The double standard for policing Capitol rioters and BLM protesters.* Bloomberg CityLab. https://www.bloomberg.com/news/articles/2021-01-07/trump -rioters-weren-t-policed-like-blm-protesters

Carlson, T. (2021, August 3). *Tucker: The mainstream media's job is to defend the ruling class.* Fox News. https://www.foxnews.com/transcript/tucker-the-mainstream-medias-job-is-to -defend-the-ruling-class

Casey, T. (2016a, October 31). *Cliven Bundy wins: Malheur verdict redefines civil disobedience.* Triple Pundit. https://www.triplepundit.com/story/2016/cliven-bundy-wins-malheur-verdict -redefines-civil-disobedience/21716

Casey, T. (2016b, February 9). *Oregon takeover update: The plot thickens.* Triple Pundit. https://www.triplepundit.com/story/2016/ortla-takeover-update-plot-thickens/28461

Center for American Women and Politics. (2022). *Women in elective office 2021.* Eagleton Institute of Politics, Rutgers University-New Brunswick. https://cawp.rutgers.edu/women-elective-office-2021

Cento Bull, A. (2009). Neo-fascism. In R. J. B. Bosworth (Ed.), *The Oxford handbook of fascism* (pp. 586–605). Oxford University Press.

Chapman, B. (1968). The police-state. *Government and Opposition, 3*(4), 428–440. http://www.jstor.org/stable/44481889

Chapman, B. (1970). *Police state.* Praeger.

Charney, M., Hagopian, J., & Peterson, B. (2021). *Teacher unions and social justice: Organizing for the schools and communities our students deserve.* Rethinking Schools.

Cheney-Rice, Z. (2020, February 10). NYC's police-union leaders are unhinged. *Intelligencer.* https://nymag.com/intelligencer/2020/02/nypd-union-war-de-blasio.html

Cherelus, G. (2018, November 13). *U.S. anti-Semitic hate crimes spike 37 percent in 2017: FBI.* Reuters. https://www.reuters.com/article/us-usa-hate-crimes-report/u-s-anti-semitic-hate-crimes-spiked-37-percent-in-2017-fbi-idUSKCN1NI2H6

Children's Defense Fund. (2021). *Income and wealth inequality.* https://www.childrensdefense.org/state-of-americas-children/soac-2021-income-inequality/

Chin, R. (2017). *The crisis of multiculturalism in Europe: A history.* Princeton University Press.

Cho, S., Crenshaw, K. M., & McCall, L. (2013). Toward a field of intersectionality studies: Theory, application, and praxis. *Signs: Journal of Women in Culture and Society, 38*(4), 785–810.

Chomsky, N. (2013). *On anarchism.* New Press.

Christiano, T. (2018). Democracy. In E. N. Zalta (Ed.), *The Stanford encyclopedia of philosophy.* https://plato.stanford.edu/archives/fall2018/entries/democracy

Churchwell, S. (2018). *Behold, America: The entangled history of "America first" and "the American dream."* Basic Books.

Cochrane, E. (2021, September 12). Six officers cited for discipline in January 6 riot. *The New York Times,* p. 32.

Cohen, D. (2021, July 7). Trump on January 6 insurrection: "These were great people." *Politico.* https://www.politico.com/news/2021/07/11/trump-jan-6-insurrection-these-were-great-people-499165

Cohen, M. (2020, July 1). Trump: Black Lives Matter is a 'symbol of hate.' *Politico.* https://www.politico.com/news/2020/07/01/trump-black-lives-matter-347051

Coles, G. (2018). *Miseducating for the global economy: How corporate power damages education and subverts students' futures.* Monthly Review Press.

Collins, C. (2021, January 25). *Updates: Billionaire wealth, U.S. job losses and pandemic profiteers.* Inequality.Org. https://inequality.org/great-divide/updates-billionaire-pandemic/

Colson, D. (2017). Propaganda and the deed: Anarchism, violence and the representational impulse. *American Studies, 55/56*(4/1), 163–186. http://www.jstor.org/stable/44982624

Congressional Black Caucus. (2018, January 11). *CBC Chairman @RepRichmond: @realDonaldTrump's "shithole" comments are further proof that his Make America Great Again agenda is really a Make America White Again agenda* [Twitter post]. https://twitter.com/TheBlackCaucus/status/951593898983477248

Conklin, H. G. (2021). Pedagogical practices and how teachers learn. In C. D. Lee, G. White, & D. Dong (Eds.), *Educating for civic reasoning and discourse* (pp. 353–396). National Academy of Education. https://naeducation.org/educating-for-civic-reasoning-and-discourse/

Corn, D. (2021, November 1). It's time to use the f-word for Fox. *Mother Jones.* https://www.motherjones.com/politics/2021/11/fox-news-tucker-carlson-documentary-fascism/

Cornejo, D. (2019, June 19). Trump's spiritual adviser prays against "demonic networks" opposing him [Video file]. *The Washington Post.* https://www.washingtonpost.com/video/politics/trumps-spiritual-adviser-prays-against-demonic-networks-opposing-him/2019/06/19/4eb98c18-8879-4df6-b77d-6110cd10fb61_video.html

Cortés, C. (2012). Media, curriculum and teaching. In J. A. Banks (Ed.), *Encyclopedia of diversity in education* (Vol. 3, pp. 1461–1463). SAGE.

Covert, B. (2017, November 6). The injustice of cash bail. *The Nation*, 12–17.

Craig, T. (2021, October 15). Moms for Liberty has turned "parental rights" into a rallying cry for conservative parents. *The Washington Post*. https://www.washingtonpost.com/national /moms-for-liberty-parents-rights/2021/10/14/bf3d9ccc-286a-11ec-8831-a31e7b3de188 _story.html

Cremin, P. (2020, July 8). School policing was designed to criminalize Black students. *Harvard Civil Rights–Civil Liberties Law Review*. https://harvardcrcl.org/school-policing-was -designed-to-criminalize-black-students-we-must-follow-black-voices-calling-for-its-abolition/

CrimethInc. (2018). *To change everything: An anarchist appeal*. https://cdn.crimethinc.com /assets/zines/to-change-everything/to-change-everything_screen_single_page_view.pdf

Dabhoiwala, F. (2020, December 3). The free speech wars review—From censorship to cancel culture. *The Guardian*. https://www.theguardian.com/books/2020/dec/03/the-free-speech-wars-review -from-censorship-to-cancel-culture

Davis, M. (2020). *Old gods, new enigmas: Marx's lost theory*. Verso.

Davis, S. (2021, March 17). *House renews Violence Against Women Act, but Senate hurdles remain*. NPR. https://www.npr.org/2021/03/17/977842441/house-renews-violence-against-women -act-but-senate-hurdles-remain

Dawsey, J., & Sonmez, F. (2022, February 3). RNC votes to condemn Cheney, Kinzinger for serving on House committee investigating Jan. 6 attack on the Capitol by pro-Trump mob. *The Washington Post*. https://www.washingtonpost.com/nation/2022/02/03/rnc-cheney-trump/

Dayen, D. (2018, September 17). Below the surface of ICE: The corporations profiting from immigrant detention. *In These Times*. https://inthesetimes.com/features/ice-abolish-immigration -child-detention-private-prison-profiting.html

de Dijn, A. (2020). *Freedom: An unruly history*. Harvard University Press.

Delgado, R. (1995). Introduction. In R. Delgado (Ed.), *Critical race theory: The cutting edge* (pp. xiii–xvi). Temple University Press.

Dennison, S. (2021, August 5). *How much is Facebook worth?* GoBankingRates. https://www .gobankingrates.com/money/business/how-much-is-facebook-worth/

DeRienzo, M. (2020, October 28). *Analysis: New and age-old voter suppression tactics at the heart of the 2020 power struggle*. The Center for Public Integrity. https://publicintegrity.org/politics /elections/ballotboxbarriers/analysis-voter-suppression-never-went-away-tactics-changed/

Descartes, J., Hardesty, M., Hoyer, J., Schreiner, M., & Shuman, B. (2020, October). Anti-fascism in the archive. *Radical History Review, 138*, 179–191. https://doi.org/10.1215/01636545-8359580

Desmond, M. (2016). *Evict: Poverty and profit in the American city*. Broadway Books.

Dewey, J. (1974). *Education and experience*. Macmillan. (Originally published in 1938)

Diamond, J. (2015, November 23). *Trump on protester: "Maybe he should have been roughed up."* CNN. https://www.cnn.com/2015/11/22/politics/donald-trump-black-lives-matter-protester -confrontation/index.html

Diamond, J. (2016a, February 23). *Donald Trump on protester: "I'd like to punch him in the face."* CNN. https://www.cnn.com/2016/02/23/politics/ortla-trump-nevada-rally-punch /index.html

Diamond, J. (2016b, January 24). *Trump: I could "shoot somebody and I wouldn't lose voters."* CNN. https://www.cnn.com/2016/01/23/politics/ortla-trump-shoot-somebody-support/index .html

Dias, E. (2021, February 8). Extremism from Whites has strong roots in U.S. *The New York Times*, A11.

Diaz, D. (2017, October 23). *Key senators say they didn't know the US had troops in Niger*. CNN. https://www.cnn.com/2017/10/23/politics/niger-troops-lawmakers/index.html

DiBranco, A. (2019, December 6). *The first anti-feminist massacre*. Political Research Associates. https://www.politicalresearch.org/2019/12/06/first-anti-feminist-massacre

DiBranco, A. (2020, February 10). *Male supremacist terrorism as a rising threat*. International Centre for Counter-Terrorism—The Hague. https://icct.nl/publication/male-supremacist -terrorism-as-a-rising-threat/

Digital History. (2021). *Virginia slave laws*. https://www.digitalhistory.uh.edu/disp_textbook .cfm?smtID=3&psid=71

Dignity in Schools. (2018). *Counselors not cops: Ending the regular presence of law enforcement in schools*. https://dignityinschools.org/take-action/counselors-not-cops/

Dinerstein, A. C. (2020). A critical theory of hope: Critical affirmations beyond fear. In A. C. Dinerstein, A. G. Vela, E. González, & J. Holloway (Eds.), *Open Marxism 4: Against a closing world* (pp. 33–46). Pluto Press.

Diouf, A. (2015, March 27). *Remembering the women of slavery*. New York Public Library. https://www.nypl.org/blog/2015/03/27/remembering-women-slavery

District of Columbia v. Heller, 478 F. 3d 370 (2008). https://www.law.cornell.edu/supct/html/07-290.ZS.html

Dogliani, P. (2009). Propaganda and youth. In R. J. B. Bosworth (Ed.), *The Oxford handbook of fascism* (pp. 185–202). Oxford University Press.

Donaghue, E. (2020, July 2). *2,120 hate incidents against Asian Americans reported during coronavirus pandemic*. CBS News. https://www.cbsnews.com/news/anti-asian-american-hate-incidents-up-racism/

Drucker, J., & Hakim, D. (2021, June 12). Private inequity: How a powerful industry conquered the tax system. *The New York Times*. https://www.nytimes.com/2021/06/12/business/private-equity-taxes.html

Dunbar-Ortiz, R. (2014). *An Indigenous peoples' history of the United States*. Beacon.

Dwoskin, E. (2020, October 9). When Trump gets coronavirus, Chinese Americans pay a price. *The Washington Post*. https://www.washingtonpost.com/technology/2020/10/09/twitter-asian-americans-discrimination/

Ecarma, C. (2021a, August 3). Tucker Carlson joining the right-wing parade to "illiberal" Hungary. *Vanity Fair*. https://www.vanityfair.com/news/2021/08/tucker-carlson-right-wing-parade-hungary?utm_source=VANITYFAIR_REG_GATE

Ecarma, C. (2021b, March 26). Tucker Carlson justifies the idea of a full-blown fascist takeover. *Vanity Fair*. https://www.vanityfair.com/news/2021/03/tucker-carlson-justifies-fascist-takeover

Eckholm, E. (2013, April 12). With police in schools, more children in court. *The New York Times*, A1, A13.

The Economist Intelligence Unit. (2021). *Democracy index* 2021: The China challenge. https://www.eiu.com/n/campaigns/democracy-index-2021/

Edwards, F., Lee, H., & Esposito, M. (2019, August). Risk of being killed by police use of force in the United States by age, race–ethnicity, and sex. *PNAS, 116*(34), 16793–16798. https://www.pnas.org/content/116/34/16793

Edwards, J. (2021, August 7). A Black Army vet toured a house with his real estate agent and teen. Police surrounded the home and handcuffed them. *The Washington Post*. https://www.washingtonpost.com/nation/2021/08/06/black-realtor-michigan-police-handcuffed/

Efrati, Y. (2019). God, I can't stop thinking about sex! The rebound effect in unsuccessful suppression of sexual thoughts among religious adolescents. *Journal of Sex Research, 56*(2), 146–155.

Eisinger, J., Ernsthausen, J., & Kiel, P. (2021, June 8). *The secret IRS files: Trove of never-before-seen records reveal how the wealthiest avoid income tax*. ProPublica. https://www.propublica.org/article/the-secret-irs-files-trove-of-never-before-seen-records-reveal-how-the-wealthiest-avoid-income-tax

Engelberg, S., & Sontag, D. (1994, December 21). Behind one agency's walls: Misbehaving and moving up. *The New York Times*. https://www.nytimes.com/1994/12/21/us/blind-eye-immigration-system-handles-discipline-special-report-behind-one-agency.html

Environmental Working Group. (2021). *Timeline: Black farmers and the USDA, 1920 to present*. https://www.ewg.org/research/black-farmer-usda-timeline/

Fabricant, M., & Fine, M. (2013). *The changing politics of education: Privatization and the dispossessed lives left behind*. Paradigm.

Fallace, T. (2017). American educators' confrontation with fascism. *Educational Researcher, 47*(1), 46–52.

Faludi, S. (1991). *Backlash: The undeclared war against American women*. Crown.

Feagin, J. R. (2012). *White party, White government: Race, class, and U.S. politics*. Taylor & Francis.

Feeding America. (2021, March). *The impact of coronavirus on food insecurity in 2020 & 2021.* https://www.feedingamerica.org/sites/default/files/2021-03/National%20Projections%20 Brief_3.9.2021_0.pdf

Feldkamp, K., & Neusteter, S. B. (2021, January 26). The little known, racist history of the 911 emergency call system. *In These Times.* https://inthesetimes.com/article/911-emergency-service -racist-history-civil-rights

Felton, E. (2017, September 25/October 2). The Department of Justice is overseeing the re-segregation of American schools. *The Nation.* https://www.thenation.com/article/archive /the-department-of-justice-is-overseeing-the-resegregation-of-american-schools/

Ferlazzo, L. (2021, July 28). When it comes to critical race theory, teachers "should go on offense with inquiry." *Education Week.* https://www.edweek.org/teaching-learning/opinion-when -it-comes-to-critical-race-theory-teachers-should-go-on-offense-with-inquiry/2021/06

Fernandez, J. A. (2020, Summer). Criminal conditions. *ACLU Magazine,* 25–29.

Fiala, A. (2018). Anarchism. In E. N. Zalta (Ed.), *The Stanford encyclopedia of philosophy* (pp. 1–41). https://plato.stanford.edu/entries/anarchism/

Finchelstein, F. (2017). *From fascism to populism in history.* University of California Press.

Finchelstein, F. (2020). *A brief history of fascist lies.* University of California Press.

Fine, B. (1938, January 16). Schools to open tolerance drive. *The New York Times.* https:// timesmachine.nytimes.com/timesmachine/1938/01/16/99531977.html?pageNumber=46

Finnegan, W. (2020, July 27). How police unions fight reform. *The New Yorker.* https://www .newyorker.com/magazine/2020/08/03/how-police-unions-fight-reform

Flag Officers 4 America. (2021). *Open letter from retired generals and admirals.* https://img1.wsimg .com/blobby/go/fb7c7bd8-097d-4e2f-8f12-3442d151b57d/downloads/2021%20Open %20Letter%20from%20Retired%20Generals%20and%20Adm.pdf?ver=1620740665549

Flavelle, C., & Goodluck, K. (2021, June 28). Native Americans feel brunt of climate change. *The New York Times,* A1, A14–15.

Fletcher, M. A. (1996, May 22). No linkage found in Black church arsons. *The Washington Post.* https://www.washingtonpost.com/wp-srv/national/longterm/churches/reaction.htm

Foner, E. (1990). *A short history of Reconstruction, 1863–1877.* Harper & Row.

Foner, E. (1995). *Free soil, free labor, free men: The ideology of the Republican party before the Civil War.* Oxford University Press.

Foster, S. J. (2000). The Red Scare: Origins and impact. *Counterpoints, 87,* 1–10.

Foucault, M. (1972). Preface. In G. Deleuze & F. Guattari (Eds.), *Anti-Oedipus: Capitalism and schizophrenia* (R. Hurley, M. Seem, & H. R. Lane, Trans., pp. xi–xiv). Viking.

Frail, T. A. (2017, January/February). The injustice of Japanese-American internment camps resonates strongly to this day. *Smithsonian Magazine.* https://www.smithsonianmag.com /history/injustice-japanese-americans-internment-camps-resonates-strongly-180961422/

Frankel, T. C. (2021, February 10). A majority of the people arrested for Capitol riot had a history of financial trouble. *The Washington Post.* https://www.washingtonpost.com /business/2021/02/10/capitol-insurrectionists-jenna-ryan-financial-problems/

Frankenberg, E. (2013). The role of residential segregation in contemporary school segregation. *Education and Urban Society, 45*(5), 548–570. doi:10.1177/0013124513486288

Franzinelli, M. (2009). Squadrism. In R. J. B. Bosworth (Ed.), *The Oxford handbook of fascism* (R. Bosworth, Trans., pp. 91–108). Oxford University Press.

Freire, P. (1970). *Pedagogy of the oppressed.* Seabury.

Freire, P. (1985). Reading the world and reading the word: An interview with Paulo Freire. *Language Arts, 62*(1), 15–21. http://www.jstor.org/stable/41405241

Freire, P. (1998). *Teachers as cultural workers: Letters to those who dare to teach* (D. Macedo, D. Koike, & A. Oliveira, Trans.). Westview Press.

Gabbatt, A. (2020, January 11). "Unparalleled privilege": Why White evangelicals see Trump as their savior. *The Guardian.* https://www.theguardian.com/us-news/2020/jan/11/onald-trump -evangelical-christians-cyrus-king

Gaddy, C. W. (2005). God talk in the public square. In C. H. Badaracco (Ed.), *Quoting God: How media shape ideas about religion and culture.* Baylor University Press.

Gandesha, S. (2020). Introduction. In S. Gandesha (Ed.), *Spectres of fascism: Historical, theoretical and international perspectives* (pp. 1–24). Pluto Press.

Gandesha, S. (2021). Identity crisis: The politics of false concreteness. In G. Albo, L. Panitch, & C. Leys (Eds.), *Socialist register 2022* (pp. 263–280). Merlin Press.

Ganor, B. (2002). Defining terrorism: Is one man's terrorist another man's freedom fighter? *Police Practice and Research, 3*(4), 287–304.

Ganser, D. (2005). Terrorism in Western Europe: An approach to NATO's secret stay-behind armies. *Whitehead Journal of Diplomacy and International Relations, 6*(1), 69–96.

Garboden, P., & Rosen, E. (2019). Serial filings: How landlords use the threat of eviction. *City & Community, 18*(2), 638–661. https://doi.org/10.1111/cico.12387

García, E. (2020, February 12). *Schools are still segregated and Black children are paying the price.* Economic Policy Institute. https://www.epi.org/publication/schools-are-still -segregated-and-black-children-are-paying-a-price/

Garcia, H., Yusta, M. Tabet, X., & Clímaco, C. (2016). Introduction: Beyond revisionism: Rethinking antifascism in the twenty-first century. In H. Garcia, M. Yusta, X. Tabet, & C. Clímaco (Eds.), *Rethinking antifascism: History, memory and politics, 1922–present* (M. Roberts, Trans., pp. 1–19). Berghahn Books.

Gardner, A., Rabinowitz, K., & Stevens, H. (2021, March 11). How GOP-back voting measures could create hurdles for tens of millions of voters. *The Washington Post.* https://www .washingtonpost.com/politics/interactive/2021/voting-restrictions-republicans-states/

Garland, C. (2018, November 9). *Uncle Sam wants you—to play video games for the US Army.* Stars and Stripes. https://www.stripes.com/news/uncle-sam-wants-you-to-play-video -games-for-the-us-army-1.555885

Garrett, H. G. (2019). Why does fake news work? On the psychosocial dynamics of learning, belief, and citizenship. In W. Journell (Ed.), *Unpacking fake news: An educator's guide to navigating media with students* (pp. 15–29). Teachers College Press.

Garza, A. (2014, October 7). A herstory of the #BlackLivesMatter movement. *The Feminist Wire.* http://www.thefeministwire.com/2014/10/blacklivesmatter-2/

Gawthorpe, A. (2019, July 31). Is this fascism? No. Could it become fascism? Yes. *The Guardian* .https://www.theguardian.com/commentisfree/2019/jul/31/is-this-fascism-no-could -it-become-fascism-yes?

Gearan, A., & Phillip, A. (2016, February 25). Clinton regrets 1996 "super-predators" after encounter with activist. *The Washington Post.* https://www.washingtonpost.com/news /post-politics/wp/2016/02/25/ortlan-heckled-by-black-lives-matter-activist/

General Assembly of Virginia. (1705). *An act concerning servants and slaves* (excerpts). www .encyclopediavirginia.org/_An_act_concerning_Servants_and_Slaves_1705

Genosko, G. (2020). Micro-fascism in the age of Trump. In S. Gandesha (Ed.), *Spectres of fascism: Historical, theoretical, and international perspectives.* Pluto Press.

German, M. (2019). *Disrupt, discredit, and divide: How the new FBI damages democracy.* The New Press.

German, M. (2020, August 27). *Hidden in plain sight: Racism, White supremacy, and far-right militancy in law enforcement.* Brennan Center for Justice. https://www.brennancenter.org /our-work/research-reports/hidden-plain-sight-racism-white-supremacy-and-far-right -militancy-law

Gingeras, R. (2010, February). Last rites for a "pure bandit": Clandestine service, historiography and the origins of the Turkish "deep state." *Past & Present, 20,* 151–174.

Giroux, H. A. (2016). When schools become dead zones of the imagination: A critical pedagogy manifesto. *The High School Journal, 99*(4), 351–359.

Giroux, H. A. (2018). *American nightmare: Facing the challenge of fascism.* City Lights Open Media.

Giroux, H. A. (2019). Trump and the legacy of a menacing past. *Cultural Studies, 33*(4), 711–739. https://doi.org/10.1080/09502386.2018.1557725

Gluckman, N. (2017, August 28). Dartmouth professors show support for lecturer after Antifa interviews. *The Chronicle of Higher Education.* https://www.chronicle.com/blogs/ticker /ortland-professors-show-support-for-lecturer-after-antifa-interviews

Goff, P. A. (2020, October 21). Trump's police state. *The New York Times*, A23.

Golby, J., & Feaver, P. (2021, May 15). Former military leaders criticize the election and the administration. That hurts the military's reputation. *The Washington Post*. https://www .washingtonpost.com/politics/2021/05/15/former-military-leaders-criticized-election -administration-that-hurts-militarys-reputation/

Goldberg, M. (2021, February 28). The campaign to cancel wokeness. *The New York Times*, SR3.

Goldman, C. A., Schweig, J., Buenaventura, M., & Wright, C. (2017). *Geographic and demographic representativeness of Junior Reserve Officer Training Corps*. Rand Corporation. https://www.rand.org/pubs/research_reports/RR1712.html

Goldstein, D. (2018, November 28). Are civics lessons a constitutional right? These students are suing them. *The New York Times*. https://www.nytimes.com/2018/11/28/us/civics-rhode -island-schools.html

Goldstein, M. (2021, August 9). The stigma of a scarlet E. *The New York Times*, B1, B3.

Goldwater, B. (1998). Goldwater's 1964 acceptance speech. *The Washington Post*. https://www .washingtonpost.com/wp-srv/politics/daily/may98/goldwaterspeech.htm

Gonsalves, K. (2017, August 2). The "long, hot summer of 1967." *The Week*. https://theweek .com/captured/712838/long-hot-summer-1967

Gordon, T. (2020, October 1). *Antifa's history and current status in Portland*. KGW8. https://www .kgw.com/article/news/local/protests/antifas-history-and-current-status-in-portland/283 -8a9d1048-69e9-4baf-879d-b59d1c93c41a

Goutam, U., & Gautam, U. (2014). Pedagogical Nazi propaganda (1939–1945). *Proceedings of the Indian History Congress, 75*, 1018–1026. http://www.jstor.org/stable/44158487

Graeber, D. (2002, January–February). The new anarchists. *New Left Review, 13*, 61–73. https:// newleftreview.org/issues/ii13/articles/ortl-graeber-the-new-anarchists

Graham, J. (2002, October 3). Bullish scenarios are emerging about war's economic impact. *Investor's Business Daily*, A1, A16.

Graham-Harrison, E., & Lindeman, T. (2022, Feb. 13). Freedom convoys: Legitimate Covid protests or vehicle for darker beliefs? *The Guardian*. https://www.theguardian.com/world/2022 /feb/13/freedom-convoys-legitimate-covid-protest-or-vehicle-for-darker-beliefs

Gray, R. (2017, August 15). Trump defends White-nationalist protesters: "Some very fine people on both sides." *The Atlantic*. https://www.theatlantic.com/politics/archive/2017/08 /trump-defends-white-nationalist-protesters-some-very-fine-people-on-both-sides/537012/

Green, E. L. (2018, April 5). National analysis sees bias in discipline. *The New York Times*, p. A17.

Griffin, R. (2018). *Fascism: An introduction to comparative fascist studies*. Polity Press.

Griffis, C. (2017). "In the beginning was the word": Evangelical Christian women, the Equal Rights Amendment, and competing definitions of womanhood. *Frontiers: A Journal of Women Studies, 38*(2), 148–172. www.jstor.org/stable/10.5250/fronjwomestud.38.2.0148

Gross, T. (2021, July 13). *Reporters reveal "ugly truth" of how Facebook enables hate groups and disinformation*. NPR. https://www.npr.org/2021/07/13/1015483097/an-ugly-truth-how -facebook-enables-hate-and-disinformation

Gumbel, A. (2018, August 6). Police violence, cliques, and secret tattoos: Fears rise over LA sheriff "gangs." *The Guardian*. https://www.theguardian.com/us-news/2018/aug/05/police -violence-cliques-and-secret-tattoos-fears-rise-over-la-sheriff-gangs

Gun Policy in America. (2020, April 22). *The effects of laws allowing armed staff in K–12 schools*. Rand Corporation. https://www.rand.org/research/gun-policy/analysis/laws-allowing-armed -staff-in-K12-schools.html

Gunter, J. (2018, February 15). *After another deadly school shooting, is it time for US teachers to carry guns?* BBC News. https://www.bbc.com/news/world-us-canada-42804741

Haaland, D. (2021, June 11). Deb Haaland: My grandparents were stolen from their families as children. We must learn about this history. *The Washington Post*. https://www.washingtonpost .com/opinions/2021/06/11/deb-haaland-indigenous-boarding-schools/

Haberman, M., & Savage, C. (2020, June 10). Trump, lacking clear authority, says U.S. will declare Antifa a terrorist group. *The New York Times*. https://www.nytimes.com/2020/05/31/us /politics/trump-antifa-terrorist-group.html

Hacker, J. D. (2020). From "20. and odd" to 10 million: The growth of the slave population in the United States. *Slavery & Abolition, 41*(4), 840–855. https://doi.org/10.1080/0144039X.2020.1755502

Hadden, S. E. (2001). *Slave patrols: Law and violence in Virginia and the Carolinas.* Harvard University Press.

Hahn, H., & Jeffries, J. L. (2003). *Urban America and its police: From the postcolonial era through the turbulent 1960s.* University of Colorado Press.

Halsall, P. (1996). *Medieval sourcebook: Urban II (1088–1099) speech at Council of Clermong, 1095, five versions of the speech.* Fordham University. https://sourcebooks.fordham.edu/source/urban2-5vers.asp

Hanebrink, P. (2018). *A specter haunting Europe: The myth of Judeo-Bolshevism.* Belknap.

Hannon, E. (2014, August 13). Police arrest two journalists covering Ferguson protests. *Slate.* https://slate.com/news-and-politics/2014/08/two-journalists-briefly-arrested-in-ferguson.html

Hardaway, A. B. (2019). Time is not on our side: Why specious claims of collective bargaining rights should not be allowed to delay police reform efforts. *Stanford Journal of Civil Rights & Civil Liberties, 15*(2), 137–199. https://papers.ssrn.com/sol3/papers.cfm?abstract_id=3264214

Harris, C. I. (1993). Whiteness as property. *Harvard Law Review, 106*(8), 1707–1791. https://doi.org/10.2307/1341787

Hayden, M. E. (2019, November 12). *Stephen Miller's affinity for White nationalism revealed in leaked emails.* Hatewatch, Southern Poverty Law Center. https://www.splcenter.org/hatewatch/2019/11/12/ortlan-millers-affinity-white-nationalism-revealed-leaked-emails

Heatherton, C. (2020, August 3). Police and the social order. *KPFA Against the Grain* [Podcast]. https://kpfa.org/episode/against-the-grain-august-3-2020/

Hedges, C. (2003). *What every person should know about war.* The Free Press.

Hernádez, K. L. (2010). *Migra! A history of the U.S. border patrol.* University of California Press.

Herzog, D. (2002). Hubris and hypocrisy, incitement and disavowal: Sexuality and German fascism. *Journal of the History of Sexuality, 11*(1/2), 3–21. http://www.jstor.org/stable/3704550

Hesse, M. (2021, February 19). Rush Limbaugh had a lot to say about feminism. Women learned how to not care. *The Washington Post.* https://www.washingtonpost.com/lifestyle/style/rush-limbaugh-feminism-feminazis/2021/02/19/3a00f852-7202-11eb-85fa-e0ccb3660358_story.html

Hill, G. (2018) *The Antifa comic book: 100 years of fascism and Antifa movements.* Arsenal Pulp Press.

Hinton, E. (2015). Creating crime: The rise and impact of national juvenile delinquency programs in Black urban neighborhoods. *Journal of Urban History, 4*(5), 808–824. https://doi.org/10.1177/0096144215589946

Hitler, A. (1999). *Mein kampf* (R. Manheim, Trans.). Houghton Mifflin. (Vol. 1 originally published in 1925, Vol. 2, 1926)

Hochschild, A. (2021, July 22). All-American vigilantes. *New York Review of Books,* 35–36.

Holloway, K. (2021, November 1). How thousands of Black farmers were forced off their land. *The Nation.* https://www.thenation.com/article/society/black-farmers-pigford-debt/

Holmes, J. (2019, June 13). An expert on concentration camps says that's exactly what the US is running at the border. *Esquire.* https://www.esquire.com/news-politics/a27813648/concentration-camps-southern-border-migrant-detention-facilities-trump/

Holmes, W. F. (1975). The demise of the Colored Farmers' Alliance. *The Journal of Southern History, 41*(2), 187–200.

Hopkins, J. P. (2020). *Indian education for all: Decolonizing Indigenous education in public schools.* Teachers College Press.

Horne, G. (2014). *The counter-revolution of 1776: Slave resistance and the origins of the United States of America.* New York University Press.

Horwitz, J., & Anderson, J. (2009). *Guns, democracy, and the insurrectionist idea.* University of Michigan Press.

House Congressional Record. (2021). Impeaching Donald John Trump, President of the United States, for High Crimes and Misdemeanors. H.R. 24, 117th Cong. https://www.congress .gov/117/crec/2021/01/13/CREC-2021-01-13-pt1-PgH165.pdf

House of Representatives. (1978). *Establishing standards for the placement of Indian children in foster or adoptive homes, to prevent the breakup of Indian families, and for other purposes* [Report no. 1386]. https://www.nicwa.org/about-icwa/

House of Representatives Subcommittee on Civil and Constitutional Rights. (1984, September 26). *Civil Rights Enforcement Record of the Department of Agriculture.* Ninety-eighth Congress. https://play.google.com/books/reader?id=vT7r4JEN6EQC&hl=en&pg=GBS.PA199

Hswen, Y., Xu, X., Hing, A., Hawkins, J. B., Brownstein, J. S, & Gee, G. C. (2021, May). Association of "#covid19" versus "#chinesevirus" with Anti-Asian sentiments on twitter: March 9–23, 2020. *American Journal of Public Health*, 111(5), 956–964. https://ajph .aphapublications.org/doi/full/10.2105/AJPH.2021.306154

Hubley, D. (2016, May 29). *Civil rights hero John Lewis to class of '16: "Get in trouble— good trouble."* Bates. https://www.bates.edu/news/2016/05/29/civil-rights-hero-john-lewis -to-class-of-16-get-in-trouble-good-trouble/

Human Rights Campaign. (2022). *Fatal violence against transgender and gender non-conforming community in 2022.* https://www.hrc.org/resources/fatal-violence-against-the-transgender -and-gender-non-conforming-community-in-2022

Human Rights Watch. (2014, October). *Submission to the United Nations committee against torture.* https://www.hrw.org/news/2014/10/20/submission-united-nations-committee-against -torture

Huntington, S. P. (2004). *Who are we? The challenges to America's national identity.* Simon & Schuster.

Immerwahr, D. (2019). *How to hide an empire: A history of the greater United States.* Farrar, Straus and Giroux.

Internet History Sourcebooks Project. (2021). *Nazi Germany: Paragraph 175 and other sexual deviance laws.* Fordam University. https://sourcebooks.fordham.edu/pwh/para175.asp

Isenberg, N. (2016). *White trash: The 400-year untold history of class in America.* Viking.

Jacobson, L. (2018, May 9). *Madeline Albright compares Mussolini, Trump on use of "drain the swamp."* PolitFact. https://www.politifact.com/factchecks/2018/may/09 /madeleine-albright/madeleine-albright-right-about-mussolini-and-drain/

Jargowsky, P. A. (2018). The persistence of segregation in the 21st century. *Minnesota Journal of Law & Inequality*, 36(2), 207–230. https://scholarship.law.umn.edu/lawineq/vol36/iss2/5

Jeansonne, G. (1996). *Women of the far right: The mother's movement and World War II.* University of Chicago Press.

Jennings, M. K. (2015). Politics and socialization. In J. D. Wright (Ed.), *International encyclopedia of the social and behavioral sciences* (2nd ed., pp. 509–511). Elsevier. https://doi .org/10.1016/B978-0-08-097086-8.93130-1

Jerusalem Declaration on Antisemitism. (2021, March 25). https://jerusalemdeclaration.org /wp-content/uploads/2021/03/JDA-1.pdf

Johnson, J. (2021, July 23). *"A huge outrage": Senate panel approves $25 billion Pentagon budget increase.* Common Dreams. https://www.commondreams.org/news/2021/07/23 /huge-outrage-senate-panel-approves-25-billion-pentagon-budget-increase

Johnson, K. R. (2019). Trump's Latinx repatriation. *UCLA Law Review*, 66(6), 1444–1504.

Johnson, V. (2019). KKK in the PD: White supremacist police and what to do about it. *Lewis & Clark Law Review*, 23(1), 205–262.

Jordan, M. (2021a, May 17). Pandemic drives new faces across U.S. border. *The New York Times*, A1, A20.

Jordan, M. (2021b, February 6,). Separated families: A legacy Biden has inherited from Trump. *The New York Times.* https://www.nytimes.com/2021/02/01/us/immigration-family-separations -biden.html

Journell, W. (2011). Social studies, citizenship education, and the search for an American identity: An argument against a unifying narrative. *Journal of Thought*, 46(3–4), 5–24. https:// www.jstor.org/stable/jthought.46.3–4.5

Journell, W. (Ed.). (2019). *Unpacking fake news: An educator's guide to navigating media with students*. Teachers College Press.

Kaba, M. (2020, June 12). Yes, we mean literally abolish the police. *The New York Times*. https://www.nytimes.com/2020/06/12/opinion/Sunday/ortl-abolish-defund-police.html

Kakel, C. P. (2019). Patterns and crimes of empire: Comparative perspectives on fascist and non-fascist extermination. *The Journal of Holocaust Research*, *33*(1), 4–12. https://doi.org/10.1080/23256249.2019.1548164

Kaplan, R. D. (2004, September 21). Indian country. *Wall Street Journal*. https://www.wsj.com/articles/SB109572689960923141

Karp, D. (2010). Unlocking men, unmasking masculinities: Doing men's work in prison. *Journal of Men's Studies*, *18*(1), 63–83. https://doi.org/10.3149/jms.1801.63

Keeler, J. (2021). *Standoff: Standing Rock, the Bundy movement, and the American story of sacred lands*. Torrey House Press.

Kelley, R. D. G. (2020). Foreword. In H. Moore & J. Tracy (Eds.), *No more fascist USA: The John Brown Anti-Klan Committee and lessons for today's movements* (pp. 11–20). City Lights Books.

Kellner, D. (1990). Critical theory and the crisis of social theory. *Sociological Perspectives*, *33*(1), 11–33.

Kendi, I. X. (2016). *Stamped from the beginning: The definitive history of racist ideas in America*. Nation Books.

Kendi, I. X. (2018, January 13). The day *shithole* entered the presidential lexicon. *The Atlantic*. https://www.theatlantic.com/politics/archive/2019/01/shithole-countries/580054/

Kershner, S., & Harding, S. (2015, October 27). Do military recruiters belong in schools? *Education Week*. https://www.edweek.org/policy-politics/opinion-do-military-recruiters-belong-in-schools/2015/10

Kingkade, T. (2021, December 16). *As parents protest critical race theory, students fight racist behavior at school*. NBC News. https://www.nbcnews.com/news/us-news/critical-race-theory-student-protests-rcna8926

Kinzer, S. (2013). *The brothers: John Foster Dulles, Allen Dulles, and their secret world war*. Henry Holt and Company.

Kirkpatrick, D. D. (2021, April 26). Police shielded by 1989 ruling on using force. *The New York Times*, A1, A13.

Klippenstein, K. (2020, August 3). Homeland Security is quietly tying Antifa to foreign powers. *The Nation*. https://www.thenation.com/article/society/dhs-antifa-syria/

Koon, D. S. (2013, April). *Exclusionary school discipline: An issue brief and review of the literature*. The Chief Justice Earl Warren Institute on Law and Social Policy, University of California, Berkeley School of Law. https://www.law.berkeley.edu/files/BMOC_Exclusionary_School_Discipline_Final.pdf

Kornfield, M. (2021, January 29). Woman charged in Capitol riot said she wanted to shoot Pelosi "in the friggin' brain," FBI says. *The Washington Post*. https://www.washingtonpost.com/dc-md-va/2021/01/29/dawn-bancroft-capitol-riot-pennsylvania-pelosi/

Lake, J., Novack, V., & Ives-Rublee, J. (2021, May 27). *Recognizing and addressing housing insecurity for disabled renters*. Center for American Progress. https://www.americanprogress.org/issues/disability/news/2021/05/27/500030/recognizing-addressing-housing-insecurity-disabled-renters/

Lange, J. (2018, October 16). 61 things Donald Trump has said about women. *The Week*. https://theweek.com/articles/655770/61-things-donald-trump-said-about-women

Laqueur, W. (2012, August 2). The Weimar union. *The New Republic*, *243*(12), 15–17.

Las Casas, B. D. (1992). *A short account of the destruction of the Indies* (N. Griffin, Trans.). Penguin. (Originally published in 1542)

Laurie, C. D. (1991). The United States Army and the return to normalcy in labor dispute interventions: The case of the West Virginia coal mine wars, 1920–1921. *West Virginia Archives and History*, *50*, 1–24. http://www.wvculture.org/history/journal_wvh/wvh50-1.html

LeBlanc, A. N. (2020, September 6). America at hunger's edge (introduction). *New York Times Magazine*, 6–13.

Ledeen, M. (1969). Italian fascism and youth. *Journal of Contemporary History*, 4(3), 137–154. http://www.jstor.org/stable/259736

Lee, C. D., White, G., & Dong, D. (Eds.). (2021a). *Educating for civic reasoning and discourse*. National Academy of Education. https://doi.org/10.31094/2021/2

Lee, C. D., White, G., & Dong, D. (2021b). *Educating for civic reasoning and discourse: Executive summary*. National Academy of Education. https://naeducation.org/wp-content/uploads/2021/04/NAEd-Educating-for-Civic-Reasoning-and-Discourse-Exec-Summary.pdf

Lee, C. D., White, G., & Dong, D. (2021c). Recommendations for practice, policy, and research. In C. D. Lee, G. White, & D. Dong (Eds.), *Educating for civic reasoning and discourse* (pp. 397–413). National Academy of Education. https://doi.org/10.31094/2021/2

Lee, M. J. (2021, January 21). *Biden inheriting nonexistent coronavirus vaccine distribution plan and must start "from scratch," sources say*. CNN. https://www.cnn.com/2021/01/21/politics/biden-covid-vaccination-trump/index.html

Legal Information Institute. (n.d.a.). *18 U.S. Code § 2331—definitions*. Cornell Law School. https://www.law.cornell.edu/uscode/text/18/2331

Legal Information Institute (n.d.b.). *First Amendment*. Cornell Law School. https://www.law.cornell.edu/constitution/first_amendment

Lemkin, R. (1944). *Axis rule in occupied Europe* (Chapter IX). Carnegie Endowment for International Peace. https://www.academia.edu/5846019/Raphael_Lemkin_Axis_Rule_in_Occupied_Europe_Laws_of_Occupation_Analysis_of_Government_Proposals_for_Redress_Chapter_IX_Genocide_

Lennard, N. (2019). *Being numerous: Essays on non-fascist life*. Verso.

Lennard, N., & Miller, J. (2020, October 21). *On fascism, non-fascism and Antifa*. Eurozine. https://www.eurozine.com/on-fascism-non-fascism-and-antifa/

Lepore, J. (2018). *These truths: A history of the United States*. Norton.

Lepore, J. (2020a, May 4). Blood on the green. *The New Yorker*, pp. 70-75.

Lepore, J. (2020b, July 20). The long blue line: Inventing the police. *The New Yorker*, 64–69.

Levin, B. (2021, April 30). *Report to the nation: Anti-Asian prejudice & hate crime—Corrected*. Center for the Study of Hate and Extremism. https://www.csusb.edu/hate-and-extremism-center

Levin, S. (2016, February 15). Oregon militia standoff: The 23 men and two women facing felony charges. *The Guardian*. https://www.theguardian.com/us-news/2016/feb/15/ortla-militia-standoff-felony-charges

Levine, R. F. (1988). *Class struggle and the new deal: Industrial labor, industrial capital, and the state*. University of Kansas Press.

Lewis, S. (1970). *It can't happen here*. Signet. (Originally published 1935)

Library of Congress. (1949, July 15). *Housing Act of 1949 (Chapter 338, § 2)*. https://www.loc.gov/law/help/statutes-at-large/81st-congress/session-1/c81s1ch338.pdf

Lichtblau, E. (2016, September 17). Hate crimes against American Muslims most since post-9/11 era. *The New York Times*. https://www.nytimes.com/2016/09/18/us/politics/hate-crimes-american-muslims-rise.html

Lifton, R. J. (2017). *The Nazi doctors: Medical killing and the psychology of genocide* (rev. ed.). Basic Books.

Lindell, C. (2021, May 7). After bitter fight, late changes and 3 a.m. vote, Texas House approves GOP election bill. *Austin American-Statesman*. https://www.statesman.com/story/news/2021/05/07/after-bitter-fight-texas-house-backs-gop-voting-bill-3-a-m-vote/4969597001/

Lineberry, A. (2019, October). Standing to challenge the lost cause. *Virginia Law Review*, 106(6), 1177–1216. https://www.jstor.org/stable/26842267

Lipset, M. S. (2003). Fascism as "extremism" of the middle class. In A. A. Kallis (Ed.), *The fascism reader* (pp. 112–119). Routledge. (Originally published in 1959)

Liptak, A. (2010, July 24). Court under Roberts is most conservative in decades. *The New York Times*. https://www.nytimes.com/2010/07/25/us/25roberts.html

Liptak, A. (2021, July 2). A Supreme Court term marked by a conservative majority in flux. *The New York Times*. https://www.nytimes.com/2021/07/02/us/supreme-court-conservative-voting-rights.html

Liptak, K., & Westwood, S. (2020). *Trump threatens military force if violence in states isn't stopped.* CNN. https://www.cnn.com/2020/06/01/politics/ortla-trump-national-address -race/index.html

Lithwick, D. (2017, August 16). Yes, what about the "alt-left"? *Slate.* https://slate.com/news-and -politics/2017/08/what-the-alt-left-was-actually-doing-in-charlottesville.html

Locke, J. (2003). *Two treatises of government and a letter concerning toleration* (I. Shapiro, Ed.). Yale University Press. (Original work published in 1690)

Loewen, J. (2005). *Sundown towns: A hidden dimension of American racism.* The New Press.

Loewen, J. (2007). *Lies my teacher told me: Everything your American history textbook got wrong* (2nd ed.). The New Press.

Lofgren, M. (2016). *The deep state. The fall of the Constitution and the rise of a shadow government.* Penguin.

Lühmann, A., & Medzihorsky, J. (2020, October). *New global data on political parties: V-party* [Briefing paper]. V-Dem Institute. http://v-dem.net/media/publications/briefing_paper_9 .pdf

Lutz, B. J., & Lutz, J. M. (2007). *Terrorism in America.* Palgrave Macmillan.

Lyons, M. N. (2018). *Insurgent supremacists: The U.S. far right's challenge to state and empire.* Kersplebeded.

Mac, R., & Lerer, L. (2022, February 15). Tech financier is kingmaker for the right. *The New York Times,* pp. A1, A13.

Mahajan, R. (2001). *"We think the price is worth it": Media uncurious about Iraq's policy's effects— there or here.* FAIR. https://fair.org/extra/we-think-the-price-is-worth-it/

Mapping Police Violence. (2020, June 30). *Police violence map.* https://mappingpoliceviolence.org/

Mareš, M., & Bjørgo, T. (2019). Vigilantism against migrants and minorities: Concepts and goals of current research. In T. Bjørgo & M. Mareš (Eds.), *Vigilantism against migrants and minorities* (pp. 1–30). Routledge.

Markwich, R. D. (2009). Communism: Fascism's "other"? In R. J. B. Bosworth (Ed.), *The Oxford handbook of fascism* (pp. 339–361). Oxford University Press.

Marx, K. (2001). *Capital: A critique of political economy* (S. Moore & E. Aveling, Trans., Vol. 1). ElecBook. (Originally published in 1887)

May, S. (2012). Critical multiculturalism and education. In J. A. Banks (Ed.), *Encyclopedia of diversity in education* (Vol. 1, pp. 472–478). SAGE.

Mayer, J. (2016). *Dark money: The hidden history of the billionaires behind the rise of the radical right.* Doubleday.

McCord, M. B. (2020, October 12). The danger of private militias. *The New York Times,* A21.

McDowell, R., & Mason, M. (2020, May 8). *Cheap labor means prisons still turn a profit, even during a pandemic.* PBS News Hour. https://www.pbs.org/newshour/economy /cheap-labor-means-prisons-still-turn-a-profit-even-during-a-pandemic

McGirt v. Oklahoma, 140 2452 (US Supreme Court 2020)

McIntire, M., & Keller, M. H. (2021, November 2). The demand for money behind many police traffic stops. *The New York Times.* https://www.nytimes.com/2021/10/31/us/police-ticket -quotas-money-funding.html

McLaren, P. (2015). *Pedagogy of insurrection: From resurrection to revolution.* Peter Lang.

McLaren, P. (2020a). Are those whiffs of fascism that I smell? Living behind the orange curtain. *Educational Philosophy and Theory, 52*(10), 101–1015.

McLaren, P. (2020b, February). Resisting fascist mobilization: Some reflections on critical pedagogy, liberation theology and the need for revolutionary socialist change. *Educational Philosophy and Theory, 53*(7), 655–668. https://doi.org/10.1080/00131857.2020.1716450

McLaughlin, M. (2014). *The long, hot summer of 1967.* Palgrave Macmillan.

McNicholas, C., Shierholz, H., & Poydock, M. (2021, January 22). *Union workers had more job security during the pandemic, but unionization remains historically low.* Economic Policy Institute. https://www.epi.org/publication/union-workers-had-more-job-security-during-the -pandemic-but-unionization-remains-historically-low-data-on-union-representation-in -2020-reinforce-the-need-for-dismantling-barriers-to-union-organizing/

McShane, J. (2021, May 7). The stealth sticker campaign to expose New York's history of slavery. *The New York Times.* https://www.nytimes.com/2021/05/07/nyregion/slavery-nyc.html

Meacham, J. (2020). *His truth is marching on: John Lewis and the power of hope*. Random House.

Means, H. (2016). *67 shots: Kent State and the end of American innocence*. Da Capo Press.

Merjian, A. H. (2001). Fascism, gender, and culture. *Qui Parle, 13*(1), 1–12. https://www.jstor.org/stable/20686134

Merrefield, C. (2021, June 29). *"Defund the police": What it means and what the research says on whether more police presence reduces crime*. The Journalist's Resource. https://journalistsresource.org/criminal-justice/defund-the-police/

Merriam-Webster. (2021). *Cancel culture*. https://www.merriam-webster.com/dictionary/cancel%20culture

Mervosh, S., & Heyward, G. (2021, August 20). Venom of political and culture battles seeps into school halls. *The New York Times*, A1, A15.

Miller-Idriss, C. (2020). *Hate in the homeland: The new global far right*. Princeton University Press.

Miller, C. (2021, February 16). *At the end of the Trump era, White nationalists increasingly embrace political violence*. Southern Poverty Law Center. https://www.splcenter.org/news/2021/02/16/end-trump-era-white-nationalists-increasingly-embrace-political-violence

Miller, R. J., Rura, J., Behrendt, L., & Lindberg, T. (2010). *Discovering Indigenous lands: The doctrine of discovery in the English colonies*. Oxford University Press.

Miscevic, N. (2020, Fall). Nationalism. In E. N. Zalta (Ed.), *The Stanford encyclopedia of philosophy*. https://plato.stanford.edu/archives/fall2020/entries/nationalism

Mishan, L. (2020, December 3). The long and tortured history of cancel culture. *New York Times Style Magazine*. https://www.nytimes.com/2020/12/03/t-magazine/cancel-cultur-history.html

Mishra, P., & Nguyen, V. T. (2020, July 24). "Free speech has never been freer": Pankaj Mishra and Viet Thanh Nguyen in conversation. *The Guardian*. https://www.theguardian.com/books/2020/jul/24/free-speech-has-never-been-freer-pankaj-mishra-and-viet-thanh-nguyen-in-conversation

Moore, H., & Tracy, J. (2020). *No fascist USA! The John Brown Anti-Klan Committee and lessons for today's movements*. City Lights Books.

Moraña, M., Dussel, E., & Jáuregui, C. A. (2008). Colonialism and its replicants. In M. Moraña, E. Dussel, & C. A. Jáuregui (Eds.), *Coloniality at large: Latin America and the postcolonial debate* (pp. 1–22). Duke University Press.

Morgan, M., & Shanahan, J. (2018). Television and the cultivation of authoritarianism: A return visit from an unexpected friend. In G. Dines, J. M. Humez, B. Yousman, L. B. Yousman (Eds.), *Gender, race, and class in media: A critical reader* (5th ed., pp. 44–52). SAGE.

Morris, M. (2016). Political curriculum concepts. *Counterpoints, 498*, 245–293. https://doi.org/10.2307/45157323

Morton, N., & Greenstone, S. (2018, October 4). For 40,000 homeless students, it's back-to-school season in Washington. *Seattle Times*. https://www.seattletimes.com/education-lab/for-homeless-students-in-rural-washington-districts-just-getting-to-school-is-hard/

Moskowitz, P. E. (2019, August 20). Everything you think you know about "free speech" is a lie. *The Nation*. https://www.thenation.com/article/archive/ortland-speech-milo-antifa-koch/

Mullen, B., & Vials, C. (2020). Introduction. In B. Mullen & C. Vials (Eds.), *The US antifascist reader* (pp. 1–22). Verso.

Mullen, L. (2018, June 15). The fight to define Romans 13. *The Atlantic*. https://www.theatlantic.com/ideas/archive/2018/06/romans-13/562916/

Murakawa, N. (2014). *The first civil right: How liberals built prison America*. Oxford University Press.

Musick, M. (2020, February 3). Meet the boy scouts of the border patrol. *The Nation*, 12–15, 26.

Na, C., & Gottfredson, D. C. (2013). Police officers in schools: Effects on school crime and the processing of offending behaviors. *Justice Quarterly, 30*(4), 619–650. https://doi.org/10.1080/07418825.2011.615754

National Academies of Sciences, Engineering, & Medicine. (2018). *Permanent supportive housing: Evaluating the evidence for improving health outcomes among people experiencing chronic homelessness*. National Academies Press. http://nap.edu/25133

National Alliance to End Homelessness. (2020). *State of homelessness: 2020 edition.* https://endhomelessness.org/homelessness-in-america/homelessness-statistics/state-of-homelessness-2020/

National Education Association. (1991). The Kanawha County textbook controversy. In R. L. Lewis & J. C. Hennen, Jr. (Eds.), *West Virginia: Documents in the history of a rural-industrial state* (pp. 308–319). Kendall Hunt. (Original work published in 1975)

National Park Service. (2021, May 2). *A legacy from the Far East.* https://www.nps.gov/gosp/learn/historyculture/a-legacy-from-the-far-east.htm

National School Resource Network. (1979). *The officer friendly program: Technical assistance bulletin 9* [ED 199862]. Author.

National Security Archive. (2002, August 1). *Memorandum for Alberto R. Gonzales counsel to the president.* nsarchive.gwu.edu/NSAEBB/NSAEBB127/02.08.01.pdf

Neumeister, L. (2018, April 5). *Muslims: Settlement will prevent illegal NYPD surveillance.* Associated Press. https://apnews.com/article/e91c450085604f3e97c6a4cdb3ab11c9

Newport, F. (2020, October 16). *Update: Evangelicals, Trump, and the election.* Gallup. https://news.gallup.com/opinion/polling-matters/322052/update-evangelicals-trump-election.aspx

The New York Times. (1924, December 21). Hitler tamed in prison. https://timesmachine.nytimes.com/timesmachine/1924/12/21/101629154.html?pageNumber=1

The New York Times. (1954, July 18). "Wetbacks" have to pay. https://timesmachine.nytimes.com/timesmachine/1954/07/19/84126671.html?pageNumber=21

The New York Times. (2010, July 7). Measuring the conservatism of the Roberts court. https://archive.nytimes.com/www.nytimes.com/interactive/2010/07/25/us/20100725-roberts-graphic.html

The New York Times. (2022, February 17). Coronavirus in the U.S.: Latest map and case count. https://www.nytimes.com/interactive/2021/us/covid-cases.html

Nierenberg, A. (2021a, January 25). After the Capitol was stormed, teachers try explaining history in real time. *The New York Times.* https://www.nytimes.com/2021/01/25/us/teaching-capitol-riot.html

Nierenberg, A. (2021b, April 21). Teachers address Derek Chauvin's guilty verdict. *The New York Times.* https://www.nytimes.com/2021/04/21/us/teachers-students-derek-chauvin-guilty-verdict-george-floyd.html

Nixon, R. (2017, January 23). Claims of corrupt contractors go unexamined, investigators say. *The New York Times.* https://www.nytimes.com/2017/01/23/us/politics/immigration-contractors-corruption-dhs.html

Noor, P. (2020, June 6). Teargassed, beaten up, arrested: What freedom of the press looks like in the US right now. *The Guardian.* https://www.theguardian.com/us-news/2020/jun/06/george-floyd-protests-reporters-press-teargas-arrested

Nowatzki, B. (2020, May 20). *Portal spotlight: Civil unrest and the Red Summer.* National Archives. https://rediscovering-black-history.blogs.archives.gov/2020/05/20/portal-spotlight-civil-unrest-and-the-red-summer/

NPR Staff. (2021, February 12). *The Capitol siege: The arrested and their stories.* NPR. https://www.npr.org/2021/02/09/965472049/the-capitol-siege-the-arrested-and-their-stories

Nuwer, R. (2021, May 4). A psychedelic drug passes a big hurtle for treating PTSD. *The New York Times,* A12.

O'Donnell, S. J. (2020). The deliverance of the administrative state: Deep state conspiracism, charismatic demonology, and the post-truth politics of American Christian nationalism. *Religion, 50*(4), 696–719. https://doi.org/10.1080/0048721X.2020.1810817

Odom, W. E. (2007, December). American hegemony: How to use it, how to lose it. *Proceedings of the American Philosophical Society, 151*(4), 440–411. https://www.jstor.org/stable/25478452

Office of Naval Intelligence. (2020). *Densho encyclopedia.* https://encyclopedia.densho.org/Custodial%20detention%20/%20A-B-C%20list/#Office_of_Naval_Intelligence.E2.80.94Navy_Department

Onion, R. (2020, August 27). Playing good cop. *Slate.* https://slate.com/human-interest/2020/08/officer-friendly-police-copaganda-history.html

Onishi, N. (2019, September 21). Man behind slogan promoting White supremacy. *The New York Times*, A6.

Onishi, N. (2022, February 15). In France, a racist conspiracy theory edges into the mainstream. *The New York Times*. https://www.nytimes.com/2022/02/15/world/europe/france-elections-pecresse-great-replacement.html

Orfield, G., & Jarvie, D. (2020, December). *Black segregation matters: School resegregation and Black educational opportunities*. The Civil Rights Project. https://www.civilrightsproject.ucla.edu/research/k-12-education/integration-and-diversity/black-segregation-matters-school-resegregation-and-black-educational-opportunity/BLACK-SEGREGATION-MATTERS-final-121820.pdf

Osnos, E. (2017, January 22). Doomsday prep for the super-rich. *The New Yorker*. https://www.newyorker.com/magazine/2017/01/30/doomsday-prep-for-the-super-rich

Oxford English Dictionary. (2021). *Rabid*. https://www-oed-com.evergreen.idm.oclc.org/view/Entry/157015

Oxford Reference. (2022). *Counter-movement*. https://www.oxfordreference.com/view/10.1093/oi/authority.20110803095643109

Palmer, E. (2022, January 14). Donald Trump won't stop peddling election fraud claims, even if it splits the GOP entirely. *Newsweek*. https://www.newsweek.com/donald-trump-election-fraud-midterms-1669108

Pape, R. A., & Ruby, K. (2021, March 12). *The face of American insurrection: Right-wing organizations evolving into a violent mass movement*. Chicago Project on Security & Threats. https://cpost.uchicago.edu/research/domestic_extremism/

Passmore, K. (2002). *Fascism: A very short introduction*. Oxford University Press.

Passmore, K. (2008). The gender genealogy of political religions theory. *Gender & History*, 20(3), 644–668.

Passmore, K. (2009). The ideological origins of fascism before 1914. In R. J. B. Bosworth (Ed.), *The Oxford handbook of fascism* (pp. 11–31). Oxford University Press.

Patnaik, P. (2020). Neoliberalism and fascism. *Agrarian South: Journal of Political Economy*, 9(1), 33–49. https://doi.org/10.1177/2277976019901029

Patterson, W. L., & Civil Rights Congress. (1951). *We charge genocide: The historic petition to the United Nations for relief from a crime of the United States government against the Negro people*. Civil Rights Congress.

Paust, J. J. (2003). War and enemy status after 9/11: Attacks on the laws of war. *Yale Journal of International Law*, 28(2), 325–335. https://digitalcommons.law.yale.edu/yjil/vol28/iss2/5/

Paxton, R. O. (2004). *The anatomy of fascism*. Knopf.

Paxton, R. O. (2009). Comparisons and definitions. In R. J. B. Bosworth (Ed.), *The Oxford handbook of fascism* (pp. 547–565). Oxford University Press.

Paxton, R. O. (2017, April 6). The future of fascism. *Slate*. https://slate.com/news-and-politics/2017/04/fascism-didnt-die-in-1945-it-evolved-and-took-new-form.html

Payne, S. (1983). *Fascism: Comparison and definition*. University of Wisconsin Press.

Payne, S. (1995). *A history of fascism, 1914–1945*. University of Wisconsin Press.

Penny, D. (2017, August 22). An intimate history of Antifa. *The New Yorker*. https://www.newyorker.com/books/page-turner/an-intimate-history-of-antifa

Perea, J. F. (2011). The echoes of slavery: Recognizing the racist origins of the agricultural and domestic worker exclusion from the National Labor Relations Act. *Ohio State Law Journal*, 72(1), 95–137. https://lawecommons.luc.edu/facpubs/151/

Perkins, G. (2007). *Expulsion in Washington*. https://www.washingtonhistory.org/wp-content/uploads/2020/04/WAExclusion.pdf

Perry, R. (2019, November 23). *Secretary Rick Perry on Gordon Sondland's impeachment testimony: He's surmising*. Fox News. https://video.foxnews.com/v/6108062048001 #sp=show-clips

Peter G. Peterson Foundation. (2021, July 21). *Discretionary spending breakdown*. https://www.pgpf.org/chart-archive/0070_discretionary_spending_categories

Peterson, B. A. (2019). Educating for social justice: A case for teaching civil disobedience in preparing students to be effective activists. *Democracy & Education*, 27(2), 1–7. https://democracyeducationjournal.org/home/vol27/iss2/

Pfosi, N., & Allen, J. (2021, June 26). *Derek Chauvin sentenced to 22-1/2 years in murder of George Floyd*. Reuters. https://www.reuters.com/world/us/ex-policeman-derek-chauvin-be-sentenced-george-floyds-murder-2021-06-25/

Phillips, A. (2020, October 30). What counts as voter intimidation? *The Washington Post*. https://www.washingtonpost.com/politics/2020/10/30/voter-intimidation/

Phillips, O. L. (1949, August). The genocide convention: Its effect on our legal system. *American Bar Association Journal, 35*(8), 623–625. https://www.jstor.org/stable/25716947

Pilisuk, M., & Rountree, J. A. (2015). *The hidden structure of violence: Who benefits from global violence and war*. Monthly Review Press.

Pitzer, A. (2017). *One long night: A global history of concentration camps*. Little, Brown, and Company.

Polanyi, K. (2001). *The great transformation*. Beacon. (Originally published in 1944)

Pollock, M., & Rogers, J. (2022, January). *The conflict campaign*. UCLA's Institute for Democracy, Education, and Access. https://idea.gseis.ucla.edu/publications/the-conflict-campaign/publications/files/the-conflict-campaign-report

Popovich, N., Albeck-Ripka, L., & Pierre-Louis, K. (2021, January 20). The Trump administration rolled back more than 100 environmental rules. Here's the full list. *The New York Times*. https://www.nytimes.com/interactive/2020/climate/trump-environment-rollbacks-list.html

Powell, J. (2019). Making "the case against the 'Reds'": Racializing communism, 1919–1920. In T. Boyce & W. Chunni (Eds.), *Historicizing fear: Ignorance, vilification, and othering* (pp. 102–121). University Press of Colorado.

Powell, J. A. (2021, February). The law and the significance of Plessy. *RSF: The Russell Sage Foundation Journal of the Social Sciences, 7*(1), 20–31. https://doi.org/10.7758/rsf.2021.7.1.02

Prasow, A. J. (2021, January 25). Declassify the post-9/11 torture program. *The Hill*. https://thehill.com/opinion/national-security/535086-declassify-the-post-9-11-torture-program

Presser, L. (2019, July 22). The dispossessed. *The New Yorker*, 28–35.

Price, A. (2020, February). *Don't fixate on the racial wealth gap: Focus on undoing its root causes*. Roosevelt Institute. https://rooseveltinstitute.org/publications/dont-fixate-on-the-racial-wealth-gap-focus-on-undoing-its-root-causes/

Prison Policy Initiative. (2020). *Louisiana profile*. https://www.prisonpolicy.org/profiles/LA.html

Provost, C., & Whyte, L. (2018, January 31). *Why are women joining far-right movements, and why are we so surprised?* openDemocracy. https://www.opendemocracy.net/en/5050/women-far-right-movements-why-are-we-surprised/

Public Broadcasting Service. (2012). *Slavery by another name*. https://www.pbs.org/show/slavery-another-name/

Pusey, A. (2015). Precedents: January 2, 1920: Palmer raids target immigrants. *ABA Journal, 101*(1), 100. http://www.jstor.org/stable/44653234

Quick, K., & Kahlenberg, R. D. (2019, June 25). *Attacking the Black-White opportunity gap that comes from residential segregation*. The Century Foundation. https://tcf.org/content/report/attacking-black-white-opportunity-gap-comes-residential-segregation/

Quijano, A. (2000). Coloniality of power, Eurocentrism, and Latin America. *Nepentla: Views from the South, 1*(3), 533–580. http://www.unc.edu/~aescobar/wan/wanquijano.pdf

Rachman, G. (2018, June 25). Donald Trump leads a global revival of nationalism. *Financial Times*. https://www.ft.com/content/59a37a38-7857-11e8-8e67-1e1a0846c475

Raj, K. (2017, October 17). *Radical right populist success in elections endangers human rights in Europe*. Human Rights Watch. https://www.hrw.org/news/2017/10/17/radical-right-populist-success-elections-endangers-human-rights-europe

Rappeport, A. (2021, May 19). Banks fight $4 billion debt relief plan for Black farmers. *The New York Times*. https://www.nytimes.com/2021/05/19/us/politics/black-farmers-debt-relief.html

Rappeport, A. (2022, February 22). Debt relief blocked, Black farmers fear ruin. *The New York Times*, pp. A1, A16.

Rappeport, A., Ngo, M., & Kelly, K. (2022, January 7). After Jan. 6, donor pause was short. *The New York Times*, pp. B1, B4.

Reece, R. L. (2020, May). Whitewashing slavery: Legacy of slavery and White social outcomes. *Social Problems, 67*(2), 304–323. https://doi.org/10.1093/socpro/spz016

Reeves, J., Mascaro, L., Woodward, C. (2021, January 10). *The unfolding of "home-grown fascism" in Capitol assault.* AP News. https://apnews.com/article/donald-trump-politics -michael-pence-nancy-pelosi-capitol-siege-db96cb1f31c02baef7957e773ac99971

Reflective Democracy. (2020, June). *Confronting the demographics of power: America's sheriffs.* https://wholeads.us/research/americas-sheriffs/

Reichardt, S. (2012). Violence and consensus in fascism. *Fascism: Journal of Comparative Fascist Studies, 1*, 59–60. https://doi.org/10.1163/221162512X631206

Reilly, R. J. (2020, August 13). Ferguson prepared America for this moment. *Huffington Post.* https://www.huffpost.com/entry/ferguson-protesters-black-lives-matter-movement_n_5eeb cb16c5b66603e671c2d7

Reisman, D. (1993). *Abundance for what?* Transaction. (Original work published in 1964).

Renton, D. (2005). "Eyes closed! Everyone face the door!" Women in Nazi Germany. *Journal of Contemporary History, 40*(2), 389–396. http://www.jstor.org/stable/30036330

Renton, D. (2019). *The new authoritarians: Convergence on the right.* Haymarket Books.

Reporters Without Borders. (2021, December 21). *Number of journalists in arbitrary detention surges 20% to 488, including 60 women.* https://rsf.org/en/news/number-journalists-arbitrary -detention-surges-20-488-including-60-women

Riccó, G. (2020, October). Teaching: It can't happen here in the Trump era. *Radical History Review, 2020*(138), 171–178. https://doi.org/10.1215/01636545-8359566

Riley, T. (2013, April 23). *Lisa Graves updates us on ALEC.* Moyers. https://billmoyers .com/2013/04/23/lisa-graves-updates-us-on-alec/

Ripley, A. (1967, November 15). Crowd reaction bolsters Wallace's hopes for 1968. *The New York Times.* https://timesmachine.nytimes.com/timesmachine/1967/11/15/issue.html

Roberto, M. J. (2018). *The coming of the America behemoth: The origins of fascism in the United States, 1920–1940.* Monthly Review Press.

Roberts, N. (2015). *Freedom as marronage.* University of Chicago Press.

Robertson, C. (2020, October 29). In rural Virginia, militia organizers push counties to give them cover. *The New York Times,* A26.

Robin, C. (2004). Fragmented state, pluralist society: How liberal institutions promote fear. *Missouri Law Review, 69,* 1061–1093.

Robin, C. (2011). *The reactionary mind: Conservatism from Edmund Burke to Sarah Palin.* Oxford University Press.

Robinson, C., & Gilmore, R. (2019). Fascism and the intersections of capitalism, racialism, and historical consciousness. In H. Quan (Ed.), *Cedric J. Robinson: On racial capitalism, Black internationalism, and cultures of resistance* (pp. 87–109). Pluto Press.

Robinson, W. I. (2014). *Global capitalism and the crisis of humanity.* Cambridge University Press.

Rogers, K. (2020, August 14). Trump, pushing racist theory, questions Harris's citizenship. *The New York Times,* A21.

Roithmayr, D. (1999). Introduction to critical race theory in educational research and praxis. In L. Parker, D. Deyhel, & S. Villenas (Eds.), *Race is . . . race isn't: Critical race theory and qualitative studies in education* (pp. 1–6). Westview.

Rosas, A. E. (2011). Breaking the silence: Mexican children and women's confrontation of Bracero family separation, 1942–64. *Gender & History, 23*(2), 382–400.

Rosenberg, C. (2021, November 1). Military jurors say torture is a moral stain. *The New York Times,* A1, A11.

Ross, A. R. (2015, September 16). *A new chapter in the fascist internationale.* CounterPunch. https://www.counterpunch.org/2015/09/16/a-new-chapter-in-the-fascist-internationale/

Ross, A. R. (2017). *Against the fascist creep.* AK Press.

Rovner, J. (2015, December). *Declines in youth commitments and facilities in the 21st century.* The Sentencing Project. https://www.sentencingproject.org/publications/declines-in-youth -commitments-and-facilities-in-the-21st-century/

Rucker, P., Parker, A., & Dawsey, J. (2021). After inciting mob attack, Trump retreats in rage. Then, grudgingly, he admits his loss. *The Washington Post.* https://www.washingtonpost.com /politics/trump-rage-riot/2021/01/07/26894c54-5108-11eb-b96e-0e54447b23a1_story.html

Rutenberg, J., Becker, J., Lipton, E., Haberman, M., Martin, J., Rosenberg, M., & Schmidt, M. S. (2021, February 1). 77 days: Trump's campaign to subvert the election. *The New York Times,* A1, A13–16.

Saad, L. (2019, November 25). *Socialism as popular as capitalism among young adults in U.S.* Gallup.   https://news.gallup.com/poll/268766/socialism-popular-capitalism-among-young-adults.aspx

Sadeghi, M. (2021, February 9). Fact check: "Deep state" theory makes false claims about martial law, arrests, pandemic. *USA Today.* https://www.usatoday.com/story/news/factcheck/2021 /02/09/fact-check-false-claims-military-takeover-mass-arrests-covid-19/4419059001/

Sakuma, A. (2015, July 1). *Six predominately Black churches burned in 10 days.* MSNBC. https:// www.msnbc.com/msnbc/six-predominately-black-church-burned-10-days-msna630381

Salter, J. (2020, July 30). *Prosecutor: No charges for officer in Michael Brown's death.* The Associated Press. https://apnews.com/38cbd0d2a9e50445bd2d875e1c48f89a

Samuels, L. (2010). Improvising on reality: The roots of prison abolition. In D. Berger (Ed.), *The hidden 1970s: Histories of radicalism* (pp. 21–38). Rutgers University Press.

Sartre, J-P. (1968). *On genocide.* Beacon.

Saull, R., Anievas, A., Davidson, N., & Fabry, A. (2015). Introduction. In R. Saull, A. Anievas, N. Davidson, & A. Fabry (Eds.), *The longue durée of the far-right: An international historical sociology* (pp. 1–20). Routledge.

Savage, C. (2022, February 11). Letter reveals C.I.A. collects data that invades Americans' privacy. *The New York Times,* p. A17.

Savell, S., & 5W Infographics. (2019, January/February). This map shows where in the world the US military is combatting terrorism. *Smithsonian Magazine.* https://www.smithsonianmag .com/history/map-shows-places-world-where-us-military-operates-180970997/

Sawchuk, S. (2020, October 14). There's no constitutional right to civics education, a federal judge reluctantly concludes. *Education Week.* https://www.edweek.org/leadership /theres-no-constitutional-right-to-civics-education-a-federal-judge-reluctantly-concludes /2020/10

Sawyer, W., & Wagner, P. (2020, March 24). *Mass incarceration: The whole pie 2020.* Prison Policy Initiative. https://www.prisonpolicy.org/reports/pie2020.html

Schleifer, T. (2015, December 22). *Donald Trump on reporters: "I would never kill them."* CNN. https://edition.cnn.com/2015/12/21/politics/trump-putin-killing-reporters

School House Connection. (2020, January 29). *Public schools report over 1.5 million homeless children and youth—all time record.* https://schoolhouseconnection.org/public-schools -report-over-1-5-million-homeless-children-and-youth/

Schwartz, S. (2021, August 11). Who decides what history we teach: An explainer. *Education Week.* https://www.edweek.org/teaching-learning/who-decides-what-history-we-teach-an-explainer /2021/08

Schwartz, S., & Pendharkar, E. (2022, Feb. 2). Here's the long list of topics Republicans want banned from the classroom. *Education Week.* https://www.edweek.org/policy-politics /heres-the-long-list-of-topics-republicans-want-banned-from-the-classroom/2022/02

Schwartzenegger, A. (2021, July 2). *Austrian World Summit 2021: Greta Thunberg speech.* https://youtu.be/m6eQwAi2U18

Security.org. (2021, April 12). *State of homelessness in 2021: Statistics, analysis, & trends.* https://www.security.org/resources/homeless-statistics/#

Sekkarie, S. (2020, August 19). *The FBI has a racism problem and it hurts our national security.* Georgetown Security Studies Review. https://georgetownsecuritystudiesreview .org/2020/08/19/the-fbi-has-a-racism-problem-and-it-hurts-our-national-security/

Semega, J., Kollar, M., Shrider, E. A., & Creamer, J. F. (2020, September). *Income and poverty in the United States: 2019, current population reports.* U.S. Census Bureau. https://www .census.gov/content/dam/Census/library/publications/2020/demo/p60-270.pdf

Shane, L. (2020, February 6). Signs of White supremacy, extremism up again in poll of active-duty troops. *Military Times*. https://www.militarytimes.com/news/pentagon-congress/2020/02/06/signs-of-white-supremacy-extremism-up-again-in-poll-of-active-duty-troops/

Shannon, D. (1985, April 19). Reagan defends cemetery visit: Says German dead are also victims of Nazis. *Los Angeles Times*. https://www.latimes.com/archives/la-xpm-1985-04-19-mn-14900-story.html

Shenk, I. (2015, October 28). Churches, Indigenous groups protest canonization of missionary priest. *Christian Century*, 132(22), 15–16.

Shephard, A. (2021, January 15). *How the GOP fell in love with cancel culture*. The New Republic. https://newrepublic.com/article/160937/gop-fell-love-cancel-culture

Sherwood, H. (2020, November 6). White evangelical Christians stick by Trump again, exit polls show. *The Guardian*. https://www.theguardian.com/us-news/2020/nov/06/white-evangelical-christians-supported-trump

Shortell, D. (2020, June 4). *Barr defends use of force at Monday's White House protest*. CNN. https://www.cnn.com/2020/06/04/politics/william-barr-news-conference-george-floyd/index.html

Shull, A. (2021, April 6). Food insecurity a problem within the US military. *The Olympian*, 5A.

Silverstein, T. (2018, December 18). *Decommodify housing without reproducing American apartheid*. Shelterforce. https://shelterforce.org/2018/12/07/decommodifying-housing-without-reproducing-american-apartheid/

Simonelli, F. J. (1995). The American Nazi Party, 1958–1967. *The Historian*, 57(3), 553–566.

Singh, N. (2006, January). The afterlife of fascism. *South Atlantic Quarterly*, 105(1), 71–93. https://doi.org/10.1215/00382876-105-1-71

Singh, N. (2017). *Race and America's long war*. University of California Press.

Sisk, A. R. (2021, May 3). Standing Rock unhappy with DAPL moves by North Dakota, Corps. *Bismarck Tribune* [North Dakota]. https://bismarcktribune.com/news/state-and-regional/standing-rock-unhappy-with-dapl-moves-by-north-dakota-corps/article_820fba0f-8e24-5e5c-b277-f7508b2e7514.html

Sloan, A., & Podkul, C. (2021, April 27). The Fed helped fuel a stock market boom that benefited wealthy Americans—and left behind everyone else. *The Washington Post*. https://www.washingtonpost.com/us-policy/2021/04/26/federal-reserve-interest-rates-inequality/

Smith, A. (2001). *The wealth of nations*. Electric Book Company. (Original work published in 1776)

Smith, M., Ballard, J., & Sanders, L. (2021, January 6). *Most voters say the events at the US Capitol are a threat to democracy*. YouGov. https://today.yougov.com/topics/politics/articles-reports/2021/01/07/US-capitol-trump-poll

Smith, S. (2021, July 20). Haven school board candidate lured into sharing racist ideology with teenage anti-fascist. *Kansas Reflector*. https://kansasreflector.com/2021/07/20/haven-school-board-candidate-lured-into-sharing-racist-ideology-with-teenage-anti-fascists/

Solender, A. (2020, September 22). Trump says police violence against journalists is "actually a beautiful sight." *Forbes*. https://www.forbes.com/sites/andrewsolender/2020/09/22/trump-says-police-violence-against-journalists-is-actually-a-beautiful-sight/

Solis, N. (2021, March 22). *LA sheriff fights subpoena over secret deputy gangs*. Courthouse News Service. https://www.courthousenews.com/la-sheriff-says-he-will-seek-to-block-subpoena-about-what-he-knows-on-secret-deputy-gangs/

Some events in the history of Mexico and the border. (1999, September). *The Journal of American History*, 86(2), 453–455. https://www.jstor.org/stable/2567039

Song, S. (2009). Democracy and noncitizen voting rights. *Citizenship Studies*, 13(6), 607–620. https://doi.org/10.1080/13621020903309607

Southern Poverty Law Center. (2020, November 16). *FBI reports an increase in hate crimes in 2019: Hate-based murders more than doubled*. https://www.splcenter.org/news/2020/11/16/fbi-reports-increase-hate-crimes-2019-hate-based-murders-more-doubled

Southern Poverty Law Center. (2021). *Anti-Muslim*. https://www.splcenter.org/fighting-hate/extremist-files/ideology/anti-muslim

Soza, J. R. (2015, July). *Teacher alienation: Reconceptualizing the educational work environment* [Dissertation, Loyola Marymount University]. https://digitalcommons.lmu.edu/etd/184

Speipel, B. (2019, April 2). Trump: "Make America Great Again" slogan "was made up by me." *The Hill.* https://thehill.com/homenews/administration/437070-trump-make-america -great-again-slogan-was-made-up-by-me

Spencer, H. (1864). *Principles of biology* (Vol. I). Williams and Norgate. https://archive.org /details/principlesbiolo05spengoog/mode/2up?view=theater

Spitzer, R. J. (2002). Lost and found researching the Second Amendment. In C. T. Bogus (Ed.), *The second amendment in law and history: Historians and constitutional scholars on the right to bear arms* (pp. 16–47). The New Press.

Spring, J. (2011). *The American school: A global context from the Puritans to the Obama era* (8th ed.). McGraw-Hill.

Stainback, K., & Tomaskovic-Devey, D. (2012, October 25). Re-segregating America's work-places. *The Washington Post.* http://www.washingtonpost.com/blogs/therootdc/post/many -american-workplaces-are-becoming-more-segregated/2012/10/25/6c86e0a6-1e15-11e 2-b647-bb1668e64058_blog.html

Stanley-Becker, I., & Narayanswamy, A. (2021, August 1). Trump has more than $100 million in political cash after first six months of 2021. *The Washington Post.* https://www.washingtonpost .com/politics/2021/07/31/trump-committees-fundraising-2021-fec/

Stanley, J. (2018). *How fascism works: The politics of us and them.* Random House.

Stearns, P. N. (1998). *Why study history.* American Historical Association. https://www .historians.org/about-aha-and-membership/aha-history-and-archives/historical-archives /why-study-history-(1998)

Steinmetz-Jenkins, D. (2020, October 29). What we call freedom has never been about being free. *The Nation.* https://www.thenation.com/article/culture/annelien-de-dijn-freedom-unruly -history-interview/

Stephens, A. (2020, June 19). *The "warrior cop" is a toxic mentality. And a lucrative industry.* The Trace. https://www.thetrace.org/2020/06/warrior-cop-mentality-police-industry/

Stephens, C. (2020, October 29). *Police wanted "a dog that would bite a Black person."* The Marshall Project. https://www.themarshallproject.org/2020/10/29/police-wanted-a-dog -that-would-bite-a-black-person

Stewart, K. (2021, January 17). The roots of Hawley's rage. *The New York Times,* 6sr.

Stockholm International Peace Research Institute. (2020, April 27). *Global military expenditure sees largest annual increase in a decade—says SIPRI—reaching $1917 billion in 2019.* https://www.sipri.org/media/press-release/2020/global-military-expenditure-sees-largest -annual-increase-decade-says-sipri-reaching-1917-billion

Stokel-Walker, C. (2021). Anti-feminism is route to alt-right. *New Scientist, 249*(3325), 12. https://www.sciencegra.com/science/article/pii/S0262407921003985

Stolberg, S. G. (2019, June 18). Ocasio-Cortez calls migrant detention centers "concentration camps," eliciting backlash. *The New York Times.* https://www.nytimes.com/2019/06/18/us /politics/ocasio-cortez-cheney-detention-centers.html

Sullivan, M. (2020, May 30). Trump has sown hatred of the press for years. Now journal-ists are under assault from police and protesters alike. *The Washington Post.* https://www .washingtonpost.com/lifestyle/media/trump-has-sown-hatred-of-the-press-for-years-now -journalists-are-under-assault-from-police-and-protesters-alike/2020/05/30/1e6b81ae-a2a3 -11ea-81bb-c2f70f01034b_story.html

Swenson, K. (2017, August 28). Black-clad Antifa members attack peaceful right-wing demon-stration in Berkeley. *The Washington Post.* https://www.washingtonpost.com/news/morning -mix/wp/2017/08/28/black-clad-antifa-attack-right-wing-demonstrators-in-berkeley/

Szalai, J. (2020, June 11). Use of "fascism" takes a new turn. *The New York Times,* C1, C4.

Tabuchi, H., & Peopovich, N. (2021, April 29). A stark inequality more harmful with each breath. *The New York Times,* A12.

Takami, D. A. (1998). *Divided destiny: A history of Japanese Americans in Seattle.* University of Washington Press & Wing Luke Asian Museum.

Taylor, A., & Smucker, J. (2021). Occupy Wall Street changed everything. *New York Intelligencer*. https://nymag.com/intelligencer/2021/09/occupy-wall-street-changed-everything.html

Taylor, C. (2011). To be a good American: The New York City Teachers Union and race during the second world war. In Taylor C. (Ed.), *Civil rights in New York City: From World War II to the Giuliani era* (pp. 10–31). Fordham University Press. https://doi.org/10.2307/j.ctt13wzxr4.5

Taylor, G. (2012). Prometheus unbound: Populism, the property question, and social invention. *The Good Society, 21*(2), 219–233.

Taylor, K.-Y. (2016). *From #BlackLivesMatter to Black liberation*. Haymarket Books.

Taylor, K.-Y. (2019). *Race for profit: How banks and the real estate industry undermined Black homeownership*. University of North Carolina Press.

Tharoor, I. (2020, June 3). Is it time to call Trump the f-word? *The Washington Post*. https://www.washingtonpost.com/world/2020/06/03/trump-protests-fascism/

Thompson, A. C. (2021, April 14). *American insurrection: Deadly far-right extremism from Charlottesville to Capitol attack. What next?* Democracy Now! https://www.democracynow.org/2021/4/14/pbs_frontline_american_insurrection

Thompson, W. (2010). *Ideologies in the age of extremes: Liberalism, conservatism, communism, fascism*. Pluto Press.

Timm, A. (2002). Sex with a purpose: Prostitution, venereal disease, and militarized masculinity in the Third Reich. *Journal of the History of Sexuality, 11*(1/2), 223–255. http://www.jstor.org/stable/3704557

Toloudis, N. (2015). Teacher unions conflict in New York City, 1935–1960. *Labor History, 56*(5), 566–586. https://doi.org/10.1080/0023656x.2015.1116805

Tompkins, L., Smith, M., Bosman, J., & Pietsch, B. (2021, February 22). Entering uncharted territory, the U.S. counts 500,000 covid-related deaths. *The New York Times*. https://www.nytimes.com/2021/02/22/us/us-covid-deaths-half-a-million.html

Traverso, E. (2016). Antifascism between collective memory and historical revisions. In H. Garcia, M. Yusta, X. Tabet, & C. Clímaco (Eds.), *Rethinking antifascism: History, memory and politics, 1922–present* (pp. 321–338). Berghahn Books.

Trump, D. (2016, October 8). Transcript: Donald Trump's taped comments about women. *The New York Times*. (Originally taped in 2005). https://www.nytimes.com/2016/10/08/us/donald-trump-tape-transcript.html

Trump, D. (2020, July 3). *Donald Trump Mount Rushmore speech transcript at* 4th *of July event*.Rev.https://www.rev.com/blog/transcripts/donald-trump-speech-transcript-at-mount-rushmore-4th-of-july-event

Trump, D. (2021, January 6). *Transcript of Trump's speech at rally before US Capitol riot*. Associated Press. https://apnews.com/article/election-2020-joe-biden-donald-trump-capitol-siege-media-e79eb5164613d6718e9f4502eb471f27

Truth and Reconciliation Commission of Canada. (2015). *Honoring the truth, reconciling for the future*. http://www.trc.ca/websites/trcinstitution/File/2015/Honouring_the_Truth_Reconciling_for_the_Future_July_23_2015.pdf

Turk, A. T. (2004). Sociology of terrorism. *Annual Review of Sociology, 30*, 271–286. https://www.jstor.org/stable/29737694

Tuser, C. (2021, April 23). The Flint water crisis: 7 years later. *Water & Waste Digest*. https://www.wwdmag.com/flint-water-crisis/flint-water-crisis-7-years-later

United Nations. (n.d.). *Ethnic cleansing*. Office on Genocide Prevention and the Responsibility to Protect. https://www.un.org/en/genocideprevention/ethnic-cleansing.shtml

United Nations. (1948). *Convention on the prevention and punishment of the crime of genocide*. https://www.un.org/en/genocideprevention/genocide.shtml

United Nations. (2013, March 12). *Indigenous youth: Identity, challenges and hope: Articles 14, 17, 21 and 25 of the United Nations Declaration on the Rights of Indigenous Peoples*. Economic and Social Council. https://daccess-ods.un.org/TMP/6907892.22717285.html

United Nations. (2020, August 12). *Mandates of the Special Rapporteur on contemporary forms of racism, racial discrimination, xenophobia and related intolerance; the Special*

Rapporteur on the human rights of migrants. https://spcommreports.ohchr.org/TMResults
   Base/DownLoadPublicCommunicationFile?gId=25476
United States v. Miller et al. (1939, May 15). U.S. Supreme Court. https://www.law.cornell.edu
   /supremecourt/text/307/174
University of California, Santa Barbara. (n.d.). *Statistics.* The American Presidency Project.
   https://www.presidency.ucsb.edu/statistics/elections
Unmasking Antifa Act of 2018, H.R. 6054, 115th Congress (2018). https://www.congress.gov
   /bill/115th-congress/house-bill/6054/text
U.S. Army Junior ROTC. (2021). *Army junior ROTC program overview.* http://www
   .usarmyjrotc.com/general/program_overview.php
U.S. Bureau of Labor Statistics. (2020, July). *A profile of the working poor, 2018.* https://www.bls
   .gov/opub/reports/working-poor/2018/home.htm#BLStable_2020_6_22_13_53_footnotes
U.S. Census Bureau. (2021, April 27). *Quarterly residential vacancies and Homeownership, first
   quarter 2021.* https://www.census.gov/housing/hvs/files/currenthvspress.pdf
U.S. Department of Agriculture (2020, September 9). *Definitions of food insecurity.* https://
   www.ers.usda.gov/topics/food-nutrition-assistance/food-security-in-the-us/definitions-of
   -food-security.aspx
U.S. Department of Education. (2013). *For each and every child: A strategy for education equity
   and excellence.* www.foreachandeverychild.org/The_Report.html
U.S. Department of Health & Human Services. (2021). *Native American youth depression
   and suicide.* Child Welfare Gateway Information Service. https://mnprc.org/wp-content
   /uploads/2019/01/suicide-ethnic-populations-1.pdf
U.S. Department of Justice. (2015a). *Investigation of the Ferguson police department.* https://
   www.justice.gov/sites/default/files/opa/press-releases/attachments/2015/03/04/ferguson
   _police_department_report.pdf
U.S. Department of Justice. (2015b). *Report regarding the criminal investigation into the shooting death of Michael Brown by Ferguson, Missouri police officer Darren Wilson.* https://
   www.justice.gov/sites/default/files/opa/press-releases/attachments/2015/03/04/doj_report
   _on_shooting_of_michael_brown_1.pdf
U.S. Department of Justice. (2017, July 28). *History of federal voting rights laws.* https://www
   .justice.gov/crt/history-federal-voting-rights-laws
U.S. Department of Justice. (2021, January 14). *Review of the Department of Justice's planning
   and implementation of its zero tolerance policy and its coordination with the Departments of
   Homeland Security and Health and Human Services.* https://oig.justice.gov/reports/review
   -department-justices-planning-and-implementation-its-zero-tolerance-policy-and-its
U.S. Department of Labor. (1965). *The Negro family: The case for national action.* University
   of Michigan Library.
U.S. Department of State. (n.d.). *The Immigration Act of 1924 (the Johnson–Reed Act).* Office of
   the Historian. history.state.gov/milestones/1921-1936/ImmigrationAct
U.S. Holocaust Memorial Museum. (2017, December 8). The United States and the Holocaust.
   Holocaust encyclopedia. https://encyclopedia.ushmm.org/content/en/article/the-united-states
   -and-the-holocaust
U.S. Holocaust Memorial Museum. (2020, December 8). Documenting numbers of victims of
   the holocaust and Nazi persecution. *Holocaust encyclopedia.* https://encyclopedia.ushmm
   .org/content/en/article/documenting-numbers-of-victims-of-the-holocaust-and-nazi
   -persecution
U.S. Holocaust Memorial Museum. (n.d.a.). Persecution of homosexuals in the Third Reich.
   Holocaust encyclopedia. https://encyclopedia.ushmm.org/content/en/article/persecution
   -of-homosexuals-in-the-third-reich
U.S. Holocaust Memorial Museum. (n.d.b.). *US ratifies genocide convention.* https://www
   .ushmm.org/learn/timeline-of-events/after-1945/us-ratifies-genocide-convention
U.S. Senate. (1989). *Report of the special committee on investigations of the select committee
   on Indian affairs.* U.S. Government Printing Office. http://libsysdigi.library.uiuc.edu/oca
   /Books2008-05/finalreportlegis10160unit/finalreportlegis10160unit_djvu.txt

U.S. Senate Select Committee on Intelligence. (2014, December 9). *Committee study of the Central Intelligence Agency's detention and interrogation program.* http://www.intelligence .senate.gov/sites/default/files/documents/CRPT-113srpt288.pdf

USA Facts. (2021, February 25). *Who are the renters in America?* https://usafacts.org/articles /who-is-renting-in-america-cares-act/

Vass, J. S., & Gold, S. R. (1995). Effects of feedback on emotion in hypermasculine males. *Violence & Victims, 10*(3), 217-226.

Vavrus, M. (2002). *Transforming the multicultural education of teachers: Research, theory, and practice.* Teachers College Press.

Vavrus, M. (2015). *Diversity and education: A critical multicultural approach.* Teachers College Press.

Vavrus, M. D. (2002). *Postfeminist news: Political women in media culture.* State University of New York Press.

Vavrus, M. D. (2019). *Postfeminist war: Women and the media-military-industrial complex.* Rutgers University Press.

Vials, C. (2014). *Haunted by Hitler: Liberals, the left, and the fight against fascism in the United States.* University of Massachusetts Press.

Vitale, A. S. (2017). *The end of policing.* Verso.

Voigtländer, N., & Voth, H. (2014, May). *Highway to Hitler* [Working paper]. University of Zurich, Department of Economics. https://econpapers.repec.org/paper/zureconwp/156.htm

Voigtländer, N., & Voth, H. (2015). Nazi indoctrination and anti-Semitic beliefs in Germany. *Proceedings of the National Academy of Sciences of the United States of America, 112*(26), 7931–7936. https://www.jstor.org/stable/26463612

Vysotsky, S. (2021). *American Antifa: The tactics, culture, and practice of militant antifascism.* Routledge.

Waldman, P., & Pope, H. (2001, September 21). "Crusade" reference reinforces fears war on terrorism is against Muslims. *Wall Street Journal.* https://www.wsj.com/articles/SB 1001020294332922160

Wallerstein, I. (2011). *The modern world system IV: Centrist liberalism triumphant, 1789–1914.* University of California Press.

Wang, A. B., & Itkowitz, C. (2021, April 16). Trump loyalists start "America First Caucus" to promote U.S. as "uniquely Anglo-Saxon." *The Washington Post.* https://www .washingtonpost.com/politics/2021/04/16/trump-loyalists-start-america-first-caucus -promote-us-uniquely-anglo-saxon/

Washington, H. A. (2007). *Medical apartheid: The dark history of medical experimentation on Black Americans from colonial times to the present.* Doubleday.

Washington, H. A. (2019). *A terrible thing to waste: Environmental racism and its assault on the American mind.* Little, Brown Spark.

Washington, H. A. (2021). *Carte blanche: The erosion of medical consent.* Columbia Global Reports.

The Washington Post. (2020, August 4). Fatal force. https://www.washingtonpost.com/graphics /investigations/police-shootings-database/

Wegner, B. (1997). SS. In C. Zentner & F. Bedurftig (Eds.), *The encyclopedia of the Third Reich* (A. Hackett, Trans., pp. 901–906). Da Capo.

Weichselbaum, S., & Schwartzapfel, B. (2017, March 30). *When warriors put on the badge.* The Marshall Project. https://www.themarshallproject.org/2017/03/30/when-warriors-put -on-the-badge

Weigel, D. (2017, August 30). Pelosi condemns "violent actions" of Antifa protesters. *The Washington Post.* https://www.washingtonpost.com/news/powerpost/wp/2017/08/30 /pelosi-condemns-violent-actions-of-antifa-protesters/

Weinger, M. (2012, November 6). Bill O'Reilly: "The White establishment is now the minority." *Politico.* https://www.politico.com/blogs/media/2012/11/bill-oreilly-the-white-establishment -is-now-the-minority-148705

Wenzelburger, J. (2021). Snaza joins 36 sheriffs backing Second Amendment, Constitution. *The Chronicle.* https://chronline.com/stories/snaza-joins-36-sheriffs-backing-second-amendment -constitution,269468?

Werthan, S. (2018, July 3). What ICE really does. *Slate.* https://slate.com/news-and-politics/2018/07/difference-between-ice-and-cbp-the-role-of-each-agency-in-family-separations-and-immigration-enforcement.html

West, C. (1995). Foreword. In K. Crenshaw, N. Gotanda, G. Peller, & K. Thomas (Eds.), *Critical race theory: The key writings that formed the movement* (pp. xi–xii). The New Press.

West, C. (2016). *Cornel West on Donald Trump: This is what neo-fascism looks like.* Democracy Now! https://www.democracynow.org/2016/12/1/cornel_west_on_donald_trump_this

Whisnant, R. (2013). Feminist perspectives on rape. In Edward N. Zalta (Ed.), *Stanford encyclopedia of philosophy.* plato.stanford.edu/archives/fall2013/ entries/feminism-rape

Whitney Plantation. (n.d.). *The field of angels children's memorial.* https://www.whitneyplantation.org/history/the-big-house-and-the-outbuildings/the-field-of-angels/

Will, M., Gewertz, C., Najarro, I., & Schwartz, S. (2021, July 15). What does the critical race theory law mean for Texas classrooms? Teachers speak out. *Education Week.* https://www.edweek.org/teaching-learning/what-does-the-critical-race-theory-law-mean-for-texas-classrooms-teachers-speak-out/2021/07

Wilson, J. (2015, January 19). "Cultural Marxism": A uniting theory for rightwingers who love to play the victim. *The Guardian.* https://www.theguardian.com/commentisfree/2015/jan/19/cultural-marxism-a-uniting-theory-for-rightwingers-who-love-to-play-the-victim

Wilson, J. (2020, January 23). Revealed: The true identity of the leader of an American neo-Nazi terror group. *The Guardian.* https://www.theguardian.com/world/2020/jan/23/revealed-the-true-identity-of-the-leader-of-americas-neo-nazi-terror-group

Wilson, J. (2021a, June 8). Amid mega-drought, rightwing militias stokes water rebellion in US west. *The Guardian.* https://www.theguardian.com/us-news/2021/jun/08/klamath-falls-oregon-protests-ammon-bundy

Wilson, J. (2021b, August 9). New movement of religious extremists push ultra-conservative vision of US. *The Guardian.* https://www.theguardian.com/us-news/2021/aug/09/deznats-religious-extremists-mormon-vision

Wilson, J. (2021c, July 21). Revealed: Assistant attorney general in Alaska posted racist and antisemitic tweets. *The Guardian.* https://www.theguardian.com/us-news/2021/jul/21/alaska-assistant-attorney-general-twitter-far-right?CMP=Share_iOSApp_Other

Wilson, J. (2021d, May 28). What is sovereignty? A conversation about American colonialism. *The Guardian.* https://www.theguardian.com/us-news/2021/may/28/sovereignty-colonialism-standoffs-us-government-jacqueline-keeler

Winau, R. (1997). Social Darwinism. In C. Zentner & F. Bedurftig (Eds.), *The encyclopedia of the Third Reich* (A. Hackett, Trans., p. 879). Da Capo Press.

Woodson, C. G. (2000). *The mis-education of the Negro.* African American Images. (Originally published in 1933)

Worth, O. (2015). The far-right and neoliberalism: Willing partner or hegemonic opponent? In R. Saull, A. Anievas, N. Davidson, & A. Fabry (Eds.), *The longue durée of the far-right: An international historical sociology* (pp. 153–172). Routledge.

Younge, G. (2013, March 27). Chicago Teachers Union plans mass demonstrations against school closings. *The Guardian.* https://www.theguardian.com/world/2013/mar/27/chicago-teachers-protest-school-closings

Yourish, K., Buchanan, L., & Lu, D. (2021, January 7). The 147 Republicans who voted to overturn election results. *The New York Times.* https://www.nytimes.com/interactive/2021/01/07/us/elections/electoral-college-biden-objectors.html

Youth.gov. (2020). *Education, employment, & the military.* https://youth.gov/youth-topics/challenges-education-employment-and-military

Zentner, C., & Bedurftig, F. (Eds.). (1997). Führer's will. In *The encyclopedia of the Third Reich* (A. Hackett, Trans., p. 308). Da Capo.

Zinn Education Project. (2022, Jan. 30). *Teachers refuse to lie to students.* https://www.zinnedproject.org/news/teachers-defy-gop-bans-on-history-lessons/

Index

About the Author

Michael Vavrus is the author of *Diversity and Education: A Critical Multicultural Approach* and *Transforming the Multicultural Education of Teachers: Theory, Research, and Practice* and coeditor of the text *Intersectionality of Race, Ethnicity, Class, and Gender in Teaching and Teacher Education: Movement Toward Equity in Education*. He is past president of the Association of Independent Liberal Arts Colleges for Teacher Education and the state of Washington Association of Colleges for Teacher Education. Vavrus is professor emeritus of interdisciplinary studies (education, history, and political economy) at The Evergreen State College in Olympia, Washington.

Printed and bound by CPI Group (UK) Ltd, Croydon, CR0 4YY

07/07/2026

14916226-0004

MULTICULTURAL EDUCATION SERIES

James A. Banks, Series Editor

For a complete list of series titles, please visit www.tcpress.com

(continued)